WITHDRAWN

GREGORY B. LEE

Troubadours, Trumpeters, Troubled Makers

Lyricism, Nationalism and Hybridity
in China and its Others

DUKE UNIVERSITY PRESS
DURHAM, NORTH CAROLINA

First published 1996

Published in the USA by Duke University Press
Durham, North Carolina

Printed in Hong Kong

Library of Congress Cataloging-in-Publication Data

Lee, Gregory B.
   Troubadours, trumpeters, troubled makers: lyricism, nationalism, and hybridity in China and its others / Gregory B. Lee.
      p. cm. — (Asia-Pacific, culture, politics, and society)
   Includes bibliographical references and index.
   ISBN 0-8223-1659-5.—ISBN 0-8223-1671-4 (pbk.)
      1. China —Intellectual life —1976-   2. Popular music —China —Text —History and criticism.   3. Chinese literature —20th century —History and criticism.   I. Title.   II. Series: Asia-Pacific.
DS779.23.L4   1995
951.05 —dc20   95-5193
                                                                      CIP

For Isabelle, Sue and Vanessa

CONTENTS

vii

PREFACE AND ACKNOWLEDGEMENTS

This book makes no claim to be an up-to-the-minute survey, even less a celebration, of modern Chinese culture. Its concerns, in any case, reach beyond the culture of China, to those which have been intertextually and contextually imbricated with China over the last century or more: the cultures of France, Britain, the United States – China's Others. Nor is the book concerned with a unitary notion of Chinese culture; it talks plurally of Chinese cultures – for example, those of Chinese people who have now created a space within the cultures of those nations that once colonised the country. These Chinese cultures are both Chinese and Other to China, just as they are Other to white culture. They are the Other in the Self, and the Self in the Other. In discussing communities and cultures that transgress borders and boundaries, this volume, similarly, is designed to be theoretically, methodologically and ideologically transgressive. If the work seems inconsistent or contradictory, that is due in part to the author's difficulty in narrating the experience and developments of both society and the author as if from some omniscient unitary perspective of arrested time.

In economic terms we live in a globalised world, but then we have done so for some time. Culturally and socially we also live in a patchwork matrix in which our responses to the material reality and 'psychic imperialism' of McDonalds' economic globalism are uneven and informed by fragmented levels and forms of understanding. New forms of patriarchal authoritarianism, fundamentalism, the interjection of new nationalisms among the old, all complicate in multiple ways the late capitalist psyche of 'the society of the spectacle' now mapped on to a socially and culturally unevenly developed world. Thus, it should not surprise us that the cultural texts, practices and histories we need to analyse are uneven, fragmented, hybrid and often contradictory and therefore demand appropriate responses. We live in a fragmented world where cultural and social developments are as uneven as those in the economic sphere, a world whose divergent and irregular formations defy even the most general manifestations of post-modern theory and metatheory.

This then would be my response to readers who detect a conflict between modernist and post-modernist tendencies, and who perceive a vacillation between what seem to be neo-Marxist and post-Marxist positions. In fact, while I still find Marxian modes of analysis useful, perhaps more so than many colleagues and contemporaries, I have always been critical of narrowly-conceived and orthodox formulations of Marxism; for this reason I suppose I find myself drawn to French radical critiques and rearticulations of Marxism. I should add that I have never been comfortable with the British tradition of political and critical thought, despite having been impressed by several British radical thinkers (especially E.P. Thompson, who has often been mistakenly identified as a 'Little Englander') and their academic projects. For historical reasons, the radical tradition in Britain was never greatly interested in theory, and thus the cultural and historical studies initiated by Raymond Williams, Thompson, Eric Hobsbawm and George Rudé constituted a welcome sea-change opening up possibilities for scores of writers and thinkers in these areas. Still, as a British colleague recently remarked to me, '1789 completely passed Britain by'. That is to say that apart from the critique that emanates from the orthodox Marxist critics, such as the Trotskyist scholar Alex Callinicos, the rebellious, revolutionary impulse of much French thought is absent from the British critical tradition. In France there is a grassroots tradition of critique which is typified by the radical journalism of the weekly magazine *Charlie Hebdo*. Thus, while many members of the fashionable intellectual élite have become part of France's packaged cultural capital, part of the increasingly globalised 'society of the spectacle', there persists a critical tradition that refuses to lose touch with everyday French life.

The theorisation of twentieth-century consumer society as spectacular society was undertaken by the late Guy Debord in the 1960s and again in the late 1980s. I suppose, like others, I have become increasingly convinced of the political and cultural astuteness of Debord's writing, and that of his erstwhile collaborator Raoul Vaneigem. The reader will note my appropriation and redeployment of their ideas throughout this book.

One further word on my critical perspective. My view of the world has always been informed by the lived experience of the marginalised community that nurtured me in childhood and youth. I hope that my references to the city of Liverpool in this book are without nostalgia or romanticism. To grow up in proximity to the kinds of social and individual deprivation, misery and injustice that existed then as now cannot fail to leave a mark. All subsequent exposure to social misery and hierarchical oppressions, such as I have experienced as an observer while living in China, the United States and Hong Kong, can only act as layered accretions or assimilations to those early experiences through which, as through a prism, all subsequent understanding has been tempered and related.

For much of the last 150 years China has been dominated and exploited by other countries: by Western countries and Japan. Much of China's cultural production has consequently been marked by the desire to participate in resistance to foreign domination, or culturally to negotiate otherwise the painful modernisation of Chinese society—a modernisation at first imposed by colonialism and then continued under a centralised, nationalistic bureaucracy which legitimated itself by means of Leninist and other ideologies. Of course, centralised, nationalistic and bureaucratic authority has not been confined to China. France has one of the most centralised bureaucracies the world has known, and its effect on cultural life, both nationally and transnationally, has been immense. Yet while French high culture has been a mainstay of that country's international reputation, it has nonetheless smothered and marginalised culturally rich non-metropolitan indigenous and immigrant traditions.

The paradox of modernity is that while it is true that we are converging into a culturally unified world, this trajectory has only been achieved by dominant societies divesting themselves of those groups in society that have not conformed to the dominant ideology and social imaginary. Indeed, one of the major concerns of this book is with the exclusion of those who are different due to race, ethnicity, or class, and how such groups have been dominated, alienated and quite simply constructed as scapegoats by those in society most responsible for the production of ideology and for the shaping of the social imaginary. In many of the chapters that follow, I discuss how lyricism has either channelled or challenged the dominant cultural practices that have tried to assimilate where possible and exclude where not. What such exclusion masks is our *mutual* exclusion: our alienation as individuals one from the other. By excluding easily distinguished groups, we conceal our own exclusion.

The excluded are often conceptualised metaphorically as being pushed to the margins of society, marginalised. However, the relationship should also be conceived vertically, hierarchically configured as a pattern of dominance. Those who are represented as different, as the Other, are also projected as inferior. This is a concern that informs this book as a whole; it is introduced in Chapter 1, the intent of which is to illustrate how even well-intentioned critiques of dominant literary practices in the West, in this case related to the consumption of poetry, can ultimately reinscribe the exclusion of the too different Other. Linked to the question of diversity are the problems of identity and authenticity, and these too are introduced in Chapter 1 in an initial discussion of the difficult issue of hybrid culture. The discourse of mainstream and 'high' culture, of 'authenticity', in harking back to past tradition only anchors us ever more firmly to the idea of an eternal present which leaves humanity with no hope. Thus in Chapter 1, and throughout the rest of the volume, the 'low', the 'bastardised' and the 'marginalised' are given a space, which I hope is a fair and equitable one, alongside more 'élite' forms of cultural expression.

Chapter 2 examines how poetry as a form of social language functions ideologically and how it can also serve to expose ideologies. Chapter 3 discusses the impact of Western, in particular French, cultural imperialism on Chinese poetry, and the resulting hybrid modernist forms of lyricism. France is perhaps unique in having been a colonial power possessing recent revolutionary credentials. That particular history has been responsible in China, and in other societies that have been subjected to outside domination, for developments in numerous emergent, and re-emergent, literatures which would surely have been produced very differently had the intrusion of metropolitan French culture not been so pervasive. While Asian and African colonies of France were to some extent 'destined' to develop hybrid, Gallicised cultures, that modern China should have done so, especially in the sphere of poetry, is due partly to the persuasive political and aesthetic ideologies of France, but also partly to a Chinese desire to gain access to emancipatory practices and thought. Chapter 4 goes on to illustrate how the supposed lack of 'authentic' Chineseness has been used as an excuse by Orientalist scholars and élitist theorists in the West to denigrate modern Chinese literary practices. Chapter 5 suggests how the 'hybrid' Chinese modernist literary practice of contemporary poetry, and modernist practices in general, might be a vital and forceful instrument of critique.

Chapter 6 departs from practices of high modernist culture and focuses on the nationalist and anti-nationalist ideologies informing popular music culture as a sub-cultural practice, particularly in mainland China and France, and as a marginalised practice in southern France (Occitania) and Hong Kong. Chapter 7 similarly represents a divergence from the discussion of élite lyric discourse, since it looks specifically at the literary production of the Chinese communities in the United States and Britain (poetry, fiction and experiential accounts), and the ways in which the Chinese diaspora itself has been represented in the newspapers, academic journals, travelogues and fiction of the dominant white majority. Everywhere in the history of modernity we stumble across narratives of exclusion and suppression.

Most of the texts discussed in this book are lyrics of one sort or another. This is not a haphazard choice. Not only in China, but also in most cultures, poetry has been the dominant literary genre. In the sphere of popular culture, lyrics are still produced, repeated and recited daily. That capitalist modernity should have constructed societies lacking poetry, yet whose political and economic powers are ready to exploit the power of lyrics, is no coincidence. In Chapter 8, it is argued that lyrical expression is essential to the establishment and maintenance of community, and that it is precisely the fact and the sense of shared community from which modernity has separated us. To reconstruct those links is no easy task and requires dramatic alteration of the nature of society. Lyrics enable us to imagine how that society might be configured. In Chapter 8, the conclusion is that there have been moments and spaces, or zones, of reconfigured reality which instructs us that a greater degree of autonomy for all individuals is possible, and that one continues to see them. That Chinese poets in exile and at home, that Hong Kong music-makers, that Occitan, latter-day troubadours and others in marginalised societies are concerned and troubled enough to continue to make poetic efforts to nurture and project moments of seeing and living otherwise, is a source of hope for us all.

The chapters of this book, then, indicate not only an interest in aspects of Chinese, European and American cultural history, but also trace an attachment, over the past few years, to often quite distinct intellectual traditions which have attempted to critique and interrogate the cultural and political condition of modern societies. The book aims consistently to put the cultures and texts discussed in historical and social context, and to do so comparatively out of the conviction that only a truly global perspective which refuses notions of authenticity and purity will enable us to effect the social and cultural changes necessary for us to live and not simply survive in the twenty-first century.

Ultimately, then, there is in my perception a coherence which weaves the various sections of this volume into a set of cogent and related concerns. If the fabrication of cracks through which optimism may leak is part of the task of creating poetry, then I hope this book has not only interpreted but emulated that task; and if such is the stuff of 'modernism', then this work must advocate that sense of modernism. I believe that what radical intellectuals ought to be about transcends the mere clever and sophisticated manipulation of modern theory. Parallel to the project of untrammelled critique of society and its cultural formations and representations should be the quest for potentially real solutions. That is why the material condition of modern society is still the most important referent of our work. At the same time, the understanding that human emancipation cannot be achieved through an obsessive economism seems increasingly clear. The necessity for the unleashing of imaginative power, for the encouragement of creativity not for commodification and recuperation but as an intrinsic means of a new way of living, is increasingly pressing.

Certain of the ideas in Chapters 1 and 2 were first aired at a University of Chicago workshop on transcultural poetry and poetics directed by Professors Paul Friedrich and A.K. Ramanujan. The latter's premature and unexpected death deeply saddened me, as it must have saddened hundreds of others. He was an honorable scholar, poet and translator, who gave me quiet but strong encouragement. Chapter 3 is a revised version of an article published in a special issue of *West Virginia University Philological Papers* (volume 39, 1993), a collection of contributions to a 1991 conference on 'The Context of Modernism'. Chapter 4 was originally written as a paper for a conference on Emergent Literatures at the University of Minnesota in April 1992, and revised for inclusion here. Chapter 5 is a somewhat altered version of a piece that appeared in *Chinese Writing and Exile*, a volume of conference papers which I edited and published through the Center for East Asian Studies, University of Chicago, in 1993; the conference, jointly sponsored by the Chicago Humanities Institute, took place in May 1991. The first draft of Chapter 6 was substantially written while I was a Chicago Humanities Institute Fellow during the autumn of 1992; it was presented at a conference on 'The Subject of China', organised by Professors Christopher Connery and John Hay and held at the University of California, Santa Cruz, in January 1993, and in a modified form to the Institute of Popular Music, University of Liverpool, in June 1993. It was subsequently published as ' "The East is Red" Goes Pop: Commodification, Hybridity and Nationalism in Chinese Popular Song and its Televisual Performance' in *Popular Music* (Cambridge University Press) 14, 1 (January 1995). Chapter 7 was presented in April 1993 to a University of Chicago Midwest Faculty Seminar, and subsequently to the University of Chicago's American Studies Workshop.

I should like to acknowledge and thank the following: David Bevington for the kind interest he took in my work; Cai Fangpei, for having taught me so much about China, and for his linguistic and technical assistance; Iain Chambers for being a generous, constructive and attentive reader; Rey Chow for all her encouragement and too frequently unheeded advice, and thus also for her indulgence and patience in the face of my stubbornness; James Chandler for his comments on an early version of Chapter 4; Christopher Connery for advice, support and camaraderie, and in particular for the 'Laughing Man'; Arif Dirlik for the strong endorsement he gave to my work; Page duBois for her warm support; Harry Harootunian, a man of great intellectual integrity and courage, for his stalwart and invaluable support, for sharing his immense knowledge and scholarship and for being a true teacher; Paul Friedrich for always having supported me in my work and for having generously shared with me his very fine graduate students; Loren Kruger, a truly radical scholar, for her warm support and comradeship; Lu Tonglin for her scholarly and attentive reading of the manuscript; Masao Miyoshi for his encouragement and enthusiasm for this book; David Pollard not for any direct input into the volume but in belated recognition of his having taught a university course in modern Chinese poetry at a time when doing so was pioneering and unorthodox; William Sibley for his affection and material support; Philip Tagg for the example of his commitment to the serious study of popular music, and his willingness to discuss it with an amateur; and Rob Wilson for his strong support of my work.

I am also very grateful to the graduate students at the University of Chicago with whom I discussed many of the ideas to be found in this book. In particular, my thanks are due to D.J. Hatfield who attentively read the manuscript and made valuable observations; likewise to Trevor Anderson who read and discussed the manuscript with me; and to those students whose participation in my seminars on modern Chinese culture provided me with much stimulation.

I should like also to thank those involved directly in the production of this book: Christopher Hurst, Michael Dwyer, Reynolds Smith and Marc Brodsky, who have all shown a remarkable degree of tolerance. I am most grateful to Ursula Starr for her kind permission to reproduce the painting *Mao Zedong in Concert* by the late Liverpool painter, Sam Walsh, among whose other twentieth-century subjects were William Burroughs, Francis Bacon, Mick Jagger, J. Edger Hoover and John Lennon. My thanks also to Geoff and Maria Brown, and Chrys Carey. In the latter stages of the revision of this book, the staff of the reference department of the university of Hong Kong Library, in particular Rebecca Yeung and Antonia Yiu, were both extremely courteous and helpful.

As usual my family have exhibited enormous tolerance and patience year in year out, and without the assistance of Isabelle the writing of this book would truly have been impossible. Finally, I should like to thank the authors of the many works that have informed and shaped this one.

1

WHITE OTHER, HYBRID OTHERS

'The famous and absurd incompatibility between East and West, that antithesis hardened by the colonizer, who thereby sets up a permanent barrier between himself and the colonized.'
—Albert Memmi[1]

'The value of an old work of art should be assessed on the basis of the amount of radical theory that can be drawn from it, on the basis of the nucleus of creative spontaneity which the creators will be able to release from it for the purposes of – and by means of – an unprecedented kind of poetry.'
—Raoul Vaneigem[2]

This chapter discusses two controversial concepts which are often treated separately, but which are in fact connected. First is the idea of alterity, of otherness. In its progressive aspect an awareness of otherness, of the difference of the Other, may imply tolerance for difference, respect for human diversity; but the naming and isolation of the Other is also essential to the exclusion of those who are racially, ethnically and otherwise different. Central to the question of alterity is the issue of identity: the important thing is 'to know how far the territory of identity extends, and where the territory of difference starts'.[3] The concept of hybridity is also essential to any

---

[1] *The Colonizer and the Colonized* (New York: Orion Press/London: Earthscan, 1990) 218. Transl. by Howard Greenfield from *Portrait du colonisé précédé du portrait du colonisateur* (Corrêa: Editions Buchet/Chastel, 1957).

[2] *Traité de savoir-vivre à l'usage des jeunes générations* (Paris: Gallimard, 1967, 1992), transl. by Donald Nicholson-Smith as *The Revolution of Everyday Life* (Rebel Press/Left Bank Books, 1983, 1994) 201.

[3] Tzvetan Todorov, *Nous et les autres: La réflexion française sur la diversité humaine*

discussion of identity, and constitutes a problematic space for
the determination of both racial and cultural difference. Both
diversity and hybridity are vexed questions, and both have
been appropriated by post-modern critics as 'liberatory alternatives' to modern cultural monoliths, while the colonial pasts
and the cultural history out of which these hybridities are
produced are forgotten, or simply disappear.[4] In thinking
about hybridity Homi Bhabha's essay on the subject, 'Signs
Taken for Wonders', can be very illuminating despite, or
perhaps because of, recent criticisms of it.

But we should start by thinking about two recent essays.
The first, by Bruce Murphy and entitled 'The Exile of Literature: Poetry and the Politics of the Other(s)', while without
doubt well intentioned, is nevertheless somewhat weakened
by its imbalanced focus on the white European Other.[5] The
second essay, 'The Postcolonial and the Postmodern', by
Anthony Kwame Appiah, attempts to work through the issues
of non-'authenticity' and hybridity in the non-Western context of modern African culture.[6] However, my common
reaction to both when I read them was: well, what about
China? While neither essay was meant to be about China as
such, it is still quite simply odd that writers feel comfortable
talking about categories like 'Communist' states or the 'Third
World' without even mentioning the largest example, in terms
of people and cultural production, in both categories. To be
fair, Kwame Appiah attempts to account for such lacunae in
writing: 'I shall speak about Africa, with confidence *both* that
some of what I have to say will work elsewhere in the so-called

(Paris: Editions du Seuil, 1989) 133. Translations of passages and poems quoted are
the present author's unless otherwise noted.

[4] Rey Chow, 'Between Colonizers: Hong Kong's Postcolonial Self-Writing in the
1990s', *Diaspora*, 2, 2(1992) 156-7.

[5] *Critical Inquiry* 17, 1, 162-73.

[6] *In My Father's House: Africa in the Philosophy of Culture* (New York and Oxford:
Oxford University Press, 1992) 137-57. The essay is a revised version of the article
'Is The Post In Post-Modern the Same as the Post in Post-Colonial?', in *Critical
Inquiry* 17, 2, 336-57.

Third World *and* that, in some places, it will certainly not.'[7]

Of course, it is also problematic even when intellectuals in the West do bother to imagine 'China' in the matrices of the Western academy's canon of 'Third World' literature, when often the effect is to relegate Chinese cultural production, and all the distinct cultures of Third World Others, to the vat of indistinguishable, multi-cultural hodgepodge. Dympna Callaghan has put it thus:

'Third World' describes diverse literatures that have been shaped by the experience of imperialism, but includes that of people of colour writing in the West, and the writing of a number of countries on the capitalist periphery. On the one hand, the term disrupts the transnational gestures of late capitalism, but on the other, it deprives cultures of autonomy in always situating them in relation to the West and to dominant white culture.[8]

Just as the sameness of 'national' cultures leaves no room for sub-cultures and regional cultures, when 'Third World' literatures are given a space, that space is homogeneous and common to the non-white Other. It is a space that 'deprives cultures of autonomy'. Only in this generalised space, in this West – Third World duality, are 'Third World' literatures allowed existence. Even then 'Third World' literature is just a background Other. The primary Other, the foregrounded Other, especially for those educated in the European intellectual tradition, has for long been the white European Other of Murphy's article.

In one aspect Murphy's article is an attempt to explain the condition of American poets and their small readership, what he calls the 'marginality of poetry in American culture'. He sees literary journals, the popular press and publishers as being to blame for privileging poets from 'Communist' countries, although I can think of only one poet from China who has received anything like the attention those from European Communist countries (such as Joseph Brodsky, Czeslaw Milosz

---

[7] Appiah 147.

[8] 'Pat Parker: Feminism in Postmodernity', in Anthony Easthope and John O. Thompson (eds), *Contemporary Poetry Meets Modern Theory* (University of Toronto Press, 1991) 129.

and Zbigniew Herbert – respectively Russian, Czech and Polish) used to receive. In short, Murphy claims it is axiomatically true that 'America is still living off its cold war dreams and the Manichaeism of east versus west, an image it shores up by exploiting the work of dissident writers', that 'the conservative projects [suffer] as an externality', or as he puts it 'the history of suffering is *their* history'. Murphy is correct in identifying America's need for an Other, and now that the only Communist state remaining that it seems to recognise as such – China mislaid again – is Cuba, the United States will have to find another Other, another demon; Iraq, Libya, Iran, Islamic fundamentalism might be substitutes; just as the African American and the excluded un-American Asian have operated as internal Others in recent American history, and as the Mexican immigrant is now. The spectre of un-American fanaticism will replace un-American totalitarianism. This will mean reverting to a weapon long since abandoned. Régis Debray, writing a decade ago when Communism was still alive if not well, stated:

In the arsenal of our 'political sciences' *totalitarianism* plays the same roles as *fanaticism* during the Enlightenment, or *totemism* in primitive ethnology: it is an alibi for ignorance and conspiracy. It permits the maintenance of constellations grouped together as exterior to the natural order, like a deviance or disorder which has no connection with our sane morality.[9]

Murphy is also probably right about the foregrounding and exploitation of poets, and their representation of suffering under the 'yoke' of Communism, being necessary to the construction of that undesirable Other. 'They are savages, we are civilised; they are sick, we are normal; they are fanatics, we are tolerant people; they are totalitarian, we are democratic. They are dangerous, we are harmless'.[10]

But the construction of the suffering Other which justifies our own social organisation and politics has it seems to be an

---

[9] Régis Debray, *Critique de la raison politique: ou l'inconscient religieux* (Paris: Gallimard, Collection Tel, 1981) 22.
[10] *Ibid.*

Other in whose place we could imagine ourselves. In other words, it has to be a white and preferably God-fearing Other. For where in the lists of Communist poets are the Chinese 'dissidents' such as Bei Dao, Duoduo, Gu Cheng, Mang Ke and the dozens of younger poets who have been arrested in China since Tiananmen Square in 1989 and noticed only by organisations like Amnesty and PEN's Writers in Prison Committee? For that matter where are the dissident Arab poets? The picture presumably would not be so dualistically neat if the mirror reflected back a person of colour. Western 'concern' over human rights abuses in China and elsewhere in the Third World has never equalled the zeal displayed over the lack of human rights in Eastern Europe during the Cold War; increasingly the expansion of capitalist markets and opportunities, often masked by such code words as 'prosperity', have displaced professed anxieties over the absence of democratic rights. It took President Clinton, however, finally to sever the linkage between human rights and capitalist trade, when he declared China's enjoyment of Most Favoured Nation status with the United States was no longer conditional on a respect for basic human rights.

That China's people are still living under a system of control at least equal to that obtaining in the Eastern Europe of the Cold War period is now being almost forgotten, not least in academic circles where the failure of China's 'socialist experiment' is viewed by many radical scholars as an embarassment. Recently, I attended a workshop organised by the journal *Critical Inquiry* at which Jacques Derrida spoke about his recent book *Spectres de Marx* (Paris: Galilée, 1993). One of the questioners enounced the standard litany of post-Communism, the death of Marxism, the end of the Soviet Union, the fall of the Wall; these were now ghosts which haunted us and whose passing we were apparently meant to 'mourn'. Of course, these particular mourners could only regret the failure of externally imagined utopias, not the lived experience of Communist régimes. China as usual was not mentioned. Perhaps China is not yet a ghost? Perhaps mourners of the Other's Marxist experiments see China as the living dead?

Now, to turn to the Kwame Appiah article, one of the enlightening points Appiah makes is that the second generation, or new wave, of modern African writers such as the Francophone Yambo Ouologuem and his novel *Le Devoir de violence* (translated as *Bound to Violence*) refuted or challenged the post-colonial realist novel, the originary 'African novel', exemplified by Chinua Achebe's *Things Fall Apart*. Ouologuem comes out against the realist novel, identifying it, indeed stigmatising it, as part of a project of nationalist legitimation, because the nationalism it sought to naturalise had by the end of the 1960s plainly failed. The national bourgeoisie's enthusiasm for nativism was, Appiah suggests, rationalisation of their urge to keep other national bourgeoisies and the industrialised nations and former colonial powers out of their way. Therefore the realist novel, the conventions of realism, are rejected whilst *post*-realism is promoted. That the author assaults the conventions of realism much of the time, and is thus anti-realist in his post-realism, means he can legitimately borrow the techniques of modernism, which are also the techniques of post-modernism; modernist 'business as usual, only *more* so'.[11]

But since this is a national bourgeoisie that is under attack, two things are quite plain. The 'nation' is of great importance, but so is capitalism. The problem of the appropriate aesthetic stems from the dual necessity to promote both nation-building ideology and an ethos protective of capitalism. What 'post-colonial' African societies are left with in cultural terms is the old, inherited 'mandarin culture' of the imperial era's high bourgeois epoch. Already in the 'developed' world this culture had been called into question by the glaring disjuncture between the old bourgeois position it espoused and the more vigorous capitalism of the commodity as yet incapable of generating its own ideology. If in advanced capitalist societies

[11] Terry Eagleton, *The Ideology of the Aesthetic* (Oxford: Blackwell, 1990) 381.

this high bourgeois aesthetic remains indispensable, as Eagleton writes, 'because the subject as unique, autonomous, self-identical and self-determining remains a political and ideological requirement of the system', how much more so in 'post-colonial' Africa where the subjecthood of nationhood also needed to be sustained and promoted.[12]

Is there any common ground between the African writer's concerns and those of the contemporary Chinese writer? Looking for institutional similarities between African nations and China will prove unfruitful, since China experienced a different form of colonial domination, marked not least by a multi-national dimension. Thus Madhava Prasad's insistence on the preservation of the Third World model – in the face of arguments for the particularism of national literatures, as for instance that strongly made by Aijaz Ahmad – leads him to claim that the 'greater visibility of the national frame of reference in Third World literature may be a function primarily of the historical conditions under which these nations came into being.'[13] This argument may be applicable to some 'nation-states' in what is understood by the 'Third World', but is not applicable without much modification to China's case. Nevertheless, Chinese and African poets find themselves otherised into the same '(Third) World literature' basket by the Euro-American literary metropolis, and by the same late capitalist book-marketing business.

African writers anxious to escape what they perceive as neo-colonialist realism that bolsters up the emergent national bourgeoisie may have championed the notion of a wider Africa, a supranationalism. In China, while during the Maoist era revolutionary romanticism was widely produced and consumed, the dominant literary mode for much of the century has been some form of realism. But for those Chinese writers who rejected the dominant realist mode of the literary estab-

---

[12] *Ibid.* 374-5.
[13] Madhava Prasad, 'A Theory of Third World Literature', *Social Text* 31/2, 78. See Aijaz Ahmad's landmark book, *In Theory: Classes, Nations, Literatures* (London: Verso, 1992).

lishment, the post-realists (and here at least 'post' certainly does
not mean 'more so' but 'less so'), there was no 'wider China'
to look to on the African model. They were already *in* the
wider China, 90 per cent dominated by the Han Chinese.
Despite efforts, largely by the Sinological academy outside
China, to construct what some have called a 'Commonwealth'
of Chinese writing (what others have called *Huawen wenxue*,
literature written in Chinese and by Chinese without regard
to territorial context, as opposed to literature which emanates
from China, *Zhongguo wenxue*), which would include con-
tinental China and Taiwan, Hong Kong, South-East Asia, the
diaspora of overseas Chinese 'settlements' and exiled individuals, most writers who come from mainland China have
rejected such a pan-Chinese notion. Indeed, trends in recent
years seem to indicate that Chinese writing may start to
fragment along the lines of the country's linguistically,
geographically distinct and increasingly economically
autonomous regions. Several contemporary Chinese writers
have expressed 'fears' at the prospect of mutually unintelligible
written Chinese literatures developing as the economic power
of dialect regions, such as Shanghai, Fujian and Guangdong,
increase.

In practice, the alternative routes out of the establishment
cultural ghetto in the Chinese context have been either to
become totally 'universalist' in the rejection of the dominant
mode of the perceived oppressor (previously and still to an
extent the Chinese cultural bureaucracy, but increasingly the
market place), or to get drawn into some vague search for an
originary ethnicity, to be found in literally peripheral folk
culture: a course that several fiction writers, poets and painters
have pursued. The universalist option, of course, may evoke
a lack of patriotism, a succumbing to the seduction of the
bourgeois West and Western civilization's cultural perceptions, and also perhaps a post-colonial return to the modernism
of the semi-colonial pre-revolutionary past. If being post-
realist meant taking on the mantle of modernism and postmodernism which could be seen as innately Western, then,

the post-Mao generation seemed to say, so be it. After all, the dominant 'ism' of the May Fourth movement, 'critical realism', was itself an import from the West, as were the influential political ideas of Social Darwinism and Marxism. The Other's ideological clothing had been exploited without hesitation by their revolutionary forebears. Neither were non-realist or modernist literary modes new to post-Mao China. Although there seems to have been some reluctance to revise modern Chinese literary history, Western and Chinese critics have now begun to recognise the existence and importance of non-realist 'isms' in the 1930s. This is true even of the anti-realist or irrealist poets of the 1970s and 1980s, who were long loath to acknowledge that they may be part of a longer tradition of counter-cultural production. Their reluctance may be explained by the imperatives of being modern: 'modernity is the always I-here-now'.[14]

There is, then, no wider China, no greater space, for Chinese writers to entertain, as there is for writers in Africa, should they still want it. The 'Chinese Commonwealth' – what an ideologically laden term – has been rejected by most. As for the notion of 'Third World', I have yet to hear of a contemporary Chinese cultural producer who accepts the concept in relation to the cultural sphere.

Whether or not we accept arguments about both African and Chinese writers being 'unwittingly' a part of a Third World literature, one striking similarity between the new wave African writer and the Chinese post-realist writer is the pessimistic nature of their writing. And without doubt post-realist writing in China does challenge the optimistic, nationalist and rationalist literary mode dominant from the 1920s to the 1960s, and the reinvented but equally stultifying realist mode unimaginatively redeployed in the 1970s and 1980s. Similarly, just as Appiah's thesis suggests there is no longer an *echt* African culture, there is likewise no *echt* Chinese culture awaiting recuperation – despite the efforts of the roots-

[14] Henri Meschonnic, *Critique du rythme. Anthropologie historique du langage* (Lagrasse: Verdier, 1982) 27.

seeking writers of the mid-1980s to delve into and reinvent the histories of the periphery. The Westernism of the twentieth-century intellectual tradition and its Maoist mutations were not by and large met by a nativist backlash (although there have been such tendencies), but rather by an even closer association with the culture of the Other; and the Other for the post-Cultural Revolution generation of new writers, as it was for those discontented with the realism of the 1930s, was the Western modernist tradition. In structuralist terms, the metaphoric polarity of the modernist mode was privileged over the metonymic of the realist mode, which by the 1970s was associated with all things objectionable in China's modern culture. This is why I contend there is no *echt* Chinese culture waiting to be saved or revived; which is not the same thing as saying that culture in China and in Chinese is not being reinvigorated; nor is it to say that the recent turn away from the realist mode has disempowered it for good. In recent years, there has been among writers, artists and intellectuals, especially those stranded abroad, a reinforced awareness of the sterile binarism of the Self and the Other. And their physical presence in the midst of China's Other induces a propulsion if not back towards the Self of the Chinese state at least towards a reassessment of Self; an oxymoronic, pessimistic aspiring for a rejuvenated China, a new Self, as opposed to the rejected old Self.

Metropolitan Chinese ideological nationalism is of interest here. The West and Japan are at once explored, studied, read, interpreted, imitated, admired and yet also mocked, criticised, resented by Marxist, *marxisant* and non-Marxist alike. But such difference is minimised when the Chinese Self is confronted by the other Others, the Arab world, Africa, the rest of Asia. Again for example, hybrid Hong Kong is largely, ignobly ignored. Contemplation of those Others can drive the intellectual and cultural Chinese Self, the post-realist Chinese writers' Self, back into the arms of the hierarchically more 'respectable' Other, the 'Foreign Self', *the* Other.

Chinese writers, like African writers, are now more than

ever dependent on and legitimated by the European-American publisher and consumer. While the products of the suffering Other are what Murphy sees as the consumable commodity in East European poetry, what Western consumers of modern Chinese culture are seeking to purchase is still the 'exoticised Other'. Painters and sculptors in particular, if their products are to be sold, learn to exploit the 'mystery of the Orient' cliché to construct their 'exotic' product; even the most experimental painters rely on a sentimentalised and mythic past, if only at the level of exploiting traditional Chinese materials. Exoticism, however, can be conjured even out of the most recent past. In the 1990s the Chinese 'exotic' may be found in the exploitation of the cult of Mao, both in mass-manufactured items and in oil paintings intended for the international market.

The depiction of the West's Other by the East European Communist era poet, according to Murphy, relied on the West's 'Mythology of our freedom, unbounded and unmediated', and our mythology 'depends precisely on this other world, on what happens over there'.[15] But can that really be the case for non-White poetry, the other Others' poetry? Orientalism is still deeply entrenched in the Western bourgeois aesthetic; the academy is still largely its authority.

Murphy casts doubt on another part of the myth, that which claims that there is, or was, a real popular audience for poetry in the East (which for Murphy is Eastern Europe, 'America's Other'). In fact, Murphy denies the existence of a popular audience in the East, and in evidence recounts the Polish poet Zbigniew Herbert's answer to the question: 'Are you aware of the fact that in Poland you practically don't exist?' The reply was reportedly: 'I know, but I cannot help it.'[16]

Murphy does indeed raise an interesting point about the consumption of poetry, and in the late capitalist era its validity is approaching global proportions. But what does Murphy

[15] Murphy 162.
[16] *Ibid.* 166.

understand by 'popular audience'? If he is referring to the man on the Clapham omnibus, then I don't think such a man generally reads much poetry any more, and he probably gets his lyrics through a Walkman attached to his ears. But if we are talking about the woman on the Beijing bicycle of a decade ago, she might have been reciting a few lines of contemporary poetry to herself. Today, however, she too might well be listening to her Walkman. However, I do know from my own acquaintance with several members of the Russian and East European urban élite that, to this day, many people can and do recite a poem by Mandelshtam and tell you what they think of Brodsky.

But Murphy's aim is to explain why Americans who read poetry read the Other's contemporary poetry and not their own. Perhaps this could be because American readers want to read poetry that they think 'means' something, that matters, that relates to lived experience. To find such poetry in the United States one generally has to turn to the works of the internal Other; to the lyrics, for example, of African Americans or Asian Americans, or of other marginalised groups such as gays.

In the China of the late 1970s, after the fall of the Gang of Four, the stature of poetry was almost that of a new and popular religion, read and quoted and recited the length and breadth of the country, at least in its cities. Poets like Bei Dao had immense audiences and readerships – for that was the era of the Chinese *samizdat* magazine, the wallposter and the cassette recorder with some Chinese poetry consumers in China listening to Bei Dao rather than reading him. It was a politically motivated audience. But that audience, for various reasons, no longer listens so intently; mainly because of the commodification of culture and the competition from newly available products. In the post-Mao 1970s, given the alternatives of Maoist rhetoric and underground poetry, the deprived would-be consumers chose the poetry. Given the choice between the underground poetry, which is now above ground, and Taiwan and Hong Kong pop music on a portable stereo with all the promise of the better, more materialistically satisfying lifestyle it symbolised, many preferred the Walkman. Nevertheless, there is still a considerable poetry-reading public and even a sense of regret on the part of the younger urban generation that they missed the 'decade of poetry'.[17] This grand political strategy of Deng Xiaoping and his allies will ultimately fail. It is failing because of the demand for a consumerist 'good life' that in the long term, assuming current capitalist initiatives are continued, is incapable of being globally satisfied. Even if the 400 million Chinese along the country's coast and in the major cities were contented consumers, that would still leave a billion people lingering on the margins of poverty. The discontent may for the moment not be expressed in the recitation of poetry, but it may be beginning to find a voice in the lyrics of popular culture. The technology of the Walkman is not restricted to entertainment songs, as demonstrated in Chapter 6 of this book.

The readership for those post-realist poets of the 1970s and 1980s, it is true, is no longer entirely the same. Internal clampdowns and enforced exile make the West the poet's main audience. But then, of course, the arrival of the modern Chinese poet on the world stage has coincided with the metanarrative which tells us that Communism is finished. What America and the West in general need now is another bogeyman. In any case, if Murphy's general thesis is correct, poets of colour could never be 'our' suffering Other. But then maybe *they* don't want to be *our* Other. Appiah in the concluding remarks to his article reminds us of Sara Suleri's frustration and weariness, recounted in *Meatless Days*, of being treated as an 'Otherness machine'.[18]

If I read Appiah correctly, running through his critique is a concern with affording space to the hybrid and consequently an intent to reveal the falseness of the idea of the authentic. These concerns are doubtless a product of the writer's own

---

[17] D.J. Hatfield, recently returned from a research trip to China, informed me that copies of poems by Bei Dao were still highly valued by students in various disciplines from economics to foreign languages.

[18] Appiah 157.

subjectivity, for while Kwame Appiah may be seen as a classic
colonial subject, he is also a hybrid subject. His mother's father
was the British statesman Sir Stafford Cripps (1889-1952), one
of a long line of liberal and independent-minded lawyers and
politicians. Appiah's father was not only an internationally
renowned lawyer and statesman, he was also the leader of his
matriclan, or *abusua*, in Ghana, and a devout Wesleyan Metho-
dist Christian; in an epilogue to his book Appiah recounts his
struggle to have his father buried in accordance with his wishes
in contravention of Asante custom.[19] Anthony Kwame Appiah
himself was educated at Cambridge University.[20] He, then,
received a priviliged upbringing perhaps, but certainly a
diverse one, and hybridity for Appiah is a lived experience as
it was for numerous former British colonial subjects.

One of the more controversial theoretical pieces of writing
on hybridity is undoubtedly that of another former British
colonial subject, Homi Bhabha. The article is 'Signs Taken for
Wonders'.[21] Attempting to describe the conditions of colonial
discourse, Bhabha analyses hybridity in a specific historical and
geographical context, that of British colonial India. Robert
Young, in a critical reading of Bhabha, claims that his attempts
to 'describe the condition of colonial discourse – 'Mimicry is
. . . ', 'Hybridity is . . . ' – seem always offered as static
concepts'.[22] Young thinks that such descriptions also tend to
result in a 'timeless characterization' of the 'concept in
question'.[23] The conclusion to be drawn, and seemingly with
good reason, from Young's critique is that hybridity is, or
perhaps hybridities are, not 'static' or timeless, but rather
dynamic and historically specific. While inclined to agree with
Young, I shall now suggest some apparent contradictions, for

[19] *Ibid.* 181-92.

[20] *Ibid.* 181.

[21] Homi Bhabha, 'Signs Taken for Wonders: Questions of Ambivalence and
Authority under a Tree Outside Delhi, May 1817', *Critical Inquiry* (Autumn 1985)
144-65.

[22] Robert Young, *White Mythologies* (New York: Routledge, 1991) 146.

[23] *Ibid.*

Bhabha's description of the effect of English colonial power seems to me legitimately universalist in its capacity to describe, in a substantially different context and period, the effect of the power of contemporary China's dominant structures of power, and the reception and subversion of regnant power by popular culture. We have to imagine for this purpose Chinese official power over the last three or four decades as being dynamic rather than static, and as itself already being a hybrid form of power, a conflation, or rather a product, of Marxist-Leninist and Chinese imperial-Confucian ideologies; a kind of imagining none too difficult for many who have lived under that authority. A type of power emerges which relies on old and new patriotisms, indigenous, traditional and Western nationalisms. It has been a power that has battled with the contradiction of the cultural 'contamination' implicit in the process of modernisation. But it has only been during the last few years that the pursuit of consumerism as a means of modernisation has been confronted by the seemingly contradictory desire to retain centralised state/party power over cultural consumption. Thus we have an already hybrid official power itself facilitating the possibilities for cultural hybridisation, and simultaneously enabling the production of a subversive potential. Bhabha's seemingly 'static' and 'timeless' descriptions here become pertinent. He is describing colonial power (the British in India), while we are dealing with an autonomous authoritarian power of a once semi-colonised state (which nevertheless has its own imperialistic tendencies). Yet if we follow Bhabha in seeing the effect of such dominant power as the '*production* of hybridization . . . then an important change of perspective occurs'. Indeed, such a change in perspective gives insight into the self-wounding and ultimately self-destructive nature of such power:

It reveals the ambivalence at the source of traditional discourses on authority and enables a form of subversion, founded on that uncertainty, that turns the discursive conditions of dominance into the grounds of intervention. It is traditional academic wisdom that the presence of authority is properly established through the non-existence of private judgment and the exclusion of reasons, in conflict with the authoritative reason.

The 'non-existence of private judgment and the exclusion of reasons, in conflict with authoritative reason' has been the basis of the practice of domination in China under Communism, the republic and the dynasties. Bhabha asks, referring to Steven Lukes's argument, if 'the acceptance of authority excludes any evaluation of the content of an utterance', and if the source of authority

disavows both conflicting reasons and personal judgment, then can the 'signs' or 'marks' of authority be anything more than 'empty' presences of strategic devices? Need they be any the less effective because of that? Not less effective but effective in a different form, would be the answer.[24]

Going on to consider what he describes as Tom Nairn's revelation of 'ambivalence between the symbols of English imperialism', Bhabha concludes that the 'production of hybridity . . . no longer simply commands authority. It gives rise to a series of questions of authority'.[25]

In the contemporary Chinese context, I should like to suggest there are manifestations of hybridity. There is, of course, the already hybrid, dominant discourse of power exercised by the party-state, official society. Then there is the hybridity of the reaction of the dominated that emerges in the appropriation and redeployment of 'signs' of Chinese state and party power – the red flag, the Great Wall, the red kerchief of the Cultural Revolution Red Guard and Young Pioneer, the Forbidden City, the sinicised once-Western trumpet used by pop musician Cui Jian, the image of Chairman Mao. Chairman Mao now seems as universal a signifier as Madonna, but with multiple semiotic readings. Pasted to a mainland Chinese bus driver's window or hanging from a cab driver's rear-view mirror, Mao's picture is a talisman to protect against misfortune; held up by students at a pop concert it is a symbolic icon,

[24] Bhabha 155.
[25] *Ibid.*

perhaps not even ironically deployed, reminding the authorities of forsaken ideals. Both dynamic and culturally specific, we may perceive in such redeployment an estrangement of the familiar symbols of Chinese ' "national" authority'; and in the appropriation of such symbols the dominated, unofficial society's 'sign of its difference'.

A serious recognition, and attempt to critique the nature, of this type of hybridity is a more appropriate response than a simplistic disavowal of electronic popular cultural forms in contemporary China because of their 'Westernness' or foreignness, or their naïveté, whether that disavowal comes from Chinese authorities or out of the élite discourse of the cultural imperialism of the Western academy.

'[I]t is not simply the content of disavowed knowledges' of a Maoist utopianism coupled with a chauvinistic nationalism —only further emaciated and emptied through recuperation and reiteration in official popular songs, and foregrounded by the strategy of redeployment that has emerged in official popular culture – which returns to be acknowledged by counter-authorities. What is also 'irremediably estranging in the presence of the hybrid . . . is that the difference of cultures can no longer be identified or evaluated as objects of epistemological or moral contemplation: they are not simply *there* to be seen or appropriated.'[26]

In the Chinese context, questions of authenticity and cultural hybridity have haunted modern China's culture(s) for a century at least. Chinese 'new poetry', a vernacular poetry which twice, in the 1920s and 1930s and again in the 1970s and 1980s, mimicked extensively modern European poetry before settling into a 'stable' hybridity, has been received unsympathetically by Chinese traditionalist and Western Sinologist alike. And yet the modern Communist orthodoxy, sometimes with great reluctance – Mao was no lover of 'new poetry' – has appropriated and sought to use this poetry as much as any other form, regardless of its 'foreignness'. As with

---

[26] *Ibid.* 156.

'new poetry', so with the pop song; as with the *fin-de-siècle* reformism, so with capitalist-nationalism; as with Maoist Marxism-Leninism, so with Dengist authoritarian consumerist capitalism. There has, however, always been more anxiety over reproducing the modern poem than over reproducing television sets or bicycles, which are perhaps more concrete forms of the legacy of foreign imperialist dominance, of cultural imperialism, of the brutal descent of modernity. However, I should emphasise that it is not my intention to romanticise pre-consumerist or pre-modern Chinese culture, no more than I wish to represent popular culture as somehow less worthy of serious attention than 'high cultural' forms. In the age of modernity, the cultural–aesthetic sphere has been a space where societies in the process of modernisation have attempted to protect and assert nativist cultural traditions, and yet the pre-modern, and thus seemingly nativist and authentic, traditional culture, literature, folk art, cuisine, the ways and arts of life, have not simply been protected as sacred, but rather frequently pressed into service as part of the nationalistic solvent for the project of modernisation. As the French social theorist Alain Touraine remarks:

> Germany and Italy, like Japan, and after them numerous other countries, have associated modernisation with the safeguarding or restoration of a national culture, for, faced with a modernity identified with British commerce or the French language, how could a nation state do otherwise, in the defence of its independence, than to mobilise non-modern resources, be they cultural, social or economic?[27]

Touraine sees this trend as having continued until the modernisation of the Islamic states, where 'the theme of national cultural renaissance has come into conflict with traditionalism as much as with liberal modernity.'[28] In China over the last century the regnant authority, Communist or otherwise, which has taken charge of the patriotic project of national salvation, deeply enmeshed in the project of modernisation,

---

[27] Alain Touraine, *Critique de la modernité* (Paris: Fayard, 1992) 161-2.
[28] *Ibid.* 162.

has wavered over this very problem of safeguarding the national culture. The spectre of non-Chinese theory and praxis hovers over modern China, and the result of the confrontation with Western capitalist imperialism and its counter-ideology is to be found in Chinese hybridity, a hybridity evidenced not only in China's cultural and political practices, but also in the presence of the Other here 'at home': the Chinese American Other in the USA. Similarly, whether it is the Arab or African in France, or the Muslim or Chinese in Britain, it is a presence which contests, challenges, weakens and ultimately invalidates the authority and legitimacy of dominant monolithic, national cultures; this is a process happening now in America, it is a process understood and viciously resisted by authorities in France. 'Hybridity intervenes in the exercise of authority not merely to indicate the impossibility of its identity but to represent the unpredictability of its presence', Bhabha writes.[29] Thus, for example, as Rey Chow has claimed, Hong Kong's hybridity indicates the 'impossibility' of China's identity.[30] Similarly, the multi-ethnic pop culture of the Toulousain Occitan region hybridised by contemporary post-colonial culture represents the 'unpredictability of its presence'.[31]

Young reads Bhabha's 'hybridisation' as 'static' and 'timeless'. Yet perhaps in its application to the practices of domination and power embedded in modernity, a wider, universal interpretive value can be afforded to Bhabha's theorising. Both dominative and subversive practices which the oppressed have to negotiate are still very much of our time. It can surely be claimed of much contemporary Chinese cultural production, whether on the mainland or in Hong Kong, that the appropriation of both present and past national 'official' culture into a 'foreign' process of mediation is a 'display of hybridity', a 'peculiar replication' which deeply disturbs Chinese regnant

[29] Bhabha 156-7.

[30] Chow 151-71.

[31] Bhabha 157. The example of hybridisation in the context of southern French, Occitan culture is discussed at greater length in Chapter 8.

authority. Yet it is doubtful whether one could claim in the case of Chinese hybrid production that it 'terrorizes authority with the *ruse* of recognition, its mimicry, its mockery'.[32]

'Hybridity' is not necessarily chic, despite fashionable posturing which, as Chow has noted, equates post-colonial with post-modern and thus somehow renders the post-colonial acceptable; 'hybridity' necessarily always bears the imprint of cultural dominance.[33] I would certainly also agree with her that 'advocates of postmodern hybridity . . . typically obliterate significant portions of the reality of a colonised culture' and that the seductiveness and deceipt in such a discourse do indeed lie in its 'invitation to join the power of global capitalism by flattening out past injustices'.[34] But 'hybridity' is today a fact of social and material reality for most of the world, and the dominance and cultural imperialism inherent in it do not prevent the subversive – which may be better described as diversive, since subversion would be brought about by diverging from the dominant discourse – and progressive from being produced out of, and through it.

At a recent international writers' forum focused on the Middle East which tackled questions of identity and of 'authenticity in borrowed Western form' and language, Edward Said spoke of accepting 'the reality of hybridity', given that now 'we are all mongrels'.

Earlier in Appiah's essay on 'The Postcolonial and the Postmodern', there is an illustration of a wooden Yoruba sculpture entitled *Man with a Bicycle*, which depicts just that – a man on a bicycle. The sculpture, Appiah notes, is 'produced by someone who does not care that the bicycle is the white man's invention'. He continues: 'It is not there . . . to be the Other to the Yoruba Self . . . it is there because it will take us further than our feet will take us; it is there because machines are now as African as novelists.'[35] And in China the poets and

---

[32] Bhabha 157.
[33] Chow 163.
[34] *Ibid.* 157.
[35] Appiah 157.

pop singers are as Chinese as the now ubiquitous bicycle. However, that stage was reached some time ago. It is in the realm of ideology that the arguments have yet to convince. Nowadays the question is one of regional identity at one extreme and of globalised, unified culture at the other, both co-existing in the same cultural context. The wooden sculpture of the bicycle has been around for some time; it will surely not be long before we see scrap metal installations made of redundant Chinese-made satellite dishes. And if the techniques of *bricolage* are available to the late twentieth-century critic and theorist, would it be for some misguided idea of political purity, or some notion of cultural authenticity, that those techniques would be denied to practitioners outside the Western academy and beyond the West?

2

THE BARRIERS OF ROUTINE AND HABIT: POETRY, PATRIOTISM, IDEOLOGY

'The first duty of a poet is not to be fooled.'

—Henri Meschonnic[1]

'But, then, patriotism is not for those who represent wealth and power. It is good enough for the people.'

—Emma Goldman[2]

'Wherever submission is demanded, the outmoded flatulence of ideology makes its way, from the *Arbeit macht frei* of the death camps to the pronouncements of Henry Ford and Mao Zedong.'

—Raoul Vaneigem[3]

'I'm not saying I will, but I could go on for hours escorting the reader . . . back and forth across the Paris-Chinese border.'

—J.D. Salinger[4]

In the Salinger story quoted above, the schoolboy fictional hero, a white child captured, mutilated and then adopted by Chinese bandits, grows up horribly deformed, himself becomes a master bandit and is soon 'regularly crossing the Chinese border into Paris, France'.[5] In this chapter, as elsewhere in this book, I too shall be escorting the reader back

---

[1] 'Le Premier devoir poétique est de ne pas être dupe.' *La rime et la vie* (Lagrasse: Verdier, 1989) 178.

[2] *Anarchism and Other Essays* (New York: Dover; London: Constable, 1969) 130.

[3] *Traité de savoir-vivre à l'usage des jeunes générations* (Paris: Gallimard, Collection Folio/Actuel, 1967, 1992) 71.

[4] J.D. Salinger, 'The Laughing Man' in *For Esmé – With Love and Squalor and Other Stories* (Harmondsworth: Penguin, 1986; published in the USA as *Nine Stories*) 50.

and forth across such borders in a spirit of wilful and necessary transgression.

The main focus of this chapter is the nexus between the lyric and ideology. In particular, I discuss in some detail the following questions: the often tortuous relationship that the modern poet has maintained with nationalism and patriotic sentiment; the confusion of socialism and nationalism; and the resultant tendency to regard first the socialist and anti-capitalist project and, more recently, the 'collapse' of socialism and the advance of capitalism as a renewal and reorientation of the project of national salvation or reconstruction. I am thinking here of the recent rise of a new kind of nationalist sentiment in China which has been revealed in a diverse range of cultural production, but which was most systematically laid out in one particular cultural text that had an enormous political impact in China in the late 1980s, demonstrating a re-emergence in a seemingly new guise of the nationalist mentality amongst intellectuals. I refer to the 1988 television documentary mini-series *River Elegy* written by Su Xiaokang and Wang Luxiang. Its agenda amounts to a demand for more rapid capitalist modernisation. Drawing an analogy between the still considerable force of feudal civilisation and the dimensions and power of the Yellow River, the series challenges established Chinese mentalities and ideologies. In particular, the narrative is critical of the kind of nationalism and patriotism that is closed to the outside world and to novelty – the innovations of the Han dynasty (206 BC–AD 220) and Tang dynasty (AD 618-907) openness are praised – but the discourse of the narrative recovers and reinvents the same kind of patriotic sentiment on which the mentalities it claims to critique also relied. Patriotism is invoked to incite the viewers to bolster economic and political reform and to shame them into action.

The programme's verbal and visual narrative is staunchly anti-feudal, anti-Confucian and strongly in favour of a Fordist,

---

[5] *Ibid.* 49.

market capitalist democracy. A central trope of the text maintains that the feudal age has lasted as long as the floods of the Yellow River, and concludes that 'China's sorrow' nowadays lies in not having developed a capitalist economy. The authors of this text are caught up in, or at least are propagating, the ideology which persists in claiming that economic 'reform' inevitably leads to democracy, understood as some form of Utopia. In countering the discourse of the traditional, the feudal, the 'official' China, *River Elegy* nevertheless tends to establish an oppositionist discourse which itself is ultimately monologic and closed.[6]

In Chapter 6 of this book, I look in greater detail at the impact of television, specifically of music television and foreign satellite television on contemporary Chinese society. But in this chapter I shall focus on the relations between modern poetry and ideology since the end of the nineteenth century to the approaching end of the twentieth.

What I mean by modern poetry is that which has complemented, conveyed or critiqued modernity as a phenomenon of the age of industrialism, the era of colonialism and neo-colonialism, the age of high capitalism, the century of Fascism, Communism, state capitalism and modern manifestations of nationalism implicated in all of the latter. By ideology I do not mean to invoke the popular sense of ideology as that which is the 'visible framework of a collective practice, identified with liberal-democratic discourse for some, with Leninist or Stalinist (indeed Maoist or Trotskyist) discourse for others, or even with fascist discourse . . . *in the very form in which they present themselves*', which imputes to the term 'almost the contrary of what it originally meant'. Rather, I refer to 'the logic of dominant ideas, removed from the knowledge of social actors

---

[6] In the West, and especially in the United States, the myth persists that 'the collapse of the Soviet bloc "proves" the failure of the collectivist, as opposed to the liberal capitalist, model', while 'all it really proves is the failure of the police state'. Louis Menand, 'Being an American: How the United States is Becoming Less, Not More Diverse', review of Christopher Ricks and William L. Vance (eds), *The Faber Book of America* (London: Faber and Faber, 1992) in *The Times Literary Supplement* 3 October 1992, p. 3.

and only revealing itself through interpretation, through the critique of utterances and their manifest connections'.[7] In other words, this is ideology as a body of received and accepted ideas, which inform and serve political projects and ambitions and the conduct of everyday lives. In advanced capitalist societies the prevalent legitimating ideology has tended to be more subtle, or invisible, as Claude Lefort describes it, 'not because it actually is, but because it seems to be organized in such a way as to blur the oppositions characteristic of the previous ideology.'[8]

There are many critics and scholars today who doubt the capacity of the pre-post-modern notion of ideology adequately to explain and account for the phenomena of 'post-modern' society. I can only agree with them. Yet the concept of ideology ought not to be abandoned because it seems outmoded, but rather re-theorised. While 'Marx could conceive of ideology only with regard to "bourgeois" ideology . . . it is incumbent upon us to recognize it in other forms and, moreover, to grasp the principle of its transformation.'[9] That Marxian conceptions of ideology and Marxist analyses of society need supplementing is beyond question. Such rethinking has been undertaken by theorists like Claude Lefort and Guy Debord, 'the Marx of consumerism'.[10]

While Gramsci imagined a gradualist scheme of undermining the political dominance of the regnant powers in society by gaining cultural and intellectual hegemony, Debord clearly illustrated how such a concept itself becomes part of the spectacular illusion, and is recuperated into the image of false optimism produced by consumer capitalism.

We cannot underestimate the importance and potency of

---

[7] Claude Lefort, *The Political Forms of Modern Society: Bureaucracy, Democracy, Totalitarianism*, ed. and intro. John B. Thompson (Cambridge, MA: MIT Press, 1986) 183.

[8] *Ibid.* 181.

[9] *Ibid.* 183-4.

[10] Carlo Freccero, 'Considérations sur le suicide de Guy Debord', *Libération* 6 December 1994, pp. 34-5.

ideology as a means of dissimulation, as a means of creating in individuals the kind of consciousness that can readily accept both the logic of television advertising (its production of desire for objects of which we have no need) and the inevitability of genocide and other war crimes, from Bosnia to Rwanda. However, it is clear that the notion of ideology as traditionally conceived is too rigid. This is particularly so after a century in which the supposedly positive ideologies of Marxism-Leninism and liberal democracy have so patently failed the majority of humanity, and so have failed us all. But the ideals of these ideologies, together with the falseness of those designed to make us blindly accept them, leave their traces in the thoughts and practices of those who experienced them, are absorbed into 'common sense', lead to the development of new social myths, become part of the web of meanings through which people communicate and live their lives. This complex of beliefs, thoughts, practices and symbols may be called the social or collective imaginary. In this century collective imaginaries have been challenged and contorted with increasing rapidity. Ordinary people are induced to re-negotiate the beliefs and re-encode the symbols they live by on an almost daily basis. Desires for stability and fixity are inevitably produced by this destabilising and alienating process, and thus the appeal of ideologies of fundamentalism and nationalism increases both in advanced capitalist societies and in those which have no possibility of ever attaining the 'enjoyment' of capitalist modernity's accelerating levels of consumption.

What, then, of the Chinese collective imaginary of the last half century and the ideologies that have underpinned it, and which in a more or less nuanced form has therefore also been the imaginary, the consciousness of the Chinese 'patriotic poet'? This imaginary, which would include Maoism at its most altruistic, has been dominated by a nationalist ideology –nationalist in the sense of anti-imperialist, but also in the sense of propagating a nostalgia for a lost greatness, coupled with a desire to re-establish that greatness. In its anti-imperialist, official orthodox manifestation, this ideology has paradoxically espoused a form of hierarchical internationalism in which the Third World, the supposedly fraternal world of the Bandung conference, is pitted against the rest. But it has been an internationalism which has relied on the paternalistic dominance of China in struggles of liberation – a paternalism graphically attested to by the central position of Mao in the widely distributed photograph of the Chairman flanked by overjoyed representatives of colour from Third World countries depicted grinning with childlike wonder and excitement in the Great Helmsman's presence. This was also a convenience internationalism which served the nationalist ends of China's official ideology. This was the 'Third World' creed, of fraternity, cooperation and peaceful coexistence developed in tandem with the aggressive expansionism of China's militaristic central authority, which in the 1950s invaded and colonised Tibet and in the early 1960s waged war with China's Third World neighbour, India. Later, in the name of Third World solidarity China's government was able to side-step revolutionary politics and turn its back on left-wing movements which it had previously encouraged, the most flagrant example being the continuance of diplomatic relations with the Chilean junta after the coup in 1973. Indeed the embassy of the People's Republic of China literally closed its doors that year on leftist friends of China seeking refuge during the CIA-sponsored right-wing military coup against the democratically elected government of President Allende who had for many years headed the Chile – China friendship society; an index of the close ties between the Chilean left and China. Similarly, in the cultural sphere close relations had developed between China and the Chilean left. Chile's leading poet, Pablo Neruda, Nobel Prize-winner and former Chilean Communist Party presidential candidate, who had lived in Asia and was very sympathetic to China, had been eulogised twenty years before the coup in Chile by China's leading Communist poet, Ai Qing, at a moment when a differently cast framework of internationalism, constituted by the socialist nationalisms of the 1950s, was the Chinese Communist Party's dominant strategy:

ON A CHILEAN HEADLAND
For Pablo Neruda

Ai Qing

May the seafarers' goddess
protect your home

....

Pablo's house
is on a promontory
outside the window
is the vastness of the Pacific

an extraordinary house
built entirely of rocks
like a small fort
bent on imprisoning the warrior

When we enter
the seafarer's home
the floor is covered with seashells
as if the tide came during the night

A much tainted carved wooden goddess
stands beside the living room door
with the devotion of a maid

....

Are you a skipper?
Or are you one of the crew?
Are you an admiral of the fleet?
Or are you an ordinary seaman?
Have you returned from a victory?
Or have you fled homewards vanquished?
Have you come to rest calmly?
Or have you run aground dangerously?
Have you lost your bearings?
Or have you hit upon a hidden rock?

None of these, none of these,
the master of this house

is the friend of the assassinated Lorca
is a witness to the suffering of Spain
is a retired diplomat
he is no admiral.

Day in day out, night after night staring out to sea
listening to waves like the sound of soughing
and like the sound of scoffing
and like the sound of defiance

Pablo Neruda
facing ten thousand acres of waves
with language brought up from the mines
declaring war on the entire old world

....

The flames in the fireplace are leaping
this evening, the sea is noisy
around the blazing fireplace
assembled here from all corners of the world
a dozen or so fellow seafarers
drinking wine, telling tales

We come from many countries
comprise many nationalities
speak different languages
but we are the best of brothers

....

Tomorrow, if the sky is clear
I'll take that brass telescope
and look out to the west
on that side of the Pacific lies my home country
I love this promontory
but I also love my homeland.[11]

---

[11] *Ai Qing quanji*, vol. 2 (Shijiazhuang: Huashan wenyi chubanshe, 1991) 186. In
1939 Neruda bought a house at Isla Negra (Black Island). The house had been built
by an old socialist sea captain. It was here that Neruda started work on *Canto
General*. The house was ransacked after the anti-Popular Front military coup in
September 1973, shortly after which Neruda died. Following his death, for many
years admirers of Neruda came to the closed and crumbling house and carved
political slogans and lines of verse on the wooden fence surrounding the property.
After the restoration of civilian government in Chile, the government renovated
and opened to the public the house at Isla Negra. Pablo Neruda was an avid collector
of shells, amassing 15,000 in all, and finally donating the collection to a museum.
   Numerous guests gathered in Chile for Neruda's fiftieth birthday celebrations.

When after the coup in Chile Neruda had his house ransacked, the very house on Isla Negra that Ai Qing had mythologised for his Chinese readers, China's authorities kept silent. In 1973 China was still governed by a régime whose ills would later be imputed to the 'Gang of Four', scapegoats for a method of governance that stemmed from the systemic, bureaucratic problems of the Chinese Communist Party's state apparatus. In 1973 Ai Qing himself was still in disgrace as a liberal and would not resurface until the late, post-Gang of Four 1970s, when he would assume his place as a grandee of modern Chinese poetry. Ai Qing is the archetypal liberal Communist patriotic poet and party loyalist who has tried his best in his populist poetry to be responsive to every twist and turn of party-government policy. The extremely militaristic and belligerent nature of the self-serving, nationalistic policies pursued by China's government, which the propagation of the Third World philosophy served to mask, have gone largely uncontested by most of China's élite. While it must be remembered that it has always been extremely perilous for Chinese individuals to voice dissent, such danger has never totally silenced it. For instance, in the realm of domestic policy Chinese intellectuals have consistently opposed, even after the events of 4 June 1989 in Tiananmen Square, the proposed construction of the Yangzi River dam. Yet very few Chinese intellectuals, Communist or not, have demurred at their government's conduct of foreign affairs. In the 1950s and 1960s most intellectuals would have been convinced that Beijing's foreign policy was conducted for the good of a China newly reunited, but still besieged by a Western anti-Communist ideology which militarily threatened the country along its borders (Korea, Vietnam). Most would have been satisfied with a quiet life 'serving the people' and helping to

---

Writers came from around the world. Besides Ai Qing, there were Ilya Ehrenburg from the Soviet Union, Deda and Kutvalek from Czechoslovakia, and numerous Latin Americans.

rebuild China. After all, that is precisely what tens of thousands of them returned from America and elsewhere in the 1950s to do, and would have continued to do had it not been for the Cultural Revolution. Supporting New China implied compromising the capacity to dissent. Yet even before the 1950s, patriotic, anti-imperialist intellectuals and cultural producers had already largely lost or surrendered their right and duty to critique. Many had in effect done so as early as the 1930s. Before the Chinese Communist Party (CCP) took control of China in 1949, left-leaning patriotic, anti-imperialist writers and other producers of culture (romanticists, modernists, critical realists, socialist realists), a majority of the creative world, admittedly not without ruffled feathers and much argument, subscribed to a discourse that was marked by the desire to see China rid of foreign powers, to be unified (there was no place for regionalism) and able to feed its people and regain national pride. There was perhaps also for those who had travelled or took an interest in other parts of the world the idea that China might stand as an example to other oppressed nations. Some lines written by Ai Qing after a visit to Latin America in 1954 attest to this mentality:

> The Chinese people are welcomed everywhere,
> The world knows well our valour and endurance,
> The six hundred million people marching ahead
> Holding high the mighty banner of peace![12]

The discourse was in the main narrowly conceived, simplistic and informed by CCP propaganda; it fell easily into place in the nationalist-patriotic ideology of the times. It was also a myth which had its impact abroad, so that the Communists were conceived of as anti-Fascists; Chiang Kai-shek was seen by many as on a par with at best Mussolini and Franco and at worst Hitler. This was the United Front Communism of the 1940s rather than the Communism of the 1930s, a Communism learnt from the Russian model of what was essentially

[12] *Chinese Literature* 4 (1955) 72, trans. Yuan Ko-chia.

a Stalinist Russian nationalism now lukewarm towards genuine revolution, whether in Spain or Asia, although still happy to expand its territorial space and influence.

I do not intend to claim that the nationalist-patriotic ideology – that has in various manifestations informed China's urban collective imaginary and thus Chinese cultural production for a century – has been a totally negative force. Nevertheless, despite good intentions and even some progressive and beneficial effects, most cultural producers have largely been manipulated by the dominant ideology. Today the nationalist ideology which was imbricated with official Communist ideology, and constructed by the CCP, is discredited, but a seemingly new nationalist ideology is being constructed, this time on a market economy capitalist base. And yet it is an ideology informed by the same discourse of nationalism and patriotism that has dominated in China for a hundred years at least.[13]

The so-called socialist states have invested heavily in the ideology of nationalism. The fact that the economic policies of what passed for socialism have now been replaced by an economics designed further to integrate their economies into the global capitalist market economy simply reveals more clearly that the more dominant of the ideologies that sustained the various national social imaginaries in those states was not

---

[13] For instance, Huang Zunxian (1848-1905), who continued to write in a classical vein while attempting to open up Chinese poetry to modern and foreign themes, wrote a poetry marked by a patriotic spirit. The turn of the century reformist intellectual Liang Qichao noted the 'practical usefulness of his patriotic poetry for kindergarten, elementary school and the army'; cited in Helmut Martin, 'A Transitional Concept of Chinese Literature 1897-1917: Liang Ch'i-ch'ao on Poetry Reform, Historical Drama and the Political Novel', in *Oriens Extremus* 20 (1973) 196.

The Chinese critic Wang Yao contributed to the recuperation and construction of Huang as a patriotic poet, when he wrote of Huang's patriotic spirit and sense of history at some length in 1951 when patriotism fuelled by anti-imperialism was at a high point; see Wang Yao, 'Wan Qing shiren Huang Zunxian' [The late Qing poet Huang Zunxian], *Renmin Wenxue*, 20 (June 1951) 68-72.

The patriotism of poets has furnished the Communist authorities with the means by which to recuperate non-Communist poets, such as Wen Yiduo, to the régime's ideology and cultural canon; even ancient poets like Qu Yuan, who lived and wrote beyond the bounds of China proper, have been reinvented as Chinese patriots.

any kind of internationalism, or socialist humanism, but nationalism. Moreover, the dilemma of such states lay perhaps in the very nationalism on which their ideologies (of both the Communist state's and its domestic opponents) were built. Certainly the socialist project was undone as soon as it started, not merely by totalitarianism, in which nationalism plays an essential part, but by the headlong dash into the modern nationalist nation-building myth. As Régis Debray has put it, 'each time a socialism confronted a nationalism we knew that it had lost (and will lose) the game.'[14] Nationalism ultimately is inimical to socialism, whereas for capitalism the nation-state sustained by nationalist sentiment constitutes the basic unit of the management and policing of markets, consumers and producers and the physical environment in which these exist. 'Democracy' or authoritarianism as the means of control of the state is irrelevant to the aims of capitalism.

One of the Chinese ideologies vying for dominance today claims to espouse 'democracy'. Perhaps again its conscious aims are laudable, but they mask another ideology that once more proves to be fundamentally vacuous. What might be the underpinning of 'democracy?' Is it merely based on anti-Communism? Is it some notion of nineteenth-century liberalism? Is it once more the democracy/market system model? For most of the people in China who have attempted to imagine a concept of democracy, it is surely as nebulous as the statue of democracy, the Tiananmen Statue of Liberty look-alike, itself has proved to be; like the image of that statue, 'democracy' has its place as myth in the counter-ideology prevalent in the collective imaginary of urban China today.[15]

There is in any event a distinction to be made between state/party ideology – an official ideology so unsure of its grip,

---

[14] Régis Debray, *Critique de la raison politique: ou l'inconscient religieux* (Paris: Gallimard, Collection Tel, 1981) 38.

[15] Is this a criticism of 'the Chinese' – if that expression is really meaningful? Not really, but I do think members of the educated élite bear responsibility, especially those who had surely unmasked at least part of the ideology that had manipulated them and others and yet failed to speak out.

of its ability to be the consciousness which dominates popular consciousness, that for decades it has sought to propagate its policies and extend its control totally even over those cultural producers who have shown allegiance to, or who were members of, the party – and an ideology which more loosely and perhaps more effectively exerts its dominance.

In terms of its literary and cultural effects, the former kind of states, ruled via what Vaneigem has called 'Eastern democratic despotism', are led by those who from Zhdanov (who denounced the dissident poet Akhmatova as 'half-nun, half-whore') to Khrushchev, from Mao (who likened the people to a blank page on which the most beautiful poem could be written) to Deng (who drew the image of a market place on that page), have had a paranoid aversion to the modern and modernist poet who very frequently has offered and represented a critique of their bureaucratic projects of modernisation.[16] The other sort of ideology, 'Western democratic bureaucracy', seemingly looser and more subtle, tends not to liquidate the ideological critique of cultural production, even irrealisms and modernisms, and can appropriate, neutralise or marginalise such production. The recuperations of anti-capitalist culture and critique have not always been seamless. Dada and Surrealism were very ill-received by the French state and bourgeoisie in the 1920s, but are now comfortably consumed. Ironically, revolutionary Surrealism was not merely feared by the bourgeois state *per se*, but was also condemned and loathed by Stalinism, not least in France. And was it any surprise that in the 1980s the so-called liberal, yet very conservative, Chinese Communist Party and its official poets were horrified at the new 'misty' or obscure poetry which challenged the cultural superstructure of the state apparatus? In Tom Stoppard's play *Travesties*, the Dadaist character remarks in a now celebrated quip: 'The odd thing about revolution is that the further left you go politically, the more bourgeois they

[16] Raoul Vaneigem, preface to the American edition, *The Movement of the Free Spirit* (New York: Zone Books, 1994) 7: translation of *Le mouvement du libre-esprit* (Paris: Editions Ramsay, 1986).

like their art.' A humorous line, but a misleading one that would have us believe that Stalinism equates with what is very left, and what is revolutionary. It is the case, however, that emergent bourgeois state-capitalist apparatuses always felt threatened by avant-garde arts.

Political Poetry and Ideology

Throughout the twentieth century, the notion has existed that there was such a thing as apolitical poetry. In Western capitalist literary cultures, indeed, the accepted nature of poetry was that it should somehow be aesthetically pleasing, occasionally didactic. From time to time, usually in periods of war and empire-building, which implies the former, patriotic poetry was called for. In China in the twentieth century, the emphasis has been weighted in the other direction. The purpose of poetic production was usually seen first and foremost as didactic, critical and often programmatic.

The notion that the natural state of poetry is apolitical, somehow uninflected by politics and ideology, is based on the idea that poetry exists in a timeless world, insulated from historical and local and social conditions. And yet when this 'apolitical poetry' is practised it is inevitably the product of a poetic subjectivity constituted by a specific consciousness, in a specific ideological context, at a specific moment in time and place, informed by the discourse of orthodoxies and unorthodoxies permitted by the imaginaries of the societies of which poets are a part. The attachment to 'apolitical poetry' is ultimately traceable to an ideal of transcendance in aesthetic thought.

However, while any idea of a truly 'pure literature' can be no more than illusionary, in China from the 1970s onwards those anti-establishment poets and pop lyricists who proclaimed an allegiance to *chun wenxue* or 'pure literature' were making a different order of statement than poets in advanced capitalist societies who claim to produce 'apolitical' poetry and thus participate in the bourgeois fiction that disguises the real social nature of 'taste'.

In China over the last fifteen to twenty years, poets have produced poetry which while sometimes claiming to be 'apolitical' is in fact extremely political in the sense that it does not observe the party's and state's blueprint for literary production, that it is written in a modernist style which runs counter to officially promoted literary modes, that it deals with dreams rather than factory chimneys. In short, a poetry has been produced which politically challenges the dominant perceptions and uses of the medium. In other words, lyricists have gone beyond a poetry that is merely cynical, apathetic and antithetical to official ideology. They have produced a literature of critique informed by the ideology of a social group, a generation, a massive stratum of society perhaps 50 to 100 million strong in the instance of both the so-called lost generation of the Cultural Revolution or the similarly populous generation of urban educated youth of the 1980s. This is not a false collectivist ideology imposed by a party machine on poetry producers, although it may be false in other ways – since it shares features of the dominant ideology and does not merely run counter to that ideology but is also informed by many of its tenets, including both the idealism of Maoism and Deng Xiaoping's consumerist myth. It is nonetheless an ideology, in the sense of a shared set of experiences and beliefs, of a collective body. In this way even the most extremely modernist poetic 'I' cannot fail to embody collective experience and thinking. As Nicole Brossard, a Canadian lesbian-feminist poet, has written: 'Anyone who encounters insult and hatred because of his or her differences from a powerful group is bound, sooner or later, to echo *we* through the use of *I*, and to draw the line between *us* and *them, we* and *they*'.[17] The post-revolutionary, alienated, modernist poet thus assumes a collective voice. This, in the manner described by Brossard, may well be either unwitting or much more direct,

---

[17] 'Poetic Politics', in Charles Bernstein (ed.), *The Politics of Poetic Form* (New York: Roof, 1990) 80.

as in the 1989 Tiananmen appropriation of the poet Bei Dao's already political poems – such as 'Declaration', which contains the celebrated refrain 'I don't believe'. Bei Dao was the first poet of the new post-Cultural Revolution generation of lyricists to come to the public's attention; his poems brought him fame at the time of the first Tiananmen incident in 1974 which followed the unofficial and anti-government mourning for Premier Zhou Enlai. The poems were revived and infused with renewed meaning by the 1989 Tiananmen student protesters, much as the pop lyrics of the singer-songwriter Cui Jian, a product of the Dengist 1980s, were employed as anti-authority songs of defiance during that moment. This is a phenomenon touched on by Gramsci when discussing popular songs which, he says, 'the people adopt because they conform to their way of thinking and feeling'. According to Gramsci, what distinguishes this sort of lyric in the popular consciousness, what brings about its adoption 'within the context of a nation and its culture is neither its artistic aspect nor its historical origin, but the way in which it conceives the world and life, in contrast with official society'.[18] In this sense the use of Bei Dao's and Cui Jian's production is not collective expression by virtue of shared experience of oppression, but appropriation more or less beyond these lyricists' control or intent, both in the way it is employed and the way it affects subsequent production.[19]

Naturally, not all Chinese poetic production has been so appropriated, and while Bei Dao's early poetry was highly popular with mass audiences, his later more self-consciously

[18] Antonio Gramsci, *Cultural Writings* (London: Lawrence and Wishart, 1985) 195.

[19] Lyotard would see it thus: 'What is important in a text is not what it means, but what it does and incites to do. What it does: the charge of affect it contains and transmits. What it incites to do: the metamorphoses of this potential energy into other things – other texts, but also paintings, photographs, film sequences, political actions, decisions, erotic inspirations, acts of insubordination, economic initiatives, etc.' *Driftworks* (New York: Semiotext(e), 1984) 9-10 (cited in Steven Best and Douglas Kellner, *Postmodern Theory* [New York: Guildford Press, 1991] 147).
Bei Dao's poetry and the way in which Western Sinologists have read it is discussed in Chapter 4, and Cui Jian and the lyricism of popular culture are discussed at length in Chapter 6.

modernistic verse has not been as well received although it should be said that the poet has been unpublished in China since 1989. Moreover, consumption of all poetry has dwindled over the last decade in inverse proportion to the increasing consumption of more recognisably popular cultural forms: pop music, magazines, television and fashion. And yet there is a still significant readership of poetry concentrated in the universities and other intellectual institutions, not a negligible readership either in terms of size or of influence. The dominant situation regarding the consumption of poetry in the capitalist West during the twentieth century was clearly understood by Benjamin Péret, a French poet, scholar and revolutionary activist who has received little critical attention compared to other Surrealist figures. Writing in 1943, he describes what, due to the effects of uneven development, has only in the last ten years or so become increasingly the case in modern China:

> The miserable existence to which society currently reduces the majority of the population cuts it off from any kind of poetic thinking, though the aspiration to poetry remains latent. The popularity of stupidly sentimental literature . . . , is a symptom of this need for poetry . . . . These days poetry has become the almost exclusive preserve of a tiny number of individuals who are the only ones left who feel more or less clearly that it is necessary.[20]

Lyric expression and 'poetic thinking' then are essential to social life, and the need for and use of the lyric lie in its capacity to defamiliarise 'the object of its discourse'. Poetry can 'engage with ideas and ideologies which shape the world we see', and can 'evoke an otherness, an alternative vision and an alternative potentiality'.[21]

The aspiration to poetic expression, the desire to have an extraordinary means of describing and explaining our lives, in part explains the production and exploitation of contemporary

[20] Benjamin Péret, *Death to the Pigs, and Other Writings*, trans. Rachel Stella (Lincoln: University of Nebraska Press, 1988); also published under the title *Death to the Pigs: Selected Writings of Benjamin Péret* (London: Atlas Press, 1988).

[21] Mike Gonzalez and David Treece, *The Gathering of Voices: The Twentieth-Century Poetry of Latin America* (London and New York: Verso, 1992) ix-x.

popular music in capitalist societies. But the popularity of 'sentimental' literary texts, whether in print or in sound, can only in part be due to the commodification of culture that is natural to capitalism. It is also surely a response to the inadequacy of what poetry is produced to meet this 'need' for lyric expression, and to the denial of a space for a more democratic practice not simply of lyrical consumption but also of production. Thus the needs for poetry are largely met, whether in China, Hong Kong or the advanced capitalist societies, by the lyrics and non-linguistic practices of popular music, ballads, heavy metal and punk rock. Of course, popular music lyrics can only respond to a need for lyrics at the level of consumption, for while pop lyrics are consumed by many, they are produced by relatively few and, except in their repetition by the consumer, now commonly in the practice of karaoke, provide no opportunity for a more lyric expression of the particular experience and concerns of individuals and their communities. It is this need for a grassroots means of expression beyond the confines of the discursive possibilities of official society that made rap so popular with excluded young African Americans. Rap needed no expensive equipment and was a means of lyric expression open to all. Its commodification by the music industry came later.

In 1989 it was a commentator's commonplace to ponder the irony that the anti-Communist wave which swept so many régimes from power left intact the CCP's hold in China, even though its authority and credibility with the urban classes had been effectively destroyed by its bloody actions and reprisals against the students and citizens of Beijing and other large cities across the country.

Whether Communist Parties were officially stripped of governmental power, or not as in China and Vietnam, the result in economic terms was the same: the triumph of market capitalism. What is also similar is the pushing to the fore of the ideology of nationalism, which had in fact always been the base of 'Communist' states' ideological structures. After Tiananmen, even the ideology that seeks to challenge official authority today in China is informed by nationalism. The same old patriotic, nationalist discourse exploited by the CCP and the nationalist Kuomintang (KMT) is also that which underpins the platform of pro-democracy activists unable to imagine a liberatory politics beyond the confines of the nation-state. Even the poets who most vehemently espoused individualism and escape from the material world rallied to the 'cause' post-Tiananmen.

Before and just after Tiananmen there were those who questioned the patriotic discourse in which the intellectual/cultural producer had engaged for the past hundred years – a discourse which privileged serving the nation and the people in materialist terms. It was a discourse which accepted that those in charge of the material interests of the nation, rather than the people themselves, should be empowered and acknowledged as the arbiters of relations of power in society. In other words, for the sake of the 'nation' – inclusive of all classes, races, both sexes and all minorities – the power of ideological critique was abandoned. The very critique which cultural production can exercise and had exercised was surrendered, only surviving publicly in a much muted form in the writings of some liberal Communists. Now, at the end of the twentieth century, the discourse of patriotism-nationalism is once again dominant, while the questionability of the nationalist project, and the place of intellectuals and producers of culture within it, is once more made marginal.[22]

The power of nationalistic 'patriotism' to sway a committed, radical writer even from his most cherished convictions is demonstrated by the testimony of George Orwell, who fought in and was radicalised by the 1936-9 Spanish Civil War,

---

[22] After a century of divergent modernisation strategies the majority in China remain materially impoverished, while the physical quality of life deteriorates for all; in 1995, of the world's ten most polluted cities, five were to be found in China, and the Chinese *nouveaux riches* now stop off at oxygen bars on their way home from the office. What is more, even if a materialist politics of production is the frame within which the country's future is imagined, is it not apparent that it is no longer possible to 'save China' without taking into consideration the ecological feasibility of doing so?

a war which attracted a number of left-wing writers, including Benjamin Péret. Both Orwell and Péret fought for the POUM battalion (the military wing of the Partido Obero de Unificación Marxista, or Workers' Party of Marxist Unification, which was anti-Stalinist and pro-Trotsky in political orientation) and witnessed the abandonment of the revolution by the established left of the Communist and Socialist parties, and their persecution of anarchists and Trotskyists.

As a socialist Orwell for several years opposed the Second World War as a capitalist war, as did most Communists, before deciding to support it. He made public his change of heart in the now celebrated piece 'My Country Right or Left', in which he recognises some, if not all, of the ideological bases of his position:

[T]he night before the Russo-German pact was announced I dreamed that the war had started. It was one of those dreams which . . . reveal to you the real state of your feelings. It taught me two things, first, that I should be simply relieved when the long-dreaded war started, secondly, that I was patriotic at heart, would not sabotage or act against my own side, would support the war, would fight in it if possible.

Given the choice between resistance and surrender to Hitler, Orwell thought that from a socialist perspective it was 'better to resist'. However, he confessed that the 'emotional basis' of his position lay elsewhere, that 'the long drilling in patriotism which the middle classes go through had done its work, and that once England was in a serious jam it would be impossible for me to sabotage.' Yet Orwell insisted that patriotism did not imply a conservative political stance:

To be loyal both to Chamberlain's England and to the England of tomorrow, might seem an impossibility, if one did not know it to be an everyday phenomenon. Only revolution can save England . . . and it may proceed quite quickly if only we can keep Hitler out . . . . I dare say the London gutters will have to run with blood. All right, let them, if it is necessary. But when the red militias are billeted in the Ritz I shall feel that the England I was taught to love so long and for such different reasons is somehow persisting.[23]

---

[23] *Collected Essays, Journalism and Letters of George Orwell*, vol. 1 (Harmondsworth: Penguin, 1970) 591.

This is a revealing and ultimately disappointing statement from a man who fought in Spain for the cause of a socialism which saw volunteers fight side by side regardless of nationality and petty nationalisms. For here Orwell, the author of the anti-imperialist *Burmese Days*, is concerned with 'little England' (England, not Wales, not Scotland, not Britain) and a very English, Anglocentric, utopian form of socialism. Orwell's is a revolution which will be achieved by cutting bourgeois throats perhaps, but which will result in a society that will stick to decent customs including English tea and scones consumed by very English revolutionaries. While not being blind to colonialism, or to class struggle, Orwell is nevertheless persistently drawn back by the ideology inculcated into him during his time at an English public school: 'To this day it gives me a faint feeling of sacrilege not to stand to attention during "God Save the King".'[24] Orwell is convinced that what he sees as the 'spiritual need for patriotism' and the emotions it engenders can be exploited and transformed in the cause of 'building a Socialist on the bones of a Blimp', which he calls 'the power of one kind of loyalty to transmute itself into another'.[25] There is nothing wrong then with Englishness as such, as long as it is transformed and reformed by socialism; a rather contorted concept, and one I suspect that has pervaded much radical cultural criticism in post-war Britain.

China's political strategists have also been adept at transmuting one kind of loyalty into another. While this particular narrative of twentieth-century patriotic sentiment might seem somewhat incommensurate with the Chinese experience, Orwell's position and his description of and explanation for the potency of patriotism are, in fact, in keeping with the sentiment produced in intellectuals in modern China, which like Britain has depended on the exploitation of this feeling to command cooperation from its population in time of war and hardship.

[24] *Ibid.* 592.
[25] *Ibid.*

Todorov has written of the 'recent manifestations' of 'patriotic sentiment' which, while it 'has existed since time immemorial', is exploited differently and extensively by the 'specifically *modern* entities' of nation and nationalism; the twentieth-century conflation of socialism and nationalism has produced an ideology which has made consistent use of such patriotic sentiment.[26] The psychological attraction of such recent manifestations of patriotic sentiment inculcated into children in the schoolrooms and via the media in word, song and image, 'the long drilling in patriotism', in Communist New China, just as in the France of the Third Republic, has produced poets and makers of culture of all sorts who, even when informed by their own lived experience of historical periods like the 1966-76 Cultural Revolution, are able, while shunning what they comprehend as socialism, to espouse the veritable backbone of Chinese Communism, – the appeal of, and to, patriotic sentiment.

The exploitation of nationalist sentiment by twentieth-century Communist authorities, it may be argued, is a corruption of the Marxist privileging of 'class' as the agent of history, and yet Marx himself emphasised the role of the nation-state in making the revolution. Engels was even more emphatic and insistent in his discussion of 'non-historic peoples', ethnicities and nations deemed incapable of self-emancipation whose only recourse was to be incorporated into larger and viable nation-states. While Lenin attempted theoretically to revalorise the political rights of smaller nations, the problem of the nation-state and the nationalist sentiment it permits must be seen as one of the greater failures of orthodox Marxist thought, and one of the contributing factors to the 'failed revolutions' of this century.

Writing in 1917, Emma Goldman wrote hopefully of an imminent challenge to the 'logic of patriotism'.[27] She understood patriotism to be 'too narrow and limited a conception

---

[26] Tzvetan Todorov, *Nous et les autres. La réflexion française sur la diversité humaine* (Paris: Éditions du Seuil, 1989) 243.

[27] *Anarchism and Other Essays* (New York: Dover, 1969) 136.

to meet the necessities of our time', and detected 'an international feeling of solidarity between the oppressed nations of the world'.[28] Goldman was right, and she was wrong. Evelyn Scott told Goldman that she was ahead of her time, and if Scott's prescience was correct, Goldman may still be proved completely right.[29]

One of the basic functions of poetry is to interpret material reality, to unmask the false, to reconfigure reality the better to demonstrate falseness, to attempt to describe what is not false, to reveal moments and images of hope, to construct landscapes of optimism and visions of a material world remade. This poetic process both includes the function of ideological critique and goes beyond it. Another use of the lyric is the propagation of ideology, of myth, of illusion, a function not unconnected with the former since engaging in critique of one ideology implies constructing another. It may also imply a conscious or unwitting masking of that substitute ideology.

This nexus between ideology and the lyric continues to be neglected by many critics and scholars, who however are perfectly able to perceive the ideological function of prose narrative. As Kristin Ross put it in her path-breaking book on Rimbaud and the Paris Commune, modern criticism, especially Marxist-inspired criticism, has

continued to reassert the traditionally dominant concern with narrative and the novel genre . . . . This hesitation on the part of Marxist critics to concern themselves with poetry can be traced back to all too traditional assumptions, themselves a development of the late nineteenth century, that regard prose as the privileged vehicle for objective or political themes, and verse for subjective or individual ones – or, put another way, to the assumption that there exists a social production of reality on the one hand, and a desiring production that is mere fantasy or wish fulfillment on the other. Despite extensive feminist critiques of such divisions between the 'personal' and the 'political', these assumptions remain largely intact and are reinscribed in Marxism as generic omission.[30]

[28] *Ibid.* 142.

[29] *Ibid.* v.

[30] Kristin Ross, *The Emergence of Social Space: Rimbaud and the Paris Commune*, Theory and History of Literature, vol. 60 (Minneapolis: University of Minnesota

The privileging of fiction over the lyric by critics and scholars is precisely what was brought about by China's discourse of national salvation from the late nineteenth century onwards. The related factor in the toppling from preeminence of the lyric genre was the structural and linguistic conservatism of the poetic practice of the ruling class; a situation that went effectively unchallenged until the early twentieth-century rupture with the poetic tradition.

The French feminist critic Hélène Cixous has written of the 'intersection between poetry and history'; in her discussion of the Russian poet Marina Tsvetaeva, she wonders how 'history makes its path in a poetic work' and also asks whether poetry is 'something stronger, something even more dangerous'.[31] Cixous poses these questions in the context of the modern poetry of Russia, which perhaps more than any recent poetry has been self-consciously historically grounded. For while, Cixous claims, history 'simply smothers and squashes', some books from the late nineteenth century 'show that one can remain poetic in the very midst of history'.[32] It seems the sense of history that Cixous is conceptualising here is akin to the kind of temporality Debray distinguishes as the kind of political history that is 'recapitulatable and programmed'.[33]

In the Chinese context I would suggest that not only contemporary Chinese poetic production, but also the interventionist production of musicians and lyricists like Luo Dayou and his Music Factory in Hong Kong, show that not merely can one 'remain poetic in the very midst of history', but that one can be historical, in the sense of a 'cumulative

Press, 1988) 11.

[31] Hélène Cixous, *Readings: The Poetics of Blanchot, Joyce, Kafka, Kleist, Lispector, and Tsvetayeva*, trans. and ed. Verena Andermatt Conley, Theory and History of Literature, vol. 77 (Minneapolis: University of Minnesota Press, 1991) 111.

[32] *Ibid.*

[33] Régis Debray, *Critique de la raison politique: ou l'inconscient religieux* (Paris: Gallimard, Collection Tel, 1981) 443. Debray distinguishes between 'non-programmable, cumulative, technical history' and 'programmed, recapitulatable [*récapitulable*], political history'.

and non-programmable' history, in the very midst of poetry.[34] Surely it is precisely the possibility of this historicity that makes the lyric 'more dangerous'.

Cixous sees a refuge from the 'noise machines' of modernity in the 'slowness . . . thought and silence' of Marina Tsvetaeva. 'The noise machines are more and more sonorous. The air in which we breathe life is given over to values which are the death of humankind, that are low-level, oriented by speculation, money, and profit.'[35] For Cixous, then, Tsvetaeva's poetry is quiet resistance not merely against life under bureaucratic Stalinism but also against capitalist modernity, which in any case the Soviet Union was pursuing in another guise. This quietist conception of the role of poetry has often led to such work being seen as mere escapism, whereas it is in fact a poetry of sonorous critique.

Tsvetaeva is an interesting poet. She stands out first of all because she is a woman, in what despite the singular stature of Anna Akhmatova was after all a poetic world dominated by men. She also, like a number of the Chinese poets discussed in this book, lived in a Marxist-Leninist state and experienced prolonged periods in exile. Also like some of the other poets mentioned in the present work, she had a highly romanticised and individualistic idea of the social role or 'vocation' of the poet. She was in many ways a rebel, often standing out against official society. When the rest of Russia, including its poets, was in a frenzy of patriotism and in a fervour of media-inspired hatred against the Prussian enemy, Tsvetaeva, for whom Germany was a 'fragrant land', a country constructed by her Romantic poets, wrote of 'Germany, my love!'[36] Tsvetaeva idealistically and firmly rejected the idea of national and nationalist poets. In this she is resembled by the outward-looking contemporary Chinese modernist poet Duoduo, whose work is discussed at length in subsequent chapters. At

---

[34] *Ibid.*

[35] Cixous 111-12.

[36] Marina Tsvetaeva, *Des poètes*, trans. Dimitri Sesemann, ed. Efim Etkind (Paris: Des femmes, Antoinette Fouque, 1992) 11.

a time when it was important to be a Russian nationalist poet, even more important than to be a people's poet, Tsvetaeva wrote to Rilke in 1926:

No tongue is a mother tongue . . . . That's why I don't understand why people talk about French poets, Russian poets, and so on. A poet may write in French, but he cannot be a French poet . . . . One becomes a poet, not to be French, Russian and so on, but to be everything. Furthermore, one becomes a poet because one is not French.[37]

But such a universalist idea of the poet has to contend with the cultural reality that there are different patterns of receptivity, different poetic cultures in different societies, which must be related to the divergent and uneven economic development of different societies. While in one society the reception of written lyrics may be enthusiastic, in other more economistically oriented societies poetry's space may have been filled by commodified cultural products. Chinese poets in the 1980s experienced this correlation between the popular consumption of their work and the changing emphases of the economic system. It was like crossing a border from one society into another. Tsvetaeva experienced the difference when exiled from Russia and living in France. She commented that she had left a world 'where for certain people my poems were as necessary as bread', and now found herself 'in a world where no-one has need of poems, neither mine nor anyone else's'.[38] These were the words of a disillusioned, displaced poet in the Paris of 1936. But surely it was at this moment and in this very place that people had need of verse. The ordinary people of France, denied access to élite poetic practices, sought to meet that need in the lyric romanticism of the movies and in the popular songs of the young and charming singer-songwriter Charles Trénet, who in 1936 penned and performed the song 'The Prince', which celebrated the virtues of ordinary people and everyday life:

[37] Rilke, Pasternak, Tsvetaeva, *Correspondance à trois*, trans. Philippe Jaccottet (Paris: Gallimard, 1983), cited in Tsvetaeva, *Des poètes* 13.

[38] Tsvetaeva 95.

> The prince had me in his bed
> The prince had me in his nest
> But me, I've had it with the prince
>
> ....
>
> He has treasures, and piles of money
> Me, I have my own lover
>
> ....
>
> I prefer my old bistro to him
> My ugly old neighborhood, people out on a Sunday
> The movies on a Saturday, the metro
> And swinging and dancing every night
> I belong to all that, ladies
> And I couldn't give a damn for the prince, gentlemen.[39]

Others, particularly Marxist critics, might say in response to Tsvetaeva that in modern societies readerships for poetry decline because poets fail to address the real concerns of those audiences and indulge in individualistic reverie. But others, including the Marxist Péret, would deny that poetry's lack of appeal has to do with its perceived flight from reality. Péret, not only a poet but an active revolutionary in 'The Dishonour of Poets', his 1945 critique of the nationalistic poetry anthology *The Honour of Poets* published by the French Communist Resistance, defends the potential of poetry and attacks its detractors who 'accuse it [poetry] of being a means of escape, a flight from reality, as if it were not reality itself, reality's essence and exaltation'.[40] What Kristin Ross would see as erroneous divisions 'between the "personal" and the "political"' constructed by certain Marxist critics, Péret sees as a misguided division between the 'useful and the useless'. For Péret, the 'enemies of poetry' have always aimed to subject it to 'their immediate ends'.[41] In a staunch attack on these

---

[39] Charles Trénet, *Le Jardin extraordinaire* (Paris: Le Livre de Poche, 1993) 59-60.
[40] Péret 201.
[41] *Ibid.*

'enemies', here to be understood as including orthodox Communists, Péret claims:

> For them, life and culture are summed up in the useful and the useless, it being understood that the useful takes the form of a pickax wielded for their benefit. For them poetry is only a luxury for the rich – the aristocrat and the banker – and if it wants to become 'useful' to the masses, it should become resigned to the lot of the 'applied', 'decorative', and 'domestic' arts.[42]

Péret's criticism of the official Communist use of poetry is not merely justified by French examples, it is also borne out by the dominant use of poetry in China both at the time he was writing and subsequently. Marxist-Leninist critics and Communist cultural bureaucrats do not have the luxury of latter-day Western Marxist critics of simply ignoring poetry, they *must* find a role for it. Péret says of the French Communist literary producers and bureaucrats of the 1940s that they sensed instinctively 'that poetry is the fulcrum Archimedes required, and they fear that the world, once raised up, might fall back on their heads'; hence their 'ambition to debase poetry, to deny it all efficacy, all value as an exaltation, to give it the hypocritical, consolatory role of a sister of charity'.[43] One has the sense that the attitude of Chinese Communist cultural bureaucrats in the 1980s and 1990s towards unofficial poetry is the same, for even though the popularity and consumption of poetry have diminished, poets are persistently harassed and arrested for attempting to publish poems that almost no-one reads.

On the whole new unofficial poetry does not aim to sloganise and mobilise; rather it aims to question quietly and to offer alternative vistas, and perhaps therein lies the fear it engenders. The revolutionary potential of poetry, according to Péret, rests in its power to engage in critique, not with its power to disseminate battle cries, fervour or comfort:

[42] *Ibid.*
[43] *Ibid.*

[T]he poet does not have to perpetuate for others an illusory hope, whether human or celestial, nor disarm minds while filling them with boundless confidence in a father or a leader against whom any criticism becomes sacrilege. Quite the contrary, it is up to the poet to give voice to words always sacrilegious, to permanent blasphemies.[44]

Such blasphemy is displayed, for instance, by the contemporary Chinese poet Duoduo in this 1982 poem:

> That's the big rock we cannot climb
> to make it
> we debated for six years
> we made it then climbed upwards
> you said it probably needed seven years more
> probably another eight
> or a longer time
> time enough for an appendicitis
> the operation took ten years
> it was just like the flash of a knife –
>   1982[45]

At first sight this poem, for Duoduo an unusually simple one, would seem so vague as to make it difficult to establish a meaningful reading, but given the context of contemporary Chinese politics an attempt at a reading is possible. For the Chinese reader, the significance of 'ten years' is immediately foregrounded. The Cultural Revolution, which officially lasted from 1966 to 1976, was subsequently dubbed the 'ten years of chaos' or the 'ten difficult years'. The 'big rock', an obstacle, has been created out of debate; before and during the Cultural Revolution people were made to engage endlessly in political debates, discussions, campaigns. Great economic plans, such as the disastrous Great Leap Forward, were launched and aborted, revolutionary schedules constantly revised, the people's aspirations and enthusiasm dulled and disappointed. I have no knowledge of the 'poet's intention' in this poem, but that such a reading is plausible for readers in China is without doubt.

Compare that mechanical and disturbing deconstruction of what I read as the Maoist mythic construction of history to

[44] *Ibid.*

[45] *The Chicago Review* (1993-4).

this supposedly proletarian poem, by Chen An'an, entitled 'Every Calendar Page a Victory Poster (Yanan Machine Casting Factory, Shanghai)', written and officially published ten years earlier during the Cultural Revolution:

> A journey of ten thousand *li* glowing in the red sunlight
> Thousands of wood shavings curl up a spring tide under the plane
> In long strides we fly across the threshold of 1971,
> Every leaf of the calendar a victory poster.[46]

The ardent revolutionary spirit of the mythic Chinese Communists' Long March of 10,000 miles to Yan'an is recuperated as a trope for factory productivity. Every leaf of the calendar of whatever year, for whatever day of the week, is a 'victory poster' of 'recapitulatable and programmed' history.[47] This kind of poem, authorised and authored by the Chinese Communist Party, is an instantiation of the type of poetry Péret is referring to when he writes that 'the enemies of poetry have always been obsessed with subjecting it to their immediate ends, with crushing it under their god.'[48] The 'god' and the cult of which it was the object in this instance were the constructions of the party and its ideology. Just as the Gang of Four cannot be held solely responsible for the ill effects of the Cultural Revolution, no more can Mao the individual be seen as the omniscient and omnipotent despot at whose door decades of misfortune can and ought to be entirely laid. Despite its lip service to Mao, it is precisely such a limitation of responsibility for past and unpopular policies that the present régime would like to achieve. Régis Debray has pointed to the mistake of locating the problem of the personality cult in the individual who is the 'object' of that cult. It is an error which merely serves to 'mask that the problem of the problems . . . does not lie in "Stalin" (Mao, Ceauşescu or Kim Il-sung), but in the "cult" '.[49]

---

[46] Kai-yu Hsu, *The Chinese Literary Scene* (Harmondsworth: Penguin, 1975) 263.
[47] Debray 443.
[48] Péret 201.
[49] Debray 18.

At the moment Benjamin Péret was writing the 'Dishonour of Poets', the bards of a particular pseudo-religious Stalinist nationalism were his specific target, but for Péret the revolutionary the 'enemies of poetry' would have included – in fact first and foremost would have been – the bourgeois readers and writers of poetry who just as surely have reduced the genre to a minor commodity and an aesthetic frill barely taken seriously even by the academy.

In the twentieth century poetry is only urged upon a popular audience when used as propaganda to bolster nationalistic, patriotic sentiment and thus the state or would-be state. What would have angered Péret was the way in which the French Communist Party during the resistance in the Second World War repeated the bourgeois tactics of the First World War by reiterating the xenophobic patriotic discourse that had dominated official ideology from the founding of the Third Republic in 1870 until the outbreak of the Great War. After France's defeat by Prussia in 1871 and the loss of the provinces of Alsace and Lorraine, the French government encouraged the instilling, particularly in schools and textbooks, of bellicose patriotic ideology. The following extract from 'Le Petit soldat' (The little soldier), a poem in which a father is represented as instructing his son in patriotic virtues, is taken from an official state elementary school textbook. These verses are typical of the lyrics taught to French schoolchildren in the period leading up to the First World War:

> Be a son and a brother to the end,
> Be my joy and my hope,
> But remember above all,
> My son, you must love France.
>
> When the drum beats tomorrow,
> May your soul yearn for war,
> For I myself shall offer you
> To our mother, *la Patrie*![50]

---

[50] V. de Laprade, *Le Livre d'un père, lectures primaires. 1er degré du cours élémentaire,*

One year into the Great War, in 1915, a more elaborate, vehemently nationalistic and militaristic verse play directly called on 'the Poet' to stir from his habitual languid condition and through his verse inspire France and her soldiers; France is always personified as a woman, even though she represents the *patrie* (fatherland). The play, *The Poet's Dream*, a 'patriotic allegory in verse' in one act comprising two scenes, was performed at Saint-Etienne in December 1915 for the benefit of the charity *Soldats au Front* and was to be performed across the length and breadth of France.[51] The play opens with the Muse appealing to the Poet to awake and break his silence, for: 'in these bad times France is going through/Leaving one's heart to lay silent is a coward's act'.

Almost immediately patriotism is linked to religion, and the sentiments and obligations understood as binding the individual and God constructed as analogous to those between individual and nation-state. The deployment of the ready-made vocabulary of Christianity is thus facilitated. Here it is invoked by the Muse:

> Poet, this is how apostles are made;
> And the best of gifts received from God,
> Is the power to feel what others feel.

This power to empathise, supposedly the province of the Poet, is to be put at the service of the fatherland. The Muse continues her tirade, denouncing the Poet as a 'man of little faith' and pleading with him to turn towards Heaven. The Poet retorts:

> Alas! I am but the herald of Death
>
> THE MUSE: Oh! Do not repeat this insolent blasphemy,
> Or I shall abandon you forever.

ed. E. Rontey, Inspecteur Primaire (Paris: Hachette, 1913), on display in the Musée de l'École de la Troisième République, Aubeterre, Charente, France.
[51] George Faure and Louis Mathieu, *Le Rêve du poète. Allégorie patriotique en vers, en un acte et deux tableaux* (Saint-Étienne: Théolier, J. Thomas, 1915).

....

> The blood that flows in you is not that of France
> If, ready to bow down under the foreign yoke,
> You are no longer the holy sower of hope,
> And of a better fate the divine messenger.

'Very moved', the Poet attempts to exculpate himself: 'I have
suffered so much, you see, from the ills of the fatherland.' To
this the Muse replies: 'Do you think that weeping will liberate
its soil?' The Poet is so affected by the imploring address of
the Muse that he starts to ascend through the firmament, until
he is so exalted that he reaffirms his 'faith' in the deified France,
the equal of God: 'France! I believe in you as I believe in
God,/With all my fervent heart and with all my soul.' The
patriotic faith of the Poet restored, the Muse and the 'Bard of
your country' depart together to the 'land of mystery/Where
a day dream becomes reality'. They are conveyed by Dream
to a 'distant palace' where 'France under the shelter of the
tricolour,/Awaits the promised hour when we shall be victors.'

In the second scene France is represented seated 'on a throne
draped in tricolours and with military attributes'. The God-
like quality of France is emphasized by the explicit references
to the gestures of religious ceremony: 'France! France! Permit
me to bow at your feet,/As in a temple where one falls to one's
knees.' Such religious fervour for the nation is interpreted by
Todorov as a modern preference for 'legitimation by the
nation, rather than by God', this preference being 'to the
detriment of universal principles'.[52] In other words, a trans-
ference of religious sentiment from God to nation implies a
shrinking of the sense of community, for the nation 'is large
enough to give to an individual the illusion of the infinite' and
thus 'bar the road of "universal sympathies" '.[53]

It is also the religious, and often quite specifically Christian,
fervour that attaches to the patriot's love of the nation, not

[52] Todorov 243.
[53] *Ibid.* 241.

least that encouraged by twentieth-century Communist states, which so impressed Régis Debray. Debray reminds us of the battle of words that accompanied the Sino-Soviet skirmishes which took place over the disputed territory along the Amur River during the 1960s. He writes that 'each of the two communist parties that one had reason to suppose were free-thinking' referred in their respective communiqués to the 'sacred territory of the fatherland'.[54] The Chinese authority's programme of nationalistic, religious fervour was meant to be consumed and reproduced not only by its own masses, but by the world. In this the Chinese state achieved a degree of success, since even 'radical' intellectuals in the West accepted and practised it. As Debray recalls: 'It was the era . . . when one of the most fantastic religious deliriums of the twentieth century – Maoism – was received and theorised in Paris by cold, thinking minds, including professors of philosophy, as the supreme stage of historic rationality.'[55] In 1970 Debray was in Bolivia, where he remembers hearing a Radio Peking broadcast in Spanish which related the story, 'not as a parable but as a true and exemplary fact', of a Tanzanian peasant woman who walked 300 kilometres to the capital to visit the embassy of the People's Republic of China, where she touched with her own hands a portrait of Mao Zedong. She died of exhaustion the next day.[56] To appreciate the follies committed across the Paris-Chinese border, perhaps it helps to be sitting in Bolivia.

While we are given to understand that an African peasant woman, having seen and touched Mao's portrait as if touching a religious relic, died happily, in the France of 1915 even the dead were not omitted from the task of the salvation of the nation. As if sacrificing life once were not sufficient, they are to be resurrected and exhorted to defend the 'fatherland' again:

---

[54] Debray 18-19.
[55] *Ibid.* 19.
[56] *Ibid.*

THE MUSE: Arise dead! Arise!

FRANCE: Arise dead! Arise!
And lead my children at the height of the battle.
Poet, what have you done? I feel my blood boil

....

POET: Look. Around about you the flags
Beat with joy to see you smile.

FRANCE: Oh my sons, oh my sons, the living and the
    dead,
To all of you whom I owe always being France,
May the benevolence of God encourage your efforts.
Look at the colours of hope in the sky.

[At this moment are heard faintly the first notes of the *Marseillaise*,
and by a trick of light, the sky adopts the hues of the tricolor.]

Recently, in one of a series of lectures on nationalism,
Benedict Anderson discussed the nationalisation of the war
dead that first took place after the First World War.[57] The
British state refused to allow any bodies to be transported back
to Britain (except for a few barrels of remains from which the
Unknown Soldier could be constituted). All the dead were to
be buried in uniform fashion. Even when dead, they belonged
not to their families and their neighbourhoods but to England,
to the state. Shortly before Anderson's lecture, I had been at
Liverpool Cemetery doing some research on Chinese in the
diaspora. Three tombstones in particular stood out. They
belonged to Chinese men who had died in 1917 in the service
of His Majesty while serving in the British Army's Chinese
Labour Corps.[58] In other words, they had been coolies in

[57] The Frederick Ives Carpenter Lectures, 'Attached Detachments: Metamorphoses
in the Nationalist Imagination', Third Lecture: 'Genesis', University of Chicago,
22 April 1993.

[58] The Chinese Labour Corps was also deployed by the British during the Second
World War. Chinese merchant seamen who refused to man ships could be deported
by both British and US authorities for conscription into the Chinese Labour Corps
formed under the aegis of the colonial administration in India. Not only were
Chinese seamen paid a fraction of the wages paid to white seamen, but they were

uniform on the battlefields, digging trenches and latrines. The three Chinese had no place alongside the white British soldiers in Flanders fields; they were 'repatriated' to the Chinese sector of Liverpool Cemetery, in England. Even in death there is discrimination, and in the columns of the Register of Deaths, appended in capitals is the additional information: 'CHINESE'. This is even though the number assigned to the gravestone makes it perfectly clear that the body is buried in the Chinese sector of the graveyard.

As for the Chinese dead in Ai Qing's patriotic 'resistance' poem 'He Has Risen', they too are conscripted into service, and as in the French verse play it is not only the warrior who is to be resurrected Christ-like, but the fatherland also:

> He has risen –
> from decades of humiliation
> from the edge of the deep pit dug by the enemy
> ....
>
> He has risen
> He has risen
> More fierce than all wild beasts
> More clever than all mankind
>
> Because he must be like this
> Because he
> Must out of the enemy's death
> Wrest back his own existence.[59]

Benjamin Péret also understood that wars between nations and the confusion they engender lead to an upsurge in religious fervour and nationalism, and the latter he saw as akin to the former. Americans need only cast their minds back a few years to recall how nationalism, equipped with Patriot missiles, and the religious nature of the fervour it engenders, can engulf society. In America, of course, God is enshrined in the constitution and in the national ideology, and therefore it was 'natural' that God, in one of the few advanced capitalist

---

also thus virtually press-ganged into service.

[59] *Ai Qing quanji*, vol. 1 (Shijiazhuang: Huashan wenyi chubanshe, 1991) 155-6.

countries where religious observance is extensive, should be on America's side. During the First World War 'the clerics of France solemnly declared that God was not German, while on the other side of the Rhine their counterparts proclaimed precisely the opposite.'[60] In the case of the Gulf War it was much more clear-cut which side the Judaeo-Christian god was on, and in war 'you never ask questions/When God's on your side'.[61] In 1982 during the Falklands/Malvinas war Britain witnessed the kind of blind jingoism that surely had not been seen since the First World War, or perhaps even since the Boer War. The war with Argentina over the territory and resources of a far-away and, to most British people before 1982, unknown remnant of empire whipped up a frenzy of patriotism. In the modern nation-state, when militarism comes to the fore, so does nationalist sentiment. In the kind of authoritarian state we see now in China, and which is re-emerging around the world from Russia to Latin America, militarism is increasingly dominant as a means of asserting national and nationalist claims.[62]

There is no doubt that where rhyme and reason seem to be lacking, rhyme and rhythm can be successfully channelled into the service of propaganda, and that is precisely why Péret attacks those on the left who so use them. Such poetic products cease to be vehicles for progress and indeed 'remain reactionary whether they are the propaganda "poetry" of fascism or anti-fascism, or religious exaltation'.[63]

Péret reserves particularly harsh criticism for former friends and comrades, the Communist poets Paul Eluard and Louis Aragon who numbered among those who had contributed to *The Honour of Poets*. He declares that they 'in no way participate in the creative thought of the revolutionaries of Year

---

[60] Péret 202.

[61] As Bob Dylan sang in 1963; *Lyrics; 1962-1985* (New York: Knopf, 1985) 93.

[62] The year 1995 opened with Peruvian and Ecuadorean armies engaged in combat over disputed territory, and continued with nationalist wars still being waged in former Yugoslavia and in the former Soviet Union.

[63] Péret 203.

II or Russia 1917', for while the latter were the 'products of a real and collective exaltation that their words translated', these 'poets' merely 'provoke a factitious exaltation in the masses'.[64] Péret even attaches greater value to the mystics or heretics of the Middle Ages, who 'expressed, then, the thoughts and hopes of an entire people imbued with the same myth or animated by the same spirit, while propaganda "poetry" aims to restore a little life to a myth in its death throes.'[65]

For Péret, the nationalistic verses in *The Honour of Poets* are 'civic hymns' exploiting rather than creating myth. The Communists' patriotic poems 'directly inherit the conservative function' of the Christian church hymn, 'or if mythical then mystical poetry creates the divinity, the hymn exploits this divinity. Just as the revolutionary of Year II or 1917 created a new society while the patriot and the Stalinist of today takes advantage of it.'[66]

While Péret's position may seem to be that there is good political poetry and bad political poetry – bad political poetry being the exaltation of narrow and ultimately reactionary nationalism, whereas good political poetry is more critical, creative and emancipatory, with a more complex comprehension of the political – such a starkly dualistic discursive distinction would be a too simplistic reading of his ideas. There is, for instance, the poetry that is not self-consciously political, yet serves a political purpose by maintaining the ideological *status quo*; and poetry which wittingly or not serves to unmask partly or fully the falseness of the image, projected by the dominant classes and cultures in twentieth-century society, of social relations and humankind's relation to Nature.

The 'poet' for Péret is a non-conformist, a heretic, who alerts the people, rather than a wielder of a blunt instrument of propaganda who speaks at the people. Indeed Péret,

[64] *Ibid.*
[65] *Ibid.*
[66] *Ibid.*

continuing his analogy with medieval religion, distinguishes between mystics,

[who] tend to consolidate myth and involuntarily prepare the conditions that will lead to its reduction to religious dogma, and heretics, whose intellectual and social role is always revolutionary because it brings into question the principle on which myth relies to mummify itself in dogma.[67]

Poetry as an expression of a genuine revolution is to be welcomed, while 'patriotic' resistance poetry like Paul Eluard's is mere propaganda exploitative of genuine revolution or myth. One of Eluard's poems from the anthology to which Péret takes exception, a poem Péret terms a 'most finished civic litany', is entitled 'Liberty':

> On the springboard of my door
> On familiar objects
> On the tide of holy fire
> I write your name.[68]

As this stanza illustrates, the poem might as well be addressed to God as to Liberty reified and deified. Indeed, Péret likens to priests the patiotic-nationalist, Communist Party-instructed producers of such litanies, because he claims 'they have the same parasitic function in relation to myth'. And in many of the poems written by those Péret calls 'supporters of fatherland and leader' the very vocabulary and myth of Christianity are indeed appropriated, just as they had been in the *Dream of the Poet* in 1915 ('France! France! Permit me to bow down at your feet,/As in a temple where one falls to one's knees'); just as graphically the image of the crucifixion was employed in a 1944 poster designed by Paul Colin and entitled 'The Liberation of France'. The poster shows the embodiment of France, Marianne, with the scars of crucifixion, but having risen again.[69] Witness also the 'Resistance' poem 'Prayer for France'

---

[67] *Ibid.*

[68] Paul Éluard, *Œuvres complètes*, v. 1 (Paris: Gallimard, La Pléiade, 1968) 1106.

[69] Stéphane Marchetti, *Affiches 1939-1945. Images d'une certaine France* (Lausanne: Edita SA, 1982) 161. The crucifix metaphor was used again by Paul Colin in a 1945 poster, 'THE NAZI CRIME', for the Nazi Crime Exhibition 'Presented by

by Loys Masson in which maternal and holy France stretches out her mutilated hands, wishing once again to be the mother of the body of Liberty, like the hands of Mother Mary embracing the body of the crucified Christ.[70]

Péret's rejection of narrow nationalistic poetry, and the insistence on a distinction between propaganda 'poetry' and revolutionary poetry, is not the usual bourgeois humanist apology for the 'apolitical' lyric. Rather he promotes a poetry that has its own means of making sense. In a case like the resistance to the Nazis in occupied France, Péret says:

> The expulsion of the oppressor and the propaganda to this end fall within the realm of political, social or military action . . . . In any case, poetry does not have to intervene in this debate *by other than its own means, by its own cultural significance, leaving poets free to participate as revolutionaries in routing the . . . adversary by revolutionary means* – without ever forgetting that this oppression corresponded to the wish . . . of all the enemies . . . of poetry understood as the total liberation of the human spirit [emphasis added].

And in a phrase redolent of Tsvetaeva, but from a much more radical and progressively internationalist perspective, indeed in a conscious paraphrasing of Marx, Péret affirms: 'poetry has no homeland because it belongs to all times and places.'[71]

Again this latter statement does not advocate a transcendental, universalist claim for an unideological, apolitical autonomy for poetry at odds with the historical specificity implicit in

the French Government under the auspices of the United Nations War Crimes Commission'; an exhibition held at the Princes Galleries, Piccadilly, London. The poster shows a young woman, her head hanging down and arms stretched above her head and nailed, Christ-like, to an enormous three-dimensional swastika.

[70]Abandoning the image of Marianne crucified, the magazine of the state-sponsored international television service, Canal France International, chose to illustrate the cover of its issue commemorating the fiftieth anniversary of the Liberation of Paris with a Marianne, recuperated from a 1940s poster, breaking free from chains of bondage. Draped in a *Tricolor* tailored to emphasise the curve of her breasts, the blonde, *maquillée*, pouting Marianne, eyes closed in the ecstasy of emancipation, offers an image of France more redolent of a 1990s commodified and consumable Hollywood film star than a nation resurrected: Marianne as Marilyn rather than Christ.

[71]Péret 205-6.

poetry as ideological critique. On the contrary, in relation to the use of easily manipulated categories like 'freedom', Péret makes an observation which is of utmost relevance:

As long as the malevolent phantoms of religion and fatherland, in whatever disguise they borrow, buffet the intellectual and social air, no freedom is conceivable. Every poem that exalts a 'freedom' willfully left undefined, even when not adorned with religious or national attributes, first ceases to be a poem and then constitutes an obstacle to the total liberation of humanity, for its deceives in presenting a 'freedom' that dissimulates new chains. From every authentic poem on the other hand, issues a breath of absolute and active freedom, even if this freedom is not evoked in its political or social aspect: in this way the poem contributes to the real liberation of humanity.[72]

The poetic 'authenticity' Péret foregrounds refers not to culturally or linguistically pure or 'genuine' poetry, but rather to a poetry determined by a commitment to a complex human emancipation and an overturning of the alienation of modernity. This is a positive poetic function surpassing the capacity to critique. It refers to active contribution to the construction of 'absolute and active freedom', a thoroughgoing 'liberation of humanity', not an illusory 'liberation' offered by a nationalist credo. But the 'authenticity' of the 'authentic poem' surely relates to its context. Whether many poems in 1990s North America or Europe are 'authentic', whether they emit a 'breath of absolute and active freedom', is debatable. However, in the context of the dominant discourses of narrowly nationalistic revolutionary romanticism or socialist realism of 1970s China, a modernist poem can both engage in critique and by virtue of its own means, 'by its own cultural significance', begin to unveil the dominant ideology of the oppressor, each authentic poem opening a window on to the possibility of attaining a meaningful freedom. I end this chapter with a passage written by Péret in exile in Mexico in 1943 but still very much relevant to lyricists writing at the end of the twentieth century:

Poets . . . can no longer be recognized as such, unless they show by

[72] *Ibid.* 206.

total non-conformity their opposition to the world in which they live. They stand against everyone, including revolutionaries who by working only in the field of politics, arbitrarily separate politics from the cultural movement in general, and advocate subordinating culture in order to achieve the social revolution. There is no poet or artist aware of his place in society who does not think this urgently-required, indispensable revolution is the key to the future. But I find it as reactionary to wish poetry and all of culture dictatorially to the political movement, as it is to exclude it completely . . . . The reactionary camps try to make poetry into the equivalent of religious prayer, while the revolutionary side all too easily confuse it with propaganda. A poet these days must be either a revolutionary or not [be] a poet, for he must endlessly launch into the unknown; one step taken one day does not let him off the next step taken the next day, because everything has to be started afresh each day . . . . Only at this price can he be called a poet and aspire to a legitimate place at the apex of the cultural movement where neither praise nor laurels are to be won, but he must work with all his strength to pull down the constantly re-growing barriers of routine and habit.[73]

---

[73] *Ibid.* 199.

3

CHINESE MODERNISM, WESTERN COLONIALISM

'It seems that each new attempt to transform the world is forced to start out with the appearance of a *new unrealism.*'
— J.V. Martin, J. Strijbosch, R. Vaneigem, R. Vienet[1]

'La réalité on ne crache pas dessus/On la transforme!'
—Rachid Boudjedra[2]

'But what does the return to the East mean, anyway? Even if the oppression has assumed the face of England or France, cultural and technical acquirements belong to all peoples.'
—Albert Memmi[3]

To the general reader Chinese poetry implies classical Chinese poetry: that of Wang Wei, Tu Fu (Du Fu), Li Po (Li Bai); of the Tang (618-907) poetic masters collected together and published during the Northern Song (960-1127) dynasty. To the English-reading public Chinese poetry perhaps implies the translations of British sinologist Arthur Waley, who wrote in a Victorian style, or of the American Kenneth Rexroth. *Modern* Chinese literature, if it means anything at all, means acquaintance with one or two writers from the modern Chinese canon; for example, Lu Xun (or Lu Hsün, essayist

---

[1] 'Response to a Questionnaire from the Center for Socio-Experimental Art', 6 December 1963, in Ken Knabb (ed.), *Situationist International Anthology* (Berkeley, CA: Bureau of Public Secrets, 1989) 147.
[2] 'You don't spit on reality,/You transform it' in Jean Sénac (ed.), *Anthologie de la Nouvelle Poésie Algérienne: Poésie 1*, no. 14 (1971) 7.
[3] *The Colonizer and the Colonized* (London: Earthscan, 1990) 218.

64

and fiction writer with a monumental reputation in China) and Lao She (known outside China mainly for his novel *Rickshaw Boy*), both adherents of the critical realist mode which developed in the 1910s and 1920s.[4] And yet China's modern poetry is almost unknown outside the country. For instance, Rexroth, who besides translating classical Chinese poetry was also a translator of the Spanish modernist poet García Lorca, translated no modern Chinese poetry.

When China entered the twentieth century, poetry was still the dominant literary genre, and if a modern vernacular literature was to take hold in this conservative and feudal land it had to be shown that a modern *poetry* was possible despite the burden of the classical tradition. This at least seems to have been the attitude of late nineteenth-century reform-minded intellectuals like Liang Qichao, Tan Sitong and Xia Zengyou, who in Shanghai in 1896 launched what they called a *shijie geming*, a 'revolution in poetry', which in reality led to very little relaxation of the constraints of classical Chinese poetry, but as least signalled a desire to see poetry re-empowered and capable of responding to social reality. At about the same time, another poet, Huang Zunxian, acknowledged by many as the predecessor of the modern Chinese poetry movement, coined the slogan: 'My hand writes what my mouth says, how can

[4] Some would describe both as modernists. In particular, Lu Xun has been recently claimed as a sort of proto-modernist preceding the modernism of the 1980s; see for example Tang Xiaobing, 'Lu Xun's "Diary of a Madman" and a Chinese Modernism', *PMLA* (*Publications of the Modern Languages Association of America*) 107 (1992): 1222-34. Although I can understand the objections to defining Lu Xun as a realist, I prefer to reserve the term 'modernism' in the Chinese context for a more specific literary production, centred for the most part on Shanghai, in the 1930s and 1940s. If a precursor of 1980s modernism is to be identified, it would surely be the cultural production of the 1930s Shanghai modernists (such as Mu Shiying, Shi Zhecun and Liu Na'ou) and of the 1940s generation of modernist poets collectively known as the Nine Leaves Poets (among whom were Chen Jingrong, Du Yunxie, Mu Dan, Xin Di and Zheng Min) who were more concerned with the alienating and dehumanisation of modernity, the employment of avant-garde techniques and the deployment of psychoanalytical critique.

It is also happily the case that thanks to the work of several translators (Howard Goldblatt stands out), contemporary Chinese fiction is becoming increasingly known to English-speaking readers.

antiquity restrain me?' This famous phrase, often quoted as heralding the preliminary and revolutionary rupture with the poetic tradition, says more about the good intentions of its author than it does of his success in crafting a malleable poetic style responsive both to modern society and to modern speech. Only when seen in the original Chinese does its failure to be modern at the linguistic level, and the difficulty scholar-poets had in breaking free of the classical idiom, become visible, for the phrase is written in the classical language rather than the vernacular: '*Wo shou xie wu kou. Gu qi neng ju qian.*'[5]

Huang was still writing in literary Chinese and his prose and poetry were still charged with allusions to the classics and celebrated poetry going back two to three thousand years. The only realm in which Huang really departed from tradition was that of subject-matter. He tackled poems dealing with foreign lands and symbols of Western modernity, like the Eiffel Tower, but always couched in a traditional poetic language and style echoing the poetry and classics of yesteryear.

Liang Qichao thought Huang the major poet of the 'poetic revolution'. Liang's own poetry displayed contradictory notions about the reform of verse, and he was evidently not convinced that it should be written in a purely vernacular language. In Liang's own poetry 'new imported things' clash with classical expression and conventional allusions.[6]

It is the latter characteristic that is also most striking in Huang's verse. And yet the fact that, despite his continued use of the traditional literary language and its accretions, literary historians perceive that Huang did make a significant contribution to the opening up of poetry to modern and foreign themes, indicates just how much Chinese poets needed to do to create a new and viable poetic medium. It also shows how

[5] Huang Zunxian, *Renjinlü shicao jianzhu*, 3 vols (Shanghai: Shangwu, 1936) *xu* 1.
[6] Helmut Martin, 'A Transitional Concept of Chinese Literature 1897-1917: Liang Ch'i-chao on Poetry Reform, Historical Drama and the Political Novel', *Oriens Extremus* 20 (1973), 196-7: 'Steamships, railways and the telegraph are introduced. A new political terminology exalting "democracy, freedom and equality" recurs. . . [and the reader encounters verses] where the new imported things are clashing with conventional allusions.'

even those who expressed a commitment to the idea of a
revolution in poetry were tied tightly to the old forms and
language. Witness the poems Huang wrote about the cities of
London and Paris. London, it should be recalled, was then the
capital not just of Britain but of its empire too, and as such was
the metropolis of the most economically and militarily powerful nation on earth, while Paris was the cultural and artistic
focus of the Western world.

In the poem entitled 'Zai Lundun xie zhen zhi gan' (Writing
a true record of London) there are numerous allusions to the
classical literary heritage: stock phrases from the poetry of Du
Fu, the *Shiji* and the *Hanshu*.[7] Are these intentional echoes?
Does the use of what might otherwise be considered clichés
merely reflect the poet's writing in the only style he could
conceive of? Or was the grip of the classical poetic style of
composition so firm that the poet employed such stock phrases
unwittingly? One would incline to the former interpretation,
for the poet would not unconsciously have employed the
wealth of literary allusions to be discovered in a poem such as
'Lundun da wu xing' (Walking in the London fog), which
employs words and phrases adapted or culled from the classical
poets Lu You and Liu Zongyuan, and from *Han Feizi*, the
Shijing or *The Book of Songs*, the *Liji*, Du Fu again, *Laozi*, the
Hou Hanshu and the poetry of Han Yu – even with this, the
list of allusions is not comprehensive. Besides classical references there also appears to be an allusion to Liang Qichao's
deployment of the dictum: 'The sun never sets on the British
Empire.'[8] While one might read the latter as a concession to
contemporary reality, it seems still to be a literary
reference used in a traditional manner. It is a measure of the
entrenched and conservative nature of contemporary poetic

---

[7] Huang Zunxian, *Renjinlü, 2, juan 6*, 13b.

[8] Huang 13a. The annotator claims Huang took the phrase as a literary reference
from Liang Qichao's record of his own travels in Europe: '*Yingguo guoqi yongyuan
hai kanbujian riluo*', Liang Qichao, *Ou you xin jing lu*. But the saying was common
currency and Huang could well have become acquainted with it at first hand. In
an English literary context, the dictum seems to be found first in *Noctes Ambrosianae*
20 (April 1829) as 'His Majesty's dominion, on which the sun never sets'.

taste that to the reader the incorporation of foreign themes and place names, even without the abandonment of Chinese metrics and recourse to allusive composition, would have been seen as an adventurous and modern departure.

Radical dissatisfaction with the classical tradition had its beginnings in the recognition that China was powerless to repel foreign colonialist aggression, in particular British imperialist ambitions. This was manifested by the defeats in the nineteenth-century Opium Wars, but dissatisfaction and heightened calls for a total social, political and intellectual break with the past reached their crescendo only after the apparent failure of the 1911 Chinese Revolution to effect real change, and most forcefully after the deplorable treatment the country received under the terms of the 1919 Versailles peace treaty. The post-war Paris conference was supposed to realise President Wilson's new world order of self-determined nation-states, but rather than reversing the imperialist powers' hundred or so years of colonialist territorial and economic encroachment as radical Chinese had hoped, the Versailles peace process entrenched and advanced it. It did so by transferring to Japan, ally of Britain and the United States in the Great War, Germany's forfeited colonies and economic rights in the Shandong Peninsula, thus providing Japan with its first major territorial foothold on the Chinese mainland. Japan had been on the side of the victors, but so had China. Thousands of Chinese coolies, enrolled in the Chinese Labour Corps, had contributed to the war effort by digging trenches and providing other support on the battlefields of Europe. That the peace treaty and the principle of self-determination were not meant to impinge on imperialist power and ambitions in Asia and Africa is clear, for Japan was not alone in profiting from Germany's defeat, being ceded German possessions in China, since France and Britain took over Germany's colonies in Africa. No victorious power conceded any overseas territory. Wilson's and the US government's double standards were also evident in the United States' own status as colonising power, which we all tend to forget, since Americans have forgotten it. The late nineteenth and early twentieth centuries constituted a moment of American imperial expansion. The United States had totally defeated Native American resistance to the colonisation of its lands by the last quarter of the nineteenth century. Having consolidated occupation of the greater part of North America, the USA started to colonise the Asian-Pacific region. Indeed, America regarded the Pacific Ocean as its own lake. In 1898 the Philippines and Hawaii were colonised; in 1900 Samoa.

At Versailles, then, there was no question of conceding self-determination to non-white peoples. If Japan, as a victor, could gain a share of the spoils, it was simply because of its industrial and military strength; a lesson not lost on China's élite. Yet paradoxically, while the verdict on Versailles from Chinese and the Western dominant liberal perspectives has tended to be strongly anti-Japanese, Japan was acting no worse, and perhaps better, than other imperialist powers after the First World War. Indeed, at the peace conference Japan had attempted to include a clause on racial equality in the Covenant of the League of Nations, the predecessor to the United Nations. The Japanese amendment, 'palpably a challenge to the theory of the superiority of the white race on which rested so many of Great Britain's imperial pretensions', was not accepted.[9] The 'West's rejection of the principle of racial equality' during the Paris peace conference 'sat uneasily alongside its affirmation of national self-determination. The tension underlined the internal incoherence of imperialist thought.'[10] But even this restricted acceptance of the principle of national self-determination deepened the crisis of imperialism:

On the basis of the European and American experience the association of nationalism with modernity was deeply embedded in Western thought. . . the national revolutions of the eighteenth and nineteenth centuries had marked the West's entry into the modern capitalist age. On the

[9] A.W. Griswold, *The Far Eastern Policy of the United States* (New Haven, CT: Yale University Press, 1966) 247, cited in Frank Füredi, *The New Ideology of Imperialism: Renewing the Moral Imperative* (London : Pluto Press, 1994) 5.

[10] Füredi 5.

basis of this experience, nationalism could not be rejected by Western thinkers, since it was identified as the most significant manifestation of modernity. . . . Imperialism could not, without renouncing its own culture of modernity, mount an attack against the claims of nationalism.[11]

Thus, while the hypocrisy of the Versailles peace settlement had made clear to China's intellectuals the intention of foreign powers to tighten their colonialist grip on the country, the nationalist road model of modernisation was reaffirmed.

After Versailles, the cultural and literary revolution that had been gaining momentum since the turn of the century assumed an even greater importance as it came to be seen by many intellectuals as the only means by which to enlighten China's populace, to enable it to engage in resistance and to relaunch the Chinese revolution. Thus from its earliest days modern literature in China was of seminal importance to the dominant nationalist, patriotic discourse to which most intellectuals, whether Communist, non-Communist or anti-Communist, subscribed. As with other dominated societies in the capitalist period, this need to assert national subjecthood was and is 'not due to internal necessity but to external pressure — it is a requirement for. . . participation in the global economy'.[12] Versailles, while denying China national integrity and autonomy, had nevertheless reaffirmed this very principle and thus, as elsewhere, in China 'the nation as a frame of reference' has been 'a constant presence in cultural production'.[13]

In fiction this led to the development of critical realism as

[11] *Ibid.*

[12] Madhava Prasad, 'A Theory of Third World Literature', *Social Text* 31/2, 78.

[13] *Ibid.* While it is extremely important to grasp, as Prasad has done, the nationalist ideological context of cultural production in dominated societies, the category of 'Third World literature' and the 'national-allegorical dimension of a literary text' (80), which Prasad seeks to defend through re-theorisation, still seems highly problematic to me. For instance, modern literature in China was not merely part of a 'counter-nationalism' to foreign imperialism, it was also defined by a previous Manchu imperialism and by China's own feudal past and its complex of traditions amongst which Confucianism was dominant. This is why the 'Third World' catch-all tag seems a somewhat specificity-free and thus problematic proposition. The issue is discussed further in Chapter 4 of the present work.

not only a vehicle for the ideological critique of society, but also as a means of imagining and representing revolutionary struggle and an alternative vision of society. There were also some modernist excursions in the genre of fiction which only in the last few years have been receiving renewed critical attention; I am thinking here in particular of the fiction of Shi Zhecun, Mu Shiying and Liu Na'ou, also known as the *Xin ganjue pai* or 'new sentiment group' after the Japanese *Shinkan-kakuha*.[14] Yet, amidst the incessant political, economic and military upheavals of the 1930s and 1940s the necessary conditions for the development of full-length modernist novels seem to have been absent.

On the other hand, extensive experimentation in poetry did take place. While there were some notable flirtations with English and German romanticism, writers seeking new structures for Chinese poetic expression focused largely on the French free verse tradition. Its technical aspects appealed to a generation of young poets seeking to break the grip of highly regulated classical verse and it facilitated the use of the new literary-language in the making, which was based on northern colloquial Chinese.

Writers on literary modernism have frequently noted its association with a break with tradition, and in China at the turn of the century the case for a break with the past was overwhelming, while the traditional, conservative cultural environment was far more overpowering and constricting than was the case in modern capitalist Western societies. In China writers were concerned less with capitalism's alienation of the individual than with the still regnant ideology of feudalism and with capitalism constructed as an external colonis-ing force acting on the country as a collectivity, rather than on Chinese individuals. In other words, Chinese society faced the need to find quickly an appropriate response to foreign industrial capitalist modernity and its colonialist designs on China's territory, resources and economic autonomy.

[14] See Dennis Keene, *Yokomitsu Riichi: Modernist* (New York: Columbia University Press, 1980) 58-130.

In the context of overturning the feudalist legacy it should be emphasised that the whole modern literary enterprise – not just modernism in the narrow sense, but romanticism, and realism too – constituted an attempt not merely to interrupt an immediate past but to break with and overturn a cultural heritage imagined as stretching back continuously over several thousand years and imbued with a fundamentally patriarchal and feudal mentality. It was a tradition which, as constructed at the beginning of the twentieth century, constituted a considerable burden and obstacle to new cultural production. If in the West, when the bourgeoisie ceased to be 'in its progressive phase' the modernist aesthetic aimed to 'pulverize traditional form and meaning, because the laws of syntax and grammar are the laws of the police', in early twentieth-century China the laws of Chinese poetry had come to be seen as laws and customs of a moribund, patriarchal order, which was still ideologically and institutionally a feudal order.[15] Indeed, the renowned Chinese scholar Wang Li refers to modern Chinese vernacular verse as 'seeking liberation' from the regulations of classical verse.[16]

What distinguished modernism in China from the other modern literary modes was its ambivalence towards the modernising, industrialising, materialist road to national salvation or regeneration which constituted the dominant narrative of progress for most patriotic Chinese intellectuals and producers of culture; an anti-imperialist narrative which can so easily become confused with national chauvinism.

Modernists in general, while rejecting much of the cultural past, were not chauvinists; they were also resistant to the utopian realism being promoted by the Communist-dominated left. Frequently, as in the fiction of Shi Zhecun and Mu Shiying, their critique centred on metropolitan modernity and the alienation and fragmentation that industrial capitalism had engendered in individual psyches and social relations. There

---

[15] Terry Eagleton, *The Ideology of the Aesthetic* (Oxford: Blackwell, 1990) 369.

[16] Wang Li, *Hanyu shulüxue* (Shanghai: Jiaoyu chubanshe, 1958, 1979) 833.

was an awareness in the cultural work of some that, in the Benjaminian sense, there are contradictory histories and that it 'can never be a question of some stark binary opposition between the dead weight of the past and some brave new present, since the past is precisely what we are made of.'[17]

The alternative critique that Western theorists would ultimately discern as latent in modernism in the West was also afforded by Chinese modernism. Modernism, then, not only supplied a critique of capitalist urban modernity and its resultant alienation of the human subject, but also foresaw the closure of emancipatory possibilities and other 'characteristics of capitalism' that orthodox Communist practice, and its attendant literary modes, would bring about.[18]

Having turned their backs on their own past, literary revolutionists looked to the world outside. They sought or found not necessarily what was 'modern' but what was 'new' and at one level all foreign literature was new. Thus in the 1920s there were poets like Guo Moruo, who assimilated Goethe, Whitman and Tagore to produce a somewhat confused, pantheistic romanticism replete with internationalist and revolutionary fervour. Dai Wangshu, later to be heralded as one of China's first modernist poets, translated not only the French symbolists but Ovid's *Amores* and the French medieval classic *Aucassin et Nicolette*. The past, it seems, was acceptable as long as it was the Other's past, a new past.[19] But it was only a matter of time before the specifically modernist foreign tradition was singled out.

The contradiction, of course, was that while the West, and Japan which had already developed its own modernist strategies and concerns, was a source of fresh ideas, texts and technologies, it was also the source of colonialist aggression, economic exploitation and China's humiliation. Such a con-

---

[17] Eagleton 378.

[18] Raymond Williams, *The Politics of Modernism* (New York: Verso, 1989) 26.

[19] For a fuller discussion of Dai Wangshu, his poetry and his translating activities, see Gregory Lee, *Dai Wangshu: The Life and Poetry of a Chinese Modernist* (Hong Kong: Chinese University Press, 1989).

tradiction led to a confused pattern of receptivity. While China was not colonised in the sense that India was, it was subjected to both territorial imperialism and neo-colonialism. Britain was the dominant colonial power, interested foremost in economic dominance. As for the French, they also were primarily interested in commerce, but failing in their bid for direct hegemonic economic exploitation, their alternative and often consciously deployed strategy was to achieve dominance in the cultural and educational fields.[20] In the China of the 1920s and 1930s, it was Shanghai which was the cultural metropolis, and it was in Shanghai that the French, who administered a major part of the city, exerted the culturally dominant influence.[21]

Unlike India, China was faced not with a unitary dominant imperialist culture but with a plethora of competing colonisers, so here a number of factors came into play. One was an aversion to the dominant imperialist 'foreign devils', the British and their culture. There was also a long-standing condescension and resentment towards Japan, which had vanquished China in the 1894-5 Sino-Japanese War, had encroached on the country's territory ever since and was soon to become the dominant imperialist aggressor in Asia.[22]

[20] See Robert Lee, *France and the Exploitation of China: A Study in Econom·_ Imperialism* (Hong Kong: Oxford University Press, 1989). The determination with which the French authorities pursued their policies of conquering minds is demonstrated by the following reference in a French school textbook published before the Second World War: 'France has also established in its colonies and abroad numerous institutions: *Maisons de France*, scientific institutes, archaeological schools, universities, *lycées*, schools, libraries. . . , centres shining with French thought. . . . At all major points of the globe, these "*foyers*" of intense culture bear witness to the intelligent and generous strength of France in the World.' J.-B. Delamarre, *La France dans le monde. Ses colonies, son empire* (Tours: 1939) 172.

[21] The Frenchness of Shanghai in the French colonialist imaginary is clear in the following paragraph on the city in Delamarre's textbook on the French colonies: 'Did you know that for a part of the city of Shanghai we practically have the right to say "France in Shanghai"? To all intents and purposes, France rules and governs over the space within the *French* Concession, which dates from 1849. . . . [M]ore than 200,000 (of which 195,000 Chinese) live in our concession, [and are] thus dependent on France.' *Ibid.* 137.

[22] However, numerous Chinese students, including Lu Xun and the Shanghai

Describing the reaction of the colonised to French colonialism in North Africa, Albert Memmi notes that with 'fury and ostentation, the colonized begins to show a preference for German cars, Italian radios and American refrigerators. He does without tobacco if it bears the colonialist's stamp!' But in China it seems to have been the British and the Japanese whose cultural products were least valued. There was a preference for the French with their seemingly more enlightened and revolutionary traditions, not to mention their educational provision for Chinese students in China and in France, and the accessibility of canonical and popular French culture in the bookshops, cinemas and cafés of the French quarter of China's cultural capital, Shanghai. The intellectual and political links had been forged at the end of the First World War when over 2,000 Chinese students left China to study in France; they comprised much of the élite of China's Communist Party, including long-time Premier Zhou Enlai and China's subsequent 'paramount leader', Deng Xiaoping. In 1931 there were approximately 1,250 Chinese students studying French and pursuing university courses in Paris, Lyon and elsewhere in France.[23] A University of Paris humanities professor wrote at the time in a report entitled 'Chinese Students in France':

There are many Chinese students in France. They are attracted not only by our culture, but also by the memory of the Revolution. They dream of a great China, established not merely in line with our methods but also in line with our principles of social justice and individual freedom. May they be doubly welcome![24]

For Chinese poets constructing a new poetic idiom, there was also the attraction to the potential formal iconoclasm of free verse and the symbolist-modernist tradition, an attraction shared by modern Japanese poets. Some odd and unexpected

---

modernist Liu Na'ou, studied in Japan, and gained access to European and American learning and literature through Japanese.

[23] George Dumas, 'Les étudiants chinois en France' in *Annales de l'Université de Paris*, January 1932, p. 11.

[24] *Ibid.* 10.

consequences result from this differentiated reception of colonial cultures. For instance, the late 1920s Chinese poets' preference for symbolism led to the atypical nineteenth-century British poet Ernest Dowson, then neglected elsewhere, being avidly read and translated, or more specifically his imitations of Verlaine were.

But the privileging of the literature of one particular colonialism did not bring wholesale and uncritical acceptance of the contemporary French canon or avant-garde anti-canon. For example, the dominant influence on the Chinese modernist Dai Wangshu in the late 1920s was not Baudelaire or Verlaine, although he had certainly read them, but the neo-symbolist rural recluse Francis Jammes.[25]

It is probable, then, that Dai Wangshu was exercising a conscious choice; he was not simply colonised by Western culture, but exercised agency in seeking out the new and the redeployable in French, Spanish and other European literatures. But as a Chinese educated in the classics, Dai Wangshu's aesthetic was also informed by the canon and practices of late Tang poetry, and Taoist thought and imagery often surfaced in his work. The fragmentation and narrative disjuncture often associated with modernism were perhaps perceived as analogous to the ease with which physical, worldly constraints are shed and reality transformed in numerous Taoist texts. These commonalties at the levels of imagination and technique would surely not have escaped a Chinese modernist practitioner acquainted with both Western modernism and Chinese Taoist texts. It is instructive that Dai's later and more extremely modernist production relies extensively on Taoist allusions to produce a synthetic or hybrid poetic imagery. While recuperating Taoist emancipatory images and tropes related to time and space, Dai Wangshu nevertheless continued

---

[25] In Japan a generation earlier, both Francis Jammes and the northern French, Lille-based, neo-symbolist Albert Samain were by far the most popular with those seeking to construct a modern Japanese poetry; yet these were just two of a whole range of European modernist poets translated by the Japanese poet Horiguchi Daigaku. The extent of the reception of French neo-symbolist poets in Japan was attested to by Oe Kenzaburo in a recent discussion with the present author.

to deploy the imagery and vocabulary of the poetic texts of the French neo-symbolist, Francis Jammes. Phrases redolent of Jammes are to be found scattered throughout Dai's poetry. For instance, in 1936 after a conversation with a friend passionately interested in astronomy, Dai wrote the following lines:

> I do not know why people give the stars
> Names they do not need
> Not understanding nor seeking fame.[26]

The poem develops this anti-positivist, anti-scientist thought, but what I wish to draw attention to is how this opening stanza is redolent of one in the poem 'Il va neiger dans quelques jours' (It will snow in a few days) by Francis Jammes:

> We've baptised the stars without thinking
> that they had no need of names, and the numbers
> which prove that beautiful comets will
> pass in the dark, will not compel them to pass.[27]

The imitation and redeployment of imagery had for millennia been part of the Chinese poetic practice, and alluding to and adapting the words of another poet a respectable element of lyric production. The response to, and reception of, a colonising culture, even when that culture is viewed as benign, are also determined by the cultural practices of the colonised, both of the colonised society and of the colonised individual. The 'failure' of the colonised to identify with and adopt the coloniser's canonical paradigms is often greeted with incredulity and condescension by the coloniser, and the fact of the coloniser's culture being rejected by the colonised or 'plagiarised' or redeployed in ways other than 'intended' raises even graver concerns over 'authenticity'. And yet even if the colonised does try to replicate the coloniser's cultural norms, in the eyes of the coloniser the colonised can only fail:

All that the colonized has done to emulate the colonizer has met with

---

[26] Gregory Lee, *Dai Wangshu* 246.
[27] Francis Jammes, *Choix de poésies* (Paris: Larousse, 1970) 50.

disdain from the colonial masters. They explain to the colonized that those efforts are in vain, that he only acquires thereby an additional trait, that of being ridiculous. He can never succeed in becoming identified with the colonizer, nor even in copying his role correctly... If he [the colonizer] is more rude, he will say that the colonized is an ape. The shrewder the ape, the better he imitates, and the more the colonizer becomes irritated.[28]

Modernism in China has been a product not necessarily of seduction by a particular colonialist culture, but rather of an appropriation of political and aesthetic ideas understood, read, reused in the Chinese context in the light of prevailing historical conditions. The multiple and simultaneous colonisation of China by foreign imperialist powers enabled Chinese cultural producers to draw on a range of cultural responses to capitalist modernity. At the level of technique, it also made available new media. The work of Berlin Dadaists Hannah Höch (whose *Dada Dance* [1922], with an African peasant head and torso superimposed on to a Western bourgeois woman's body clad in a ball gown, illustrates the gulf between the coloniser's industrial and bourgeois culture and the condition of the colonised), Raoul Hausmann and John Heartfield (pseudonym of Helmut Herzfelde, whose *War and Corpses –Last Hope of the Rich* [1932], depicting a snarling leopard sporting a top hat astride a battlefield of corpses, exemplifies the group's concern with exposing the interdependence of capitalism and modern war) illustrated how capitalist modernity's self-images, the object of their social critique, could by employing the technique of photomontage become the very means of critique.[29] For the Chinese visual artists Luo Gusun and Feng Zili, photomontage makes possible a strong and immediate illustration of the contrast between wealth and poverty, metropolitan bourgeois comfort and the suffering of the war-ridden hinterland. The employment of fragments of familiar photographic images out of their original context

[28] Memmi 190.

[29] Kenneth Coutts-Smith, *Dada* (London: Studio Vista; New York: Dutton, 1970) 78, 92.

interrogates and reconstructs the 'truth' represented by the newspapers' and advertisers' use of photography. Luo Gusun in a two-page photomontage, *The Material City and the Bankrupt Village*, illustrates the duality of Chinese material existence by splitting his montage between photographs of the paradise of modern, Western consumer goods and lifestyle available to the wealthy city-dweller, and the ragged, war-torn, disaster-ridden, beggarly reality of rural China.[30]

Some Western modernist practices were less immediately relevant and assimilable to the Chinese experience. For instance, in literary production it was not until the late 1940s that the English-language modernism of Pound and Eliot gained some popularity with poets. That Pound should have had an impact on the modern practice of a poetic culture whose tradition he had earlier appropriated surely fits precisely the Orientalist presumptions of European modernity: the East, and the Third World in general, provides the tradition to be exploited and reinvented as the modern, and then offered back to the East as the 'new', the Western, the superior. That the East should mimic the West is taken as an indication of a lack of originality and authenticity; that the West should recuperate the East is glossed as the inventive creativity of high modernist genius.

By the late 1940s the ideological climate in mainland China precluded further modernist experimentation. Modernism would remain dormant and its potential in the Chinese context unfulfilled until the 1970s, when from underground writers with limited access to Western literature and pre-Communist-era modern Chinese poetry, a deliberately anti-realist, modernist poetry re-emerged.

Since the end of the 1970s, practitioners of modernist poetry have once again been exposed to foreign literatures and cultures, no longer perceived, at least not by those who write poetry, as manifestations of colonialism. And while modernism is now a major literary mode, certainly of unofficial

[30] Scott Minick and Jiao Ping, *Chinese Graphic Design in the Twentieth Century* (London: Thames and Hudson, 1990) 82.

writing, it is still an oppositional, anti-establishment mode. Although by the 1940s the new literary language had finally attained aesthetic and cultural authority, the standardising and conformist literary policies of the Communist apparatus, especially during the Cultural Revolution of 1966-76, led to what has recently been termed the Maoist mode, a linguistic discourse so dominant as to determine some of the most avidly anti-Maoist writing. In the writing of poetry, even as late as 1978, young official poets would write lines like these in praise of electric lighting: 'Now our commune's power plant towers high,/The pearls fall into our village from the sky.'[31]

It was the 'unofficial' poetry of the 1970s and 1980s – contemptuously dismissed by the authorities as *menglong shi* or 'Misty Poetry', a designation nevertheless readily accepted by its practitioners – which attempted to break the Maoist domination of lyrical writing and construct a new idiom. At the end of the Cultural Revolution, new poetry already had a relatively large following in urban China. And while the economic changes effected by Deng Xiaoping and the resulting commodification of culture led to a comparative decline in the reading of poetry and an increasing interest in popular music, television soap operas and fashion, the appeal and the power of poetry as a practice of both writing and reading remains much more significant, especially in the universities and other intellectual institutions, than is the case in America or Britain.

The poet Duoduo, born in 1951 and thus a member of the Red Guard generation, wrote secretly throughout the first half of the 1970s, not knowing when or whether his poems might be published. In 1972, while Mao and his clique still dominated the party-state bureaucracy, Duoduo wrote a poem entitled 'At Parting':[32]

---

[31] Jiang Zhou, *Shikan* 11, 1978: 59-60, trans. Kai-yu Hsu, in Bonnie S. McDougall (ed.), *Popular Chinese Literature and the Performing Arts* (Berkeley: University of California Press, 1984) 264.

[32] Duoduo, *Looking Out From Death: From the Cultural Revolution to Tiananmen Square*, trans. Gregory Lee and John Cayley (London: Bloomsbury, 1989) 21.

The green fields are like constructions of the mind which have
   suddenly
collapsed, like an unending, boundless twilight
where the future's serried ranks keep marching on
You, you are like someone pushed onto an unfamiliar path,
walking down a side alley, grown older
  – those lights from countless dwellings and one shadow of
   loneliness.
There is only a shepherd, tightly gripping his scarlet switch:
  – he is watching the darkness,
           he is watching over the darkness.

Even in this very early example of contemporary Chinese modernist poetry we find a complication of the accepted descriptions of modernist writing. Eagleton, for instance, writes of the 'self-generative nature of modernist writing', of a text which 'authorizes its own discourse'.[33] But Duoduo's poem, so strikingly different to the official products, is a negotiation of real social life, grounded in and meditating on reality. The individual is alienated not materially by commodity capitalism, but ideologically by a modern social formation claiming to be socialism, the kind of social organisation Régis Debray describes as 'a society of commemoration', whose major commodity is ceremony. This poem describes a society experienced by the poet and his fellow dominated beings, whose future can only be imagined in relation to its historicised present as 'an unending, boundless twilight/where the future's serried ranks keep marching on.' Social life is constructed not simply as uniform, but as mundane and alienating. Clearly, in 'At Parting' the exposure of the social isolation of the individual, 'one shadow of loneliness', constitutes at least a partial unveiling of the ideology which had dominated and duped and whose distorted truth offered the only ultimate release from an alienation represented here by the metaphors of solitude and divergence 'on an unfamiliar path'.

We read a great deal about the psychological terror of the Cultural Revolution in China, and indeed such fear has been one of the most undeniable aspects of 'actually existing

[33] Eagleton 140.

socialism', yet one of the most pernicious marks of that system has surely been boredom, not least that of the repetitiously performed cultural products of the Great Proletarian Cultural Revolution (in the main, the films and sound recordings of the strictly limited number of revolutionary model operas).[34] Boredom was in part constitutive of the alienation from the power that was supposed to have emancipated people from the alienatory effects of capitalist social relations. Socialism was meant to release the subject from the numbing relations of capitalism, since, as we are given to understand in Marx's *1844 Manuscripts*, the goal of history is the overcoming of alienation, 'the complete, conscious return of man to himself as social man'.[35]

   In the context of the historical moment of its production, it is compelling to read the image of the solitary 'shepherd, tightly gripping his scarlet switch', the omniscient warder, as a figure of the régime's authority: 'he is watching the darkness,/he is watching over the darkness.' Such a reading is possible, but I would tend to see this more as a metaphor for the alienation of members of society bereft of remedy, with an ideological lack looming before them as black as the darkness itself. Throughout the Cultural Revolution, Mao was likened to the sun; people organised themselves into 'sunflower' groups to study Mao's works. When the sun dims you find yourself in the 'twilight'; when it has ceased to shine you are confronted by darkness. *Pace* Eagleton's description of modernism, then, I do not find modernist poetry in this particular context 'self-generative'. There is in this kind of verse an attempt to establish, against official poetic practice, which in this instance is an instrument of society's regnant authority, a type of aesthetic autonomy, although of a sort that still provides a critique of social life. It is not, then, strictly an autonomy that is a 'kind of negative politics'; for art at this

---

[34] Régis Debray, *Critique de la raison politique: ou l'inconscient religieux* (Paris: Gallimard, Collection Tel, 1981) 21-2.

[35] Cited in Henri Lefebvre, *Pour connaître la pensée de Karl Marx* (Paris: Bordas, 1961) 120.

stage is not 'turning in upon itself' but rather responding to dominant social formations.[36]

The separation between the text and extra-literary reality, which has been noted as a modernist trait, is frequently absent in Chinese modernist texts. The twentieth-century Chinese patriotic-nationalist discourse which has nursed writerly commitment, and the modern Chinese socio-political context in which politics and ideology have not merely been dominant but hegemonically intrusive on a daily basis, have led to a modernistic poetry which *is* frequently more clearly marked by an extra-literary context than may be the case in other modernist lyrical practices. It is possible to overemphasise the extent to which modernist poetry in the post-Mao era has functioned as a mode of resistance against the dominant ideology of Chinese Communism, which under Deng Xiaoping has been transformed into so-called 'socialism with Chinese characteristics', which can be translated as 'capitalism with authoritarian characteristics'. However, the political import and ideological context of this modernism are undeniable.

While it ought to be perverse to apply critically the theory of 'dominant ideology', as theorised by the French Communist Party thinker Althusser, to a socialist society which claims to have constructed a new society along Marxist lines, in the instance of China's supposedly 'Marxist' society it appears to be both valid and appropriate. If there is a paradox here, it does not merely lie in applying such a Marxist critique to the culture of a self-proclaimed Marxist state, but also relates to Althusser's own flirtation with Maoism. Raymond Tallis in his book *In Defence of Realism* points to Althusser's failure to address consciously deployed state ideologies in Marxist-Leninist states.[37] Similarly Terry Eagleton, discussing Foucault's 'secret refusal of régime as such', remarks on the dangerous elision of 'distinctions between, say, fascistic and liberal capitalist forms of society' and notes also that Althusser's

---

[36] Eagleton 370.

[37] Raymond Tallis, *In Defence of Realism* (London: Edward Arnold, 1988) 90.

'concept of "ideological state apparatuses" refuses as purely legalistic the vital difference between state-controlled and non-state ideological institutions'.[38] Of course, it is true that unlike other theorists working in France at that time, such as Cornelius Castoriadis and Guy Debord, Althusser failed to develop a clear-sighted critique of bureaucratic society in its non-Western manifestations, and yet, from the perspective of this end of the twentieth century, whether the difference now seems so 'vital' is questionable. To what extent can the now regnant capitalist forms of society sustain the qualification 'liberal'?

While doubts about contradictions between Althusser's theory and the experience of the 'socialist' societies are justified, they do not necessarily support the kind of 'defence' of realism mounted by Raymond Tallis. When Tallis poses the question 'Is there any reason why in principle that realm of real relations [identified by Althusser as lying beyond that of imaginary relations] should not be intelligible?', my answer would be: in principle, perhaps not, but in contemporary Chinese practice, yes. While realism is or has been *capable* of representing reality so as to expose ideology, in the instance of twentieth-century Chinese realism, despite an early capacity for ideological critique, it has so far been so closely identified with the dominant ideology, has indeed so often inscribed it and been its instrument, that in the light of that ideology's explicit self-exposure during the Cultural Revolution, and more recently in the crushing of dissent in 1989, realism's credibility and ability to represent reality have been seriously impaired. And so for many Chinese writers a degree of 'unintelligibility' or 'meaninglessness' *has* been the only way to represent or mediate reality, and thus counter misconstruction of that reality by the dominant ideology of Maoism and the metanarrative of modernity. 'Meaninglessness' is not merely what in the end the 'bourgeoisie cannot take'.[39] It is also what

---

[38] Eagleton 386-7.
[39] *Ibid.* 370.

bureaucratic, authoritarian and Fascistic régimes cannot take, as the spate of detentions of young experimental poets in China over the last few years illustrates.

In recent years, however, most noticeably in fiction, the oppositionism of the counter-realist trend has taken on some ugly dimensions, not least in the barely concealed misogyny that has marked some of this production. Women's rights were supposed to have been a major facet of the Communist revolution. There were indeed some initial gains, not least in combating remnant feudalistic and patriarchal practices. However, despite the pious propaganda that described women as holding up half the sky, in reality women remained after thirty years of Mao's rule very much dominated by an authority constituted overwhelmingly of men. Since the death of Mao and the new capitalist-oriented politics of Deng Xiaoping, their situation has hardly improved, unless the 'freedom' for men to parade women in beauty contests, to sell them into prostitution and to drown them at birth has somehow liberated women. Unfortunately the male-dominated literary world, while at times seeking to critique these new practices, has nevertheless simultaneously reinscribed women in the new fiction as the objects on which are played out repressed and now liberated masculinist desires, and as the dominated in a reinvigorated patriarchal relationship. It seems appropriate to ask whether women are being made to pay for their seemingly privileged position in the old Communist Party ideology.[40] These are some of the negative effects of the revolt against

---

[40] The contemporary cinema industry, held by many to be anti-hegemonic and resistant to official ideology, has profited most from the commodification of women. While ordinary Chinese women may have benefited little from this exploitation, the film star Gong Li, who has become almost as much an archetype of Chinese woman for foreign audiences as Catherine Deneuve has become the archetypal French woman, has grown not only famous but wealthy; she is reported (*South China Morning Post International Weekly*, vol. 2, no. 28, 30-1 October 1993, p. 1) to have earned 1 million *yuan* for a television commercial advertising air conditioners. More recently she appeared on the winners' podium in Tiananmen Square between the two victorious drivers of the Hong Kong-Beijing car rally, the sponsor's 555 cigarette logo emblazoned across her chest (*Yin Doi Yat Bo* [Xiandai ribao]/*Hong Kong Today*, 29 October 1994, p. 47).

official realism. Yet what can be said of modernism in general is certainly specifically pertinent to much Chinese modernist practice from the 1970s to 1980s: 'By interrupting a discourse . . . we are implicitly claiming the right to participate in and even change that discourse; we are insisting on our right to speak and write.'[41]

Lest this writer's position be taken as a defence of anti-communist rhetoric, let me reiterate that much of Chinese modernist practice seems to be revolting against more than just the authoritarianism of what has been called Confucian-Leninism.[42] It is revolting against the modernising, totalising, monumental and postitivist discourse altogether, a discourse which is closely associated with the nationalist-patriotic project monopolised for the last half-century by the Chinese Communist Party. In other words, as elsewhere, it has been the discourse of industrial modernity itself against which Chinese modernism has revolted. Whether or not sustainable as a description of modernism in general, the proposition that modernism 'is the other [of] modernity', 'modernity held in abeyance', is certainly true of much Chinese modernist poetic practice, both in the first half of the twentieth century and in the past two decades.[43]

That this poetic discourse of opposition, especially when latterly operating against the Maoist mode, should be seen as dependent on Western cultural models might seem to reek of cultural imperialism; indeed that is the very charge the Chinese Communist Party makes when it employs the code words 'spiritual pollution' and 'bourgeois liberalism' in its frequent campaigns against the spread of foreign (in other words Western) influence. But, in that case, were not the nationalis-ing and standardising ambitions of Marxist-Leninist-Maoist

---

[41] Astradur Eysteinsson, *The Concept of Modernism* (Ithaca, NY: Cornell University Press, 1990) 241.

[42] For a discussion of what Lucian Pye has termed Confucian-Leninism, see his *The Mandarin and the Cadre: China's Political Cultures* (Ann Arbor, MI: Center for Chinese Studies, University of Michigan, 1988).

[43] Eysteinsson 240.

anti-colonialism reinforced by, if not derived from, that same alien political and philosophical culture? And is not that materialist, modernising and hence Westernising and now ultimately capitalist impulse also a legacy of Western colonialism? Such questions are central to the 'drama' of the dominated subject 'who is a product and victim of colonisation'.[44] The reaction against the Western colonisers' culture when taken to its fanatical extreme results in tragedies like the Cultural Revolution and the relentless assassinations of thousands of intellectuals in Algeria in the mid-1990s. Writing in 1957, Albert Memmi foresaw the effects of what he called 'the period of revolt': 'We must await the complete disappearance of colonization – including the period of revolt.'[45] For the sake of narrative closure it would not be difficult to construct the Chinese Cultural Revolution as that 'period of revolt', and yet such a construction of history would be to avoid the reality of late capitalism. Colonisation has not disappeared but rather transformed itself into a generalised global dominance with new kinds of relations of dependence; and in the formerly formally colonised societies, the effects of colonisation, not least in the realm of aesthetic ideology, remain. Citing the example of visual aesthetics in his description of the dilemma of the colonised, Memmi writes:

Colonized painting. . . is balanced between two poles. From excessive submission to Europe resulting in depersonalization, it passes to such a violent return to self that it is noxious and esthetically illusory. The right balance not being found, the self-accusation continues. Before and during the revolt, the colonized always considers the colonizer as a model and antithesis. He continues to struggle against him. He was torn between what he was and what he wanted to be, and now he is torn between what he wanted to be and what he is making of himself.[46]

In the Chinese context, literary practice, even at its most 'Westernised', has the mask of the Chinese language with

---

[44] Memmi 206.

[45] *Ibid.* 207.

[46] *Ibid.* 206.

which to conceal itself. It is after all a synthesis, a hybrid product that emerges, even in the most literal translation from one language to another. But in the visual arts the situation is more stark. Over the last ten years Chinese plastic arts have become increasingly and extremely 'avant-garde', as was evidenced by a recent exhibition of work by artists, of whom the majority are now living outside China. The exhibition, 'New Art from China', was mounted in Britain at the Museum of Modern Art (MOMA), Oxford.[47] It was in two parts. The first, 'Silent Energy', consisted largely of installations; the second, 'China Avant-Garde', of paintings, videos and installations. Some but not all of the work displayed was marked by being in some way *about* China; a very few of the artists made use of traditional Chinese techniques or materials. Several of the artists were at pains to avoid 'the stereotypes of calligrapher' and determined 'not to make a contemporary version of ancient art'.[48] The art on show was, like much avant-garde production, highly élitist. Furthermore, almost all of the artists present, despite throwaway remarks such as 'art has no commercial value', made their living out of selling their work or being paid to 'install' it in exhibition spaces. What was interesting, however, was that while the majority of the artists were practitioners of avant-garde or (post-)modernist art, and mostly claimed to subscribe to post-modernist aesthetics, both their work and their explanation of it clung closely to an intended meaning relating to Chinese society.[49] Chen Zhen stated that his installation, a sloping plywood

[47] *New Art from China*, MOMA, Oxford. Part 1: 27 June-29 August 1993 'Silent Energy', work by Cai Guoqiang, Chen Zhen, Gu Wenda, Guan Wei, Huang Yongping, Wang Luyan, Xi Jianjun, Yang Jiechang; Part 2: 5 September-24 October 1993 'China Avant-Garde', work by Ding Yi, Fang Lijun, Geng Jianyi, Gu Dexin, Liu Wei, Ni Haifeng, Wang Guangyi, Yan Peiming, Yu Hong, Yu Houhan, Zhang Peili, Zhao Bandi. Exhibition curated by Lydie Mepham and David Elliot. My thanks to the latter and to Julian May who made my visit and conversations with the artists possible, and to Sally Dunsmore of MOMA who was most generous with information and materials.

[48] Chen Zhen publicity material.

[49] Tape-recorded conversations during installation of the exhibition, 24 June 1993, with Yang Jiechang, Chen Zhen, Gu Wenda, Wang Luyan.

terrace in which a number of holes had been cut and mounds of newspaper were burnt to become black ash, was 'not really a Chinese piece', and that there was 'nothing to show I'm Chinese'. However, the artist went on to say that the work was situated in the 'country where I live now [France]' and in the 'context of my country, China'. It was five years since he had left China, Chen emphasised, and he now wanted 'to dialogue with as large a public as possible'.[50] Chen's own statement on his installation claimed that the work was 'based on the traditional rice terraces of ancient China covered by the lost ashes of lost learning, knowledge, hope and communication'.[51]

The work of Gu Wenda, 'Oedipus Refound II: The Enigma of Birth', was more problematic. His installation consisted of a series of babies' cots, or cradles, several of which had been sprinkled with dried and milled human placentas and then covered with glass cases. These were reminiscent of the *vitrine* works of the radical German artist Joseph Beuys, who exhibited his works in glass display cases as if they were scientific specimens.[52] 'The art objects I make', stated Gu, 'include human materials and have no element of illusion in them; they are as real as the people who look at them. The materials I use reject the idea of the body as object and penetrate through to a sense of spiritual presence.'[53] Two of the cots were meant to represent 'normal' births, one a deformed birth, one an aborted foetus – so the blanket was blank – and one stillborn. Gu Wenda claimed to be making the object, the body, into the material. He had left China six years previously and throughout his work has progressed from 'Chinese images' to a Chineseness 'buried in the work – invisible'.[54] His aim was to challenge 'ready-made civilization'

---

[50] Chen Zhen in conversation.

[51] Chen Zhen publicity material.

[52] For instance, 'Fat Battery' (1963), arranged by Beuys in a vitrine at the Tate Gallery, London, in 1984, and exhibited in 1993–4 at the Tate, Liverpool.

[53] Gu Wenda publicity material.

[54] Gu Wenda in conversation.

which was 'like a cage'. He added, 'I want to make the work be about morality', and he wanted the spectator 'to know what we don't know.' As for this particular work, it was 'not only a women's issue' for him, but 'a universal issue'.[55]

As with all avant-garde artists, Chen's and Gu's ambition is to break free from bourgeois aesthetics. As was the case with Dada, these artists produce politically significant work. With Chen, although his audience is bound to be largely non-Chinese, there is a message from and about China contained in his own reading of his installation. Gu Wenda too claims to be engaged in producing an art which is universalist. It too is highly political since it concerns not merely the politics of the body, but the politics of women's bodies. Gu is concerned with traditional art's creating illusions. He claims he is against the trend of 'using Asian callousness in order to amaze the West, as for instance Zhang Yimou [director of *Red Sorghum*, *Judou* and *To Live*] does in his movies. I choose the placentas from China only because of one technical problem: I'm not able to get this material from the US.'[56] In fact, since the placenta powder comes from China, it specifically concerns Chinese women's bodies and how men may use them in that society. Gu's argument that he is dealing with an issue of universal concern marginalises the immediate political issue of women's control over their bodies.

The issues Gu Wenda raises are not unimportant. He desires to challenge and interrogate the discourse of the body that became so dominant in the nineteenth century. Other artists working in the West have attempted to draw attention to this 'illusion' and to the politics of body and blood, which has become increasingly important since the advent of AIDS. The British artist Marc Quinn, for instance, made the object, blood, into the medium when he filled a life cast of his own head with blood. The difference from Gu Wenda's work was that the blood was his own.[57] The work 'Self' cannot fail to

[55] *Ibid.*

[56] Gu Wenda, letter to Julia F. Andrews, Ohio State University, 16 June 1993.

[57] Marc Quinn, 'Self', *Young British Artists 11*, Saatchi Collection, London, 1993.

shock, but also to critique and perhaps make the viewer reflect upon society's *idées reçues* and *idées forces* about the body and body fluid. As one critic has written: 'To make the decision to work with blood in the age of AIDS points to at least an awareness of the political nature of the body in the dying decade of the twentieth century.'[58] It is generally accepted that 'the avant-garde's response to the cognitive, ethical and aesthetic is quite unequivocal. Truth is a lie; morality stinks; beauty is shit.'[59] In the late 1960s in Britain examples of conceptualist art presented the medium of excreta itself as beautiful. Faced with both the continuance of an official ideology which is a tortuous hypocrisy and lie, and a moribund official aesthetic, one would not be surprised to witness a Chinese avant-garde which took a similar position; the Chinese examples I have discussed would tend to support such a view, with the proviso that many Chinese cultural producers continue to use artistic practice as a critical tool with which to pursue a commitment to some notion of truth and morality.

Both Chen Zhen and Gu Wenda want to distance themselves from the Chinese discourse of cultural nationalism. In this they are only partially successful, and while such a move constitutes a welcome interruption of a twentieth-century cultural tradition, it is also dependent on the acceptance of their work by comparatively wealthy Western consumers who commodify it not for its qualities of 'universality' but for its Chineseness.

So, then, is Chinese modernism, along with other counter-realist trends, a result of Western cultural dominance? If all modern Chinese literature may be seen as part of the cultural response to imperialist domination, which included in its ideological baggage the cultural imperialism that accompanies the invasion of imperialist capital, then Chinese modernism is a function of that dominance. But the very fact that capital was not coherent, that it was also divided by competing

[58] Sean Olson, 'Art of the Body', *ARTSPOOL*, vol. 2 (Summer 1993) 19.
[59] Eagleton 372.

nationalist, imperialist ambitions resulting in two world wars, facilitated and produced differentiated cultural responses. Given the reality of capitalist imperialist ambitions and the need to counter them in the cultural sphere, it is not at all clear why the mimicry of the Western modernists and avant-garde, which had previously enjoyed a critical capacity, should be any less a progressive strategy than the adoption of Russian realism or French naturalism. The appropriation of Western modernist techniques and ideas does not necessarily make Chinese modernism a 'lackey' of Western bourgeois culture. If an appreciation of the political and social importance of Baudelaire, Lorca, Marina Tsvetaeva or Sylvia Plath would not necessarily indicate a reactionary bourgeois viewpoint in the Western academy, why should such texts read in the Chinese context by a Chinese reader indicate that she or he is a victim of Western cultural imperialism? Why after all should Western progressive critics ground their own judgement, as many have done since the founding of the People's Republic, in that of a 'Marxist-Leninist' culturally conservative bureaucracy which peddles a hypocritical and damaging ideology, and which is afflicted by a narrow-minded conception of politics? That such an authority has despotically declared these modernist poets, Western or Chinese, to be 'bourgeois' is rather an index of that authority's political and intellectual corruption.

At the end of the twentieth century in China the 'society of commemoration' has now yielded to the 'consumer society', and while the oppressive character of the former hegemonic ideology has not been displaced, social and economic conditions all too familiar to cultural producers in the advanced capitalist societies have been established. And yet it should be remembered that the hegemony cultural producers, of the 1970s and 1980s in particular, faced was only indirectly produced by external forces. Their and society's primary oppression derived from the cultural and social stasis of an authority that suppressed the all-important function of continuous critique and replaced it with self-congratulatory 'ritualised festival'.

4

CONTEMPT FOR THE CONTEMPORARY: ORIENTALISTS, WESTERN MARXISTS AND CHINESE POETRY

'The demonisation of the Third World is conducted not only in the press. Academics have often played a full part.'
—Frank Füredi[1]

'Man lives from choice in the framework of his own experience, trapped in his former achievements for generations on end.'
—Fernand Braudel[2]

My main concern in this chapter is to discuss the very negative reception that has been afforded to modern Chinese literature, and in particular modern Chinese poetry, by certain critics in the Western academy.

The Harvard sinologist Stephen Owen in a review article of the contemporary Chinese poet Bei Dao's *August Sleep-walker*, entitled 'What is World Poetry? Poets Who Write to be Read in Translation are a Curious Breed, as Bei Dao Shows', made a generalised attack on modern Chinese poetic practice throughout the twentieth century but especially over the last two decades.[3] In fact, Owen seems simply to have quite forthrightly articulated views shared by many in the Sinological academic world. His main claims are that modern Chinese poetry is but a pale imitation of Western modernist poetry and

---

[1] *The New Ideology of Imperialism: Renewing the Moral Imperative* (London and Boulder, CO: Pluto Press, 1994) 2.
[2] *Capitalism and Material Life 1400-1800* (New York: Harper and Row, 1975) 25.
[3] Stephen Owen, *The New Republic* 19 November 1990: 28-32. A second subtitle, 'The Anxiety of Global Influence', is also given.

that 'it' lacks Chineseness – that is authenticity and ethnicity – especially when compared with the grandeur of the classical Chinese poetic canon of which Owen, a professor of classical Chinese poetry, is an interpreter, translator and custodian. Owen further claims that except for the occasional splash of local colour contemporary Chinese poetry is now a barely indistinguishable strand of 'world poetry' which he describes as 'provincial'.

Apart from a number of comments that indicate a rather simplistic narrative of the historical changes in twentieth-century poetic practice, and the nature of the impact of Western poetry, Owen's critique is hurtful and gratuitous. Let me first deal with the misunderstandings and inaccuracies.

Owen conflates, in a totalising and Orientalising manner, varied and distinct poetic practices and histories, when he states that China's poetic 'encounter' with the West was no less severe than the 'upheaval in the poetries of many other great Asian cultures'.[4] Yet the reader is told nothing further about any other Asian poetry. Ascribing agency to Western poetic practices, as though alluding to some sort of gracious muse, Owen claims that 'Western poetry, in most cases Romantic poetry, entered these traditions like a breath of fresh air', and specifies that romantic poetry was 'China's particular poetic import'.[5] It was not. Owen is doubtless alluding to Xu Zhimo (1897-1931) and Wen Yiduo (1899-1946), and per-haps to others of the Crescent Moon School, who certainly were avid readers of English romantic poetry. However, these are just a few of the dozens of poetic practitioners in the pre-Communist, pre-1949 era, who were significant for their part in the process of experimentation and practice that constructed the modern poetic idiom. Many of these ex-perimenters specifically and consciously rejected the Anglo-American poetic tradition, and many again invested in French poetic practices, as Owen in part acknowledges in the claim

[4] *Ibid.* 29.
[5] *Ibid.* 30.

that some 'world poetry' is but a 'version of Anglo-American or French Modernism'. He emphasises, however, that 'an essentially local tradition (Anglo-European) is widely taken for granted as universal', and that duped 'Third World' poets are blindly, unconsciously engaged in producing 'world poetry', ignorant of its 'local' and specific genesis:

[A]lthough it is supposedly free of all local literary history, this 'world poetry' turns out, unsurprisingly, to be a version of Anglo-American modernism or French modernism, depending on which wave of colonial culture first washed over the intellectuals of the country in question. This situation is the quintessence of cultural hegemony, when an essentially local tradition (Anglo-European) is widely taken for granted as universal.[6]

Owen also claims that since 'Romantic poetry usually arrived in translation, or through an imperfect knowledge of the original languages', it therefore 'came to China, as to other countries, with little sense of the weight of the cultural and literary history that lay behind it', and thus 'appeared as a poetry free of history'.[7] What are we to understand by this? Is it that in China some of the essential 'Europeanness' of romantic poetry was lost? Was this perhaps because China was not a fully constituted European colony? As Albert Memmi asserts, the price the colonised pays for such 'assimilation' into the coloniser's culture is high, and the benefit dubious. Referring to the French colonies of North Africa, he writes of the colonised child who has the fortune to receive an education rather than rot in the streets:

The memory which is assigned to him is certainly not that of his people. The history which is taught him is not his own. He knows who Colbert or Cromwell was, but he learns nothing about Khaznadar; he knows about Joan of Arc, but not about El Kahena. Everything seems to have taken place out of his country. . . . In other words with reference to what he is not: to Christianity, although he is not a Christian; to the West which ends under his nose, at a line which is even more insurmountable than it is imaginary.[8]

[6] *Ibid.* 28.

[7] *Ibid.* 30.

[8] Albert Memmi, *The Colonizer and the Colonized* (London: Earthscan, 1990) 171. Jean-Baptiste Colbert (1619-83) was the principal minister of Louis XIV; Mustafa

Such is the effect of a colonialist education. Throughout the British Empire millions were subjected to a similar educational experience. Did they learn the 'correct' way to read romantic poetry, I wonder? Is there only one 'correct' way to read romantic poetry? Is it essential to be equipped with the entire ideological and cultural apparatus of a nineteenth-century white bourgeois reader to read romantic poetry as it 'should' be read? Moreover, what is constitutive of the 'literary history' of a poem: the history of its production alone, or also the history of its reception, a history that changes with every reader that reads that poem? Surely these Chinese poets as consumers of European poetry were *part* of its history, just as Professor Owen is part of the history of Chinese classical poetry.

Nor is the claim that Chinese consumers and re-transmitters of European poetic production somehow mistransmitted the product due to an 'imperfect knowledge of the original languages' substantiated by the facts. Apart from a number of celebrated translators of foreign poetry, many of whom were poets in their own right, the prominent redeployers of romanticism, Wen Yiduo and Xu Zhimo, were both educated in the West; Wen in the United States and Xu Zhimo at the London School of Economics and King's College, Cambridge, in England. Both had good English. Unlike those in the post-Mao generation, many poets active before 1949 had studied abroad and many had excellent and multiple foreign language skills, their translations being still valued today.

The importance of the English romantic tradition is over-privileged in Owen's narrative. German, Spanish and, in particular, French poetic practices also informed the production of modern Chinese poetry. French poetry, *pace* Owen, has had a much greater impact on the formal and conceptual development of Chinese poetry than English romanticism. Indeed, writers seeking new structures for Chinese poetic

---

Khaznadar the principal minister of two of the rulers or *beys* of nineteenth-century Tunisia; El Kahena, or Al Kahina, a semi-legendary Berber queen who defeated the Arabs in battle.

expression related mainly to the French free verse tradition. As has already been mentioned, the technical aspects of free verse seemed preferable to a generation of young poets seeking to break the grip of highly regulated classical verse, and free verse facilitated the use of the new literary language in construction. There were several probable reasons for this Francophile tendency, particularly in 1920s and 1930s Shanghai, China's modern cultural metropolis. In Shanghai, administered in part by the French, cultural dominance was exercised through a number of institutions such as French schools and universities, often Jesuit-run, and French-language presses and book stores. The French government funded preparatory courses for study in France and established a Franco-Chinese Institute at the University of Lyon to house Chinese students. All of this can be seen as a sort of Althusserian ideological state apparatus mapped on to colonised Shanghai and other French 'treaty ports' and 'spheres of influence'. In cultural terms it was an apparatus designed to impress and win for France the Chinese intellectual, and in the sphere of poetry it was doubtless the potentially revolutionary iconoclasm and idealism of modern French free verse that seduced those engaged in reinventing Chinese lyricism.

While Wen Yiduo experimented with a constrictive metre based on English poetic metre – which itself mimicked the 'classical' metre of Latin poetry associated with the imperialist project of Rome – most Chinese poetic experimenters who sought to break free of the formal constraints of their own feudal and imperial tradition were averse to such repressive mechanisms. Surely the modern Chinese poets were right to reject such a restrictive and regressive move, for, as Adorno notes, those who adhere to metre and reject the potential of free verse, 'stop their ears to history by which free verse is stamped. . . . Not without reason was the epoch of free-rhythms that of the French Revolution, the solemn entrance of human dignity and equality.'[9]

Having dealt cursorily with modern Chinese poetry of the

---

[9] Theodor W. Adorno, *Minima Moralia* (London: Verso, 1991) 221-2.

pre-Communist era, Owen moves on to a critique of the work of the 'representative' contemporary poet under review, Bei Dao. Taking two lines out of context, he writes:

I wince when Bei Dao begins a poem:

> A perpetual stranger
> am I to the world

I thought I destroyed the only copy of that poem when I was 14, a year after I wrote it. I thought we all did.[10]

There is a whole book full of poems from which to quote. Owen could for example have chosen to quote from 'Declaration' in which Bei Dao simply but powerfully commemorates his deceased friend, the anti-authority activist Yu Luoke:

> The still horizon
> Divides the ranks of the living and the dead
> I can only choose the sky
> I will not kneel on the ground
> Allowing the executioners to look tall
> The better to obstruct the wind of freedom[11]

Or from 'An End or a Beginning':

> Here I stand
> Replacing another, who has been murdered
> So that each time the sun rises
> A heavy shadow, like a road
> Shall run across the land
>
> ....
>
> I have lied many times in my life
> But I have always honestly kept to
> The promise I made as a child
> So that the world which cannot tolerate
> A child's heart
> Has still not forgiven me

[10] Owen 30.

[11] Bei Dao, *The August Sleepwalker*, trans. Bonnie S. McDougall (New York: New Directions Press, 1989) 62.

Here I stand
Replacing another, who has been murdered.[12]

I doubt that Professor Owen wrote or threw away lines like
that when he has fourteen.

Bei Dao, it is true, has spent much time in distancing himself
from the Chinese tradition, from respect for old books and
artefacts. Indeed, he has expended energy and time pursuing
his interest in Western modernism – in particular with the
Scandinavian modernist poet, Tomas Tranströmer. Bei Dao
has also translated Seamus Heaney into Chinese. Naturally,
then, he is at odds with Owen's nostalgia for the Chinese
tradition.

Owen's critique pointedly betrays the mundane Orientalist
discourse of which it is a part when it finds 'the new poetries
of Asia. . . thin and wanting, particularly in comparison to the
glories of traditional poetry'. Edward Said has it exactly when
he isolates the Orientalist narrative that foregrounds 'feelings
of emptiness, loss, and disaster that seem thereafter to reward
Oriental challenges to the West; and also the lament that in
some glorious past Asia fared better.'[13]

Owen articulates a distaste for the chimaera which is twen-
tieth- century poetry that is equal only to the fear of the hybrid
expressed by the cultural custodians of China's own conservative regnant authority. 'Authenticity' is paramount in
Owen's construction of a lyric loss in the newly wrought
Chinese literature:

[I]s this Chinese literature, or literature that began in the Chinese language?. . . Success in creating a 'world poetry' is not without its costs.

[12] *Ibid.* 63.

[13] Edward W. Said, *Orientalism* (New York: Vintage Books, 1979). Said's critique
of Orientalism has been subjected recently to some intense criticism, the most
rigorous of which has come from Aijaz Ahmad in his book *In Theory: Classes,
Nations, Literatures* (London and New York: Verso, 1992). While sympathising
with the latter's doubts about Said's construction of a 'seamless and incremental
history' (181) of Orientalist discourse, I nevertheless find that the main thrust of
Said's observations on the ideology and workings of Orientalism remains incisively
perceptive, perhaps just because they are commensurate with the Orientalist's
attempt to construct a pre-modern 'seamless and incremental' history of Asia.

Bei Dao has, by and large, written international poetry. Local colour
is used, but sparsely. . . . These could just as easily be translations from
a Slovak or Estonian or a Philippine poet.[14]

This is a problematic charge for Bei Dao and others who
have not only turned against the Marxist-Leninist politics and
ideology of the party-state, but who also continue to operate
within a century-old revolutionary discourse of literary anti-
traditionalism. It is certainly the case that much of the production of Bei Dao and his cohort of fellow poets, many of whom
are in exile, is largely consumed in English translation. Is the
outrage at Owen's review article that emanates from Chinese
poets and their promoters partly generated by some of the
partial truths of his critique? Owen wonders about 'the power
and the consequences of the approval of the international, that
is, the Western audience':

I have in mind the way in which the attention of a Western audience
is a function of successful advertising. Bei Dao is a well-known contemporary poet in China, but he is by no means pre-eminent. By
writing a supremely translatable poetry, by the good fortune of a gifted
translator and publicist, he may well attain in the West the absolute
pre-eminence among contemporary Chinese poets that he cannot quite
attain in China itself. And the very fact of wide foreign (Western)
recognition could, in turn, grant him pre-eminence in China.[15]

This is an opinion that has also been articulated by Chinese
critics. But whatever kind of aesthetic reading the critics may
have of Bei Dao's poetry, his 'pre-eminence' in China, his
reputation as the most prominent poet of the last twenty years,
is beyond doubt and is due to his rise to fame before and during
the Democracy Movement of 1978-9, when several of his
poems became popularised. That kind of 'pre-eminence' was
not manufactured by advertisers or propagandists, but was a
function of the popular appropriation of his poems. That
'reputation' and popularity are not so easily undone. Yet it is
also the case that there are many in China who accuse Bei Dao
of exploiting his reputation, and the events of 1989, to his own

[14] Owen 31.
[15] *Ibid.* 32.

advantage. I believe such charges are unfair and unjustified, but Owen has touched upon a sensitive issue.

One 'positive' aspect of Bei Dao's work to which Owen does give credit is his 'welcome move. . . away from a narrowly defined and obvious version of political engagement'. Despite poems which display 'overt opposition' to the state, for Owen Bei Dao's 'heroism lies, rather, in his determination to find other aspects of human life and art that are worthy of a poet's attention.' Owen here is critical of a 'narrowly defined' version of politics. If he means by that a restriction of the political to the politics of economism and the state, then I would agree. The politics of human life is much more complex than that; the restrictive nature of what we are made to believe is 'political' is what alienates us from society and deprives us of our will and power to critique and change 'other aspects of human life'. The monotonous propaganda literature that sought to eulogise the misery of the Cultural Revolution was the antithesis of critique; and the experience of that kind of cultural production, far from obviating the need for the social and political engagement of literary production, made it essential. However, it is precisely that group of Bei Dao's poems that responded to the absence of human life during the Cultural Revolution that Owen criticises most stringently. While accepting that 'a truly apolitical poetry is impossible in such a highly politicized world, that an ostensibly apolitical poetry is itself a strong political statement', Owen nevertheless maintains that Bei Dao has indulged in the production of 'poems that demonstrate his "political correctness" in opposing the regime', which he finds regrettable since Bei Dao is 'capable of more'.[16] For Owen, then, the ideal goal of lyric production is an 'apolitical' poetry. Professor Owen is the expert in matters of pre-modern poetry, but surely the centrality of politics in much pre-modern Chinese poetry over the last two millennia cannot be denied?

The relationship of lyric production to society in an histori-

[16] *Ibid.* 31.

cal period like that of the post-Maoist 1970s and 1980s is bound to be much more complex. Ideology, as Adorno reminds us in his essay 'On Lyric Poetry and Society', is not coterminous with politics. Politics and engaged or committed lyric production are not bound to be false. While ideology understood as 'untruth, false consciousness, deceit. . . manifests itself in the failure of works of art, in their inherent falseness', that which makes cultural products successful 'consists solely in the fact that they give voice to what ideology hides. Their very success moves beyond false consciousness, whether intentionally or not.'[17]

There is an important general point here about the use of, and need for, the lyric in society, which may help us understand why and how it re-emerged as an important practice in post-Mao China. Adorno's remarks on the opposition of lyric poetry to society are useful to an understanding of the function of 'unofficial' poetic production in post-Cultural Revolution, late 1970s China:

You experience lyric poetry as something opposed to society, something wholly individual. Your feelings insist that it remain so, that lyric expression, having escaped from the weight of material existence, evoke the image of a life free from the coercion of reigning practices, of utility, of the relentless pressures of self-preservation. This demand, however, the demand that the lyric word be virginal, is itself social in nature.[18]

This presages the remarks of the poetic practitioner Nicole Brossard about the presence of the collective 'We' in the poet's 'I' when the poet belongs to an oppressed group.[19] It also reminds us that despite any individualistic 'demand that the lyric word be virginal', and precisely because poets are social beings they construct a collective, social voice of a refashioned,

---

[17] Theodor W. Adorno, *Notes to Literature*, vol. 1 (New York: Columbia University Press, 1991) 39.

[18] *Ibid.*

[19] 'Poetic Politics', in Charles Bernstein (ed.), *The Politics of Poetic Form* (New York: Roof, 1990) 80. If the poet stood on the side of the dominant group, the oppressed group would be seen as 'laughable, insignificant, or used as a scapegoat'.

but social, language. This demand, as Adorno explains it, 'implies a protest against a social situation that every individual experiences as hostile, alien, cold, oppressive'. Further, Adorno's remark that 'the lyric's spirit's idiosyncratic opposition to the superior power of material things is a form of reaction to the reification of the world, to the domination of human beings by commodities' is a particularly appropriate description of the spirit of 'unofficial' 1970s poetic production, a poetry decried as 'misty' or 'obscure' by those parts of the state apparatus charged with official poetic production and criticism.[20]

Since a 'collective undercurrent provides for all individual lyric poetry', the social and political importance of the lyric is twofold and inescapable. When the production of a poet such as Bei Dao 'bears the whole in mind. . . participation in this undercurrent is an essential part of the substantiality of the individual lyric as well'. Even when lyricists seem to make a move away from the collective, as the poets Bei Dao and Duoduo do in their more recent poetry, when they 'abjure any borrowing from the collective language', they still 'participate in that collective undercurrent by virtue of their historical experience'.[21] In the modern era, 'when individual expression. . . seems shaken to its very core in the crisis of the individual, the collective undercurrent in the lyric surfaces in the most diverse places'.[22]

Another Sinologist who has engaged in a generalised critique of contemporary Chinese poetic practice is William Jenner, who for many years produced numerous translations of modern vernacular Chinese writing and was a frequent visitor to New China, with whose aims he seemed to express a degree of sympathy. What made his interest in contemporary China unusual was the fact that Jenner trained in the very Oriental Institute at Oxford University to which Said refers in *Orientalism* as one of the major institutions promoting an Orientalist ideology that constructs the Eastern past as a

[20] Adorno *Notes* 39–40.

[21] *Ibid.* 45.

[22] *Ibid.* 46.

halcyon age, while dismissing contemporary Asia as culturally decadent, aesthetically moribund.[23] Having striven to counter British Sinology's historical tendency to privilege the 'glory' of the past over the 'dullness' of the present, Professor Jenner has arrived at a critical stance towards modern and contemporary literary production which echoes Owen's negative evaluation of modern Chinese poetry. In fact, Jenner too has targeted Bei Dao's *August Sleepwalker*.[24]

Jenner believes the modern Chinese written language to be inadequate to the task of lyric production. Others too have pointed to the adverse effect of Maoist linguistic dominance over the production of all texts in post-1949 China. But Jenner means to go further; he points to what amounts to the inability of the modern Chinese 'mind' to produce *echt* poetry, 'great poetry', for he suggests that even those Chinese beyond the control of Communist China – in Taiwan, in Hong Kong, throughout the diaspora – have failed to produce poetry of 'literary quality'. A typical Orientalist narrative of an ur-culture of China in terminal decline is retold when he suggests that the situation is deteriorating and that 'even' the poetic production of the first half of this century was better than that of the second:

There is a devil's argument about contemporary Chinese poetry that is very hard to refute: great poetry can no longer be written in Chinese. The negative evidence is crude but telling: no really memorable Chinese verse has been written for the last forty years, and not so very much was created in the half century before that. If explanations are looked for in the Maoist and post-Maoist politics, that still leaves tens of millions of Chinese living beyond the reach of Communist power who have also failed to match the poetry of much smaller populations living in difficult times, such as the Irish of the Six Counties. So why is it that a culture that once produced so much outstanding poetry cannot do so any more?[25]

What emerges is a bourgeois humanist critique dependent

[23] Said 53.

[24] W.J.F. Jenner, review of *The August Sleepwalker* by Bei Dao, trans. Bonnie McDougall, *Australian Journal of Chinese Affairs* 23 (1990): 193-5.

[25] *Ibid*. 193-4.

on the ideology of Eurocentrically, 'liberally' educated men who have narrow and stilted notions of what poetry *ought* to resemble. What poetry ought to resemble for many educated men in Britain is the sort of anodyne verse canon organised into school anthologies which children were forced to learn by rote – which surely in part accounts for poetry's enduring unpopularity with the mass of people who baulk at bourgeois aesthetics.

The level of generalisation in Jenner's review is disturbing. The assertion of professional opinions is meant to be enough to convince the targeted First World reader of the worthlessness of modern Chinese poetry: 'no really memorable Chinese verse has been written for the last forty years.' Sadly, of course, many will accept Jenner's judgement. How can the Chinese poet, the producer of the object of critique, refute this? She or he is not expected to, of course. Does not the monologic white voice enunciating his verdict from the dominant heights of Western and largely white academe resonate with the echoes of colonialism? There is a definite resentment in Jenner's, as in other modern Sinologists' discourse, that goes further than Orientalism. For several decades after the Second World War there emerged a cohort of scholars who believed in the Chinese revolution, not merely as a social and economic revolution but as a Chinese Renaissance, a 'rebirth' of China's cultural 'greatness'. This is analogous to the chauvinistic, nationalist idea that modernisation will restore China to its 'rightful' pre-eminence in the hierarchy of nations. Those scholars who believed that they were somehow involved in this cultural 'reconstruction' now appear to feel doubly disappointed. The revolution was supposed to restore China's former cultural glory and has failed to do so.

The Chinese poet is, however, exculpated by the British professor, for how can the culturally impoverished be expected to exercise agency and *change* their own material existence, their own means of expression? 'Perhaps the contemporary language itself specially in its written form, gives poets difficulties that are even greater than those faced by writers of Chinese prose or poets working in many other languages'.[26] The language, the means by which the patriotic intellectuals of the beginning of the century sought to 'enlighten' and defend China against the West, has failed to equal the fetishised 'glory' of the Sinological literary canon: the lyric. Jenner continues in a similar vein:

> The language available to Bei Dao is too weak to carry much of a burden. This is not the poet's fault: it was bad luck to be born into a period when the resources of China's literary tradition were out of reach, and the culture was left with a written code that while purporting to reflect living speech could in fact only be used to its full effect by people soaked in the concise but daunting written code of the past.[27]

This 'written code', whose 'literary tradition', the means of decoding, is now only accessible to the Sinologists who have delved into the deep inner mysteries of the past, is denied to those who had the misfortune to be 'sent down' to the countryside rather than graduate from university. Yet even the 'classically educated', like the poet Wen Yiduo, a romanticist whom Jenner evidently favours but who nevertheless is 'not up there with Auden and Yeats', who studied abroad and discovered that the West only valorised the genuinely ancient in China, 'have found it almost impossible to create poetry in the vernacular that is better than quite good.'[28]

This level of generalisation ignores the fact that by the end of the 1940s, as witness the poetry of the Nine Leaves poet Mu Dan, the language of modernist poetry was capable of great complexity and nuance, attributes revealed again in much of the poetry of the post-Mao era. But Jenner's 'evaluation' of the suitability of the Chinese language seems to relate to more generally held ideological notions about

---

[26] *Ibid.* 194.

[27] *Ibid.*

[28] *Ibid.* Such 'total condemnation' of recent Chinese cultural production by the Orientalists, and the privileging of the ancient, was noted by Walter Benjamin in a 1938 article on Chinese painting, reproduced in Walter Benjamin, *Ecrits français* (Paris: Gallimard, NRF, 1991) 260. See 195-6 of present work.

language and poetry. Henri Meschonnic, for one, has observed that there is generally held to be a connection between national characteristics and languages; English is, for example, deemed to be concrete, French to be abstract. For Charles Bally, German is 'motivated, synthetic, dynamic, precise', while French is 'arbitrary, analytical, static, clear'.[29] French is reputed to have no rhythm' and thus is unsuited to poetry, while German, on the contrary, is the language of 'dream, poetry, philosophy'.[30] But what such notions elide is that we 'are in our own language in the same way that we are in our own skin. That's why naively we believe it says more than it does: illusion, and truth, together'. In fact there is only identity, and the disregard for otherness and diversity, so that again and again the same illusion is repeated.[31] Meschonnic reminds us that the 'narcissistic' naming of ourselves and others 'condemns the Other to silence' – 'The *barbarians* did not speak Greek', and 'in nahuatl, *nahuatl* means "speak clearly"'.[32]

We are in our language as we are in our skins, because quite simply each of us 'has had, still has, his childhood in the language'.[33] Surely, then, the linguistic and poetic conventions which are instilled into us during our childhood have a major place in our cultural reproduction. It is true for Bei Dao. It is true for Professor Jenner. They are both ideologically situated, and surely Jenner's narrative, while coming to a wrong conclusion, nevertheless perceives this.

Jenner would have us believe that Bei Dao and his cohorts (Duoduo, Mang Ke and others) were denied the grounding of an education in classical literature. This is only partly true, since although they did not attend university, before the start of the Cultural Revolution these poets had benefited from an

---

[29] Henri Meschonnic, *La rime et la vie* (Lagrasse: Verdier, 1989) 30. Meschonnic is referring to opinions expressed by Charles Bally in his *Linguistique générale et linguistique française* (Bern: Francke, 1965).

[30] Meschonnic 30-1.

[31] *Ibid.* 31.

[32] *Ibid.*

[33] *Ibid.*

élite and élitist high-school education in the metropolis in the
nation's best schools. It was no Confucian training, but they
were certainly not culturally illiterate. Bei Dao and his cohort
elected to reject the tradition. Bei Dao tells a story that after
numerous guided tours around British Sinological hallowed
halls – the British Museum, the Ashmolean, the Cambridge
University Far Eastern library – and after having numerous
volumes of 'precious' Chinese books and artefacts displayed
under his nose, he finally turned to his hosts and told them
that he was not interested in the slightest in pre-modern
Chinese texts and objects. This was sacrilege, no doubt, to the
Sinologists whose whole training teaches them veneration for
the past and its hierarchical classification, and further evidence
of the worthlessness of a contemporary culture alienated from
the tradition. Moreover, such disdain for ancient civilisation
constitutes an even greater reason for the Western academy to
enshrine and protect, on behalf of the Chinese, their national
heritage, and especially the lyric.

'Memorability' ranks high in Jenner's index of literary
qualities. Thus while Bei Dao's 'stories work, even in translation',
his poems 'are less memorable, even in the original'. Here again
Jenner is alluding to this undefined measure of 'literary quality'.
(What is it precisely that defines 'literary quality'? Whose
literary quality is it? What colour is it, and what class?) The
fact that much of Bei Dao's poetry was 'memorised', was read
in public over and over again and distributed by audio cassette
in the 1970s by tens of thousands of people, and was appropriated
by the student protesters at Tiananmen Square in 1989, will
not make it 'memorable' for the Sinologist. Bei Dao's poetry
will simply not bear comparison with the Sinologist's received
and untheorised idea of 'literary quality'. The latter is based
on a particularly narrow reading of some body of texts drawn from
the Western or the indigenous canon; or, as Professor Jenner
has it, 'Bei Dao's lines rarely have the inevitability, the weight,
the structure, the authority of *real* poetry [emphasis added].'[34]

---

[34] Jenner 194.

It must be recalled that these generalisations, like Owen's, are called forth by what is supposed to be a reading of one collection of poems by one 'representative' poet; other contemporary poets are not discussed. While I am sure that Jenner, at least, has read more than one volume of contemporary poetry, this selectivity does indicate an unwillingness to become involved, to get acquainted with more contemporary poetry. This practice of sampling and selecting may well be inherited from the Sinological, Orientalist practice, exemplified by the editorial and translating policy of Arthur Waley, who selected for the general reader of English only the handful of pre-modern Chinese poets he considered of literary worth; moral character seems also to have been a consideration, since Waley is thought not to have approved of drunken poets. This reductionism masks the centuries of varied poetic activity involving tens of thousands of poets and frequently drawing on anonymous folk ballads and similar collective lyric production, so that now only a handful of anthologised 'greats' of Chinese poetry may be commonly read by anyone except the Orientalist *cognoscenti*.

Many Sinologists, like many traditional Orientalists, are fixated on the canon, and modern literature (let us leave aside the marginalised and unmentioned practices of mechanically and electronically reproduced mass or popular culture) to be acceptable must be canonised. Even the anti-canonical 'unofficial' poetry must be confined by a canonising discourse capable of producing respectable, representative poets, and of marginalising or demoting the unsettling, the inconvenient. The resulting poetic canon ideally ought to display 'literary quality', that is at least to the extent that a literary practice ranked at the bottom of a literary hierarchy can display such 'quality'. In this instance, the poet chosen for the honoured place at the head of the sub-canon, a poet whom certain Sinologists even promoted on to the Nobel Prize short-list, has ultimately been found wanting.

While the Sinological community may believe that the Chinese traditional narrative canon cannot 'compete' with that of the West, it proudly takes its construction of the lyric

tradition to be at least the equal of both modern and pre-
modern Western poetry. Bei Dao's poems, with the spectre
of the lyric tradition nurtured and privileged by modern and
modernised Sinologists looming over them, merely conceal 'a
disillusioned intelligence looking for words and forms to
express itself, but in vain'. While Bei Dao is credited with
rejecting 'the politically degraded language of the Mao era',
Jenner claims that 'not much is left' and that the poems 'do
not lose all that much' in translation 'because there is not much
in the original language to be lost'.[35]

Jenner's dismissal of modern Chinese lyric production as
not being 'real poetry', and the construction of contemporary
Chinese poetry as some sad shadow of 'real poetry', a bastard
descendant of the pre-modern tradition, alert us to the underlying élitist and Orientalist basis of this argument. In this
Orientalist-Sinological discourse, modern Chinese poetry is
seen not as an emergent, or re-emergent (if we think of
contemporary poetry as in some sense resuming the project of
pre-Communist poetic production of the first half of this
century), lyric discourse being constructed out of a new set of
socio-economic realities, but rather a pathetic tail-end of a
once great poetic tradition, the faintest glimmer of an il-
lustrious 'great poetry that can no longer be written in
Chinese'. It should be recalled that the Chinese literary language, persistently held up for praise, and against which the
modern idiom is judged, is a classical and dead language; not
classical and kept alive like Arabic, but defunct and no longer
employed as an active and productive language. It has a
relation to modern literary Chinese similar to that of Latin to
French, and not as close as that of classical to modern Greek.
Edward Said's comments on the significance attached to
language by the Orientalist is pertinent here, for it is indeed
the case that the 'exaggerated value heaped upon [language]
permits the Orientalist to make [it] equivalent to mind,
society, history, culture, and nature'. Just as for the Orientalist-

---

[35] *Ibid.*

Arabist 'the language *speaks* the Arab Oriental, not vice versa', for the Orientalist-Sinologist classical Chinese speaks the Chinese Oriental.[36] Whereas classical Chinese could produce authenticity, modern Chinese is deemed incapable of so doing.

Both the conviction that the modern Chinese language and its poetry are but the tail-end of a great linguistic and literary tradition, and the contradictory belief in the power of individual agency over language, are held out at the conclusion to Jenner's critique in which he claims to discern in Bei Dao's last poem in the collection under review the 'possibility that Bei Dao has it in him to produce words that will put life into the dying language'. In this narrative of despair for a once-great culture, a solitary poet may yet rejuvenate the language which, 'too weak to carry much of a burden', has so far failed not only the poet, but the nation and, let us not forget, the Sinologist.

Jenner's narrative elides the fact that, throughout the course of Chinese cultural history, élite producers of culture have time and again raided the lyrics and stories produced by the people. Poets may manipulate language, but language itself is social. If Chinese poetic language is altered, it will be as a result of drawing on society's linguistic practices which are, as with all languages, in constant flux. Jenner's criticisms are also based on the premise that if poetry is to matter, it can only do so insofar as it meets criteria of 'literary quality' established by literary critics of the dominant classes. A poetry valorised in such terms is a poetry alienated both from society and from the needs of society. Whether in children's ditties, in remnants of folk songs, in snatches of appropriated 'high poetry' or in electronically reproduced pop lyrics, those others

who not only stand alienated, as though they were objects, facing the disconcerted poetic subject but who have also literally been degraded to objects of history, have the same right, or a greater right, to grope

[36] Said 321.

for the sounds in which sufferings and dreams are welded. This inalienable right has asserted itself again and again, in forms however impure, mutilated, fragmentary, and intermittent – the only forms possible for those who have to bear the burden.[37]

It is not the Orientalist scholar alone who devalorises the literary production of Asia, or more generally the Third World; even enlightened, progressive humanists have done so, some of them quite famously. Fredric Jameson's writings on 'Third World literature' have been ably critiqued by Aijaz Ahmad, and I do not wish to restate the case against Jameson's totalising interpretation of so-called Third World texts as nationalist allegories; I agree with Ahmad that 'societies in formations of backward capitalism are as much constituted by the divisions of classes as are societies in the advanced capitalist countries'.[38] Rather, I should like to discuss some specific questions relating to Jameson's reading of modern Chinese literature, while bearing in mind his remark that the 'third world novel will not offer the satisfactions of Proust or Joyce'.[39]

There has already been much discussion of Jameson's narrative of 'Third World literature', but it seems the only real difference between his and the Sinologist's critique of Chinese, and more generally Asian, modern poetry is that Jameson assigns a redemptive function to 'Third World literature'.[40]

For Owen, modern Chinese literary production in the traditionally and hierarchically supreme and dominant genre of the lyric is merely a slave to the master which is Western modernism, or at best a minor strand in the hybrid fabric of international poetry. For Jameson, while 'Third World literature' fails to offer the satisfactions of First World modernist masters, it yet has a residual function as standard bearer for

---

[37] Adorno, *Notes* 43.

[38] Ahmad, *In Theory* 103.

[39] Fredric Jameson, 'Third World Literature in the Era of Multinational Capitalism', *Social Text* 15 (1986) 65.

[40] See Robert Young, *White Mythologies* (New York: Routledge, 1990) 114–15; Aijaz Ahmad, 'Jameson's Rhetoric of Otherness and the "National Allegory"', *Social Text* 17 (1987) 3–25; and Ahmad, *In Theory*.

a Utopia which can no longer be imagined in the First World. Within the category Third World, Jameson seems to permit China a separate, even elevated position and identity; but then so, of course, did Mao.

The fact that a major scholar and theorist of mainstream literary studies took the time and effort to read some modern Chinese literature, and I understand to learn to read some Chinese, is both remarkable and admirable. Yet Jameson's exposure to Chinese modern literature is naturally limited to a small number of texts, amongst which are the 1936 realist novel by Lao She (1899-1966), *Camel Xiangzi*; the fiction of the establishment writer who has exploited 'modernist techniques', Wang Meng; and some texts of the patriarch of modern Chinese literature, Lu Xun (1881-1936). Jameson in his critique of modern Chinese literature seems to make a number of allowances for the kind of aesthetic lack he has criticised in other literatures. For instance, in 1984 he wrote that when 'we turn to socialist countries, we are dealing with a much more recent and chronologically limited tradition from which new and original categories may ultimately be expected to emerge, and in which inherited Western categories risk being rather misleading'.[41] Indeed, 'Western categories', such as 'Third World literature', may not merely be misleading but epistemologically impossible.[42] But what is most striking here is the unproblematic acceptance of the People's Republic of China as a 'socialist' country, and that such 'socialist' countries provide culturally utopian possibilities unavailable to societies with other forms of social organisation. Jameson describes the modernisation of China as the 'specific situation of socialist construction'. All seems permissible to the cultural producers of this 'socialist' state. 'Modernism' is suddenly rehabilitated as it is revealed that

it seems *perfectly appropriate* to consider that Wang Meng's work is 'modernist' in its structure. But it should also be evident that modernist

---

[41] Fredric Jameson, 'Literary Innovation and Modes of Production: A Commentary', *Modern Chinese Literature* (1984) 1: 77.

[42] Ahmad, *In Theory* 105.

'techniques' in this sense need carry no suggestion of some foreign export product which is borrowed or imported into a different socio-economic context.[43]

It is as if the mere suggestion of 'imported' modernism as anything other than techniques would somehow sully the Third World 'socialist' purity and new authenticity of official modern Chinese cultural production. Jameson's concern is redolent of the conservative Chinese bureaucracy's paranoid fears of foreign 'spiritual pollution'. Worse is the erroneous idea that the dominant socio-economic context in China resembled anything anyone in the Western Marxist tradition, like Jameson himself, would recognise as socialism. What others had for decades recognised in China, however, was a bureaucratic, state-capitalist, nationalistic and authoritarian country. Yet it is in this 'socialist' chapter of 'Third World literature' that Jameson has placed his faith. But if such optimism was to be invested anywhere, surely it was not in the official Chinese cultural bureaucrats such as the hack poet-critic Xu Chi, in whose dismal analytical work Jameson perceives an 'interesting correlation of cultural modernism with the Four Modernizations'.[44] These four modernisations (of agriculture, industry, national defence, and science and technology) were never anything more than an economic strategy designed by a faction of the state-party apparatus to accumulate capital and further nationalist ambition. For suggesting a fifth modernisation, democracy, the Chinese dissident radical Wei Jingsheng has spent much of the last two decades in gaol.

While seeming to encourage China's emergent new literature, Jameson in fact valorises 'official' party-state-sponsored literary production. The literature that was truly revolutionary at the time Jameson wrote his article was and is the largely 'unofficial' literary production, as much at odds with officially sanctioned 'modernism' as it was with 'socialist realism' and

[43] Jameson, 'Literary Innovation' 77.
[44] *Ibid.*

'revolutionary romanticism'. The modernism that brought critique to bear on contemporary Chinese society and its regnant authority opposed the dehumanising effects of modernisation and the domination of nature by humanity, a domination still today graphically and monumentally attested to by the Chinese state's continuing determination to dam the Yangzi River gorges despite the near-certainty of devastating ecological consequences and increased human misery.

The critical work performed by much contemporary Chinese poetry has been one of its most significant characteristics. It is interesting to observe how the majority of those Sinologists who have defended contemporary Chinese poetry (perhaps they could be described as modernised Sinologists) have stressed 'purity' and lack of 'politicality' in contemporary Chinese poetic production. Perhaps they harbour an understandable aversion to the ultimately bankrupt Maoism that for long dominated not only Chinese literary production but also its critique in the Western academy. However, thankfully 'politics' is more than parties and state apparatuses want us to believe. Contemporary Chinese poetry is embedded in politics, both as traditionally conceived and in its wider, more emancipatory sense. The fact that poetic practitioners reject 'politics' and deny the politicality of their work merely serves to affirm that politics is the history and context of contemporary Chinese poetry. The academic critique of literary production may appear to be a 'defence' of the producers, as perhaps in this chapter, but it is not meant to replicate or promote the producer's own critique or 'intentions'.

The rejection of 'politics' by the 'unofficial' (*buguanfang*) cultural producers of the 1970s was a political reaction to the ideology that had become dominant and institutionalised in the structures and organs of the state and party since the founding of the People's Republic of China. The reaction emanated from and was constitutive of counter-ideologies which were necessarily marked by many of the official ideology's features. These oppositional or subordinate ideologies maintained nationalist and populist positions and rarely questioned the unity of the nation-state or the dominance of the Han ethnic majority. They offered critiques of official society, in particular by foregrounding corrupt officialdom and mendacious Communist Party propaganda. Frequently, and especially in the sphere of unofficial literary practices, 'politics' – direct engagement with dominant political thought and practice – itself was refused in the attempt to account for history and to reimagine modes of living. This 'rejection' of politics was of the utmost political importance. Such poetic strategies were designed not only to purge the psyche or to resist oppression, but to imagine living as even more important now that in China, and globally, 'the economic machine has begun to expose the cynical nakedness of its component parts.' For the economic system 'designed to ensure the survival of human beings at the expense of living', the 'illusions and subterfuge' of ideology have become increasingly unnecessary.[45] More and more people see the economy for what it is, but the lingering effect of its ideology is that they are convinced of their incapacity to change it. However, the state, for so long the policing and facilitating agent of the economic system, now weakened by the globalisation of capitalism, still desperately clings to myth and ideology to sustain itself, as do those power formations which oppose it on its own terms. Over the last two decades, Chinese society has experienced just such a process. During the 1970s and 1980s, since there had been no sustained 'underground' theoretical preparation for the post-Maoist moment, the modernist or irrealist strategies employed by unofficial lyricists which served to challenge and critique the discredited official cultural practices were not informed by any substitute normative alternative ideology. There was simply a reliance on the cultural and ideological forms which harked back to a sort of pre-Maoist, Gramscian 'common sense'.

While the work of contemporary cultural producers has

[45] Raoul Vaneigem, *The Movement of the Free Spirit: General Considerations and Firsthand Testimony Concerning Some Brief Flowering of Life in the Middle Ages, the Renaissance and, incidentally, Our Own Time* (New York: Zone Books, 1994) 18.

demystified, exposed and defied the myths of the ruling bureaucratic class in China, it has also frequently reinscribed the 'common sense' thinking of the pre-Communist era patriarchal hegemony, its ethnic-chauvinist and masculinist ideology now reauthorised by once Western, now global, Ramboesque and Music Television (MTV) heavy metal cultural role-models. Just as problematic is the discourse of a totalising nationalism, a facet of the Chinese identity projected by both official and oppositional ideologies. For instance, many of the poets who have produced a discursive practice whose very existence is a defiance of official literary discourse and state-party ideology would almost certainly subscribe to the idea of a 'free' yet united China, a unitary motherland. Many lyric producers of northern China, including certain popular music lyricists, possess a centralised, capital-centric view of China and Chineseness. Ethnic or regional entitlement to local modern cultures does not seem to be a concern. This is not to say that poets have ignored the periphery; on the contrary, like contemporary Chinese painters, fiction writers and film-makers, they have often actively exploited an exoticised minority ethnic, non-Han periphery in a paradoxical search to reauthenticate modern Han (the majority Chinese) poetry, to create for it a non-Western matrix. Employing a strategy redolent of colonialism and Orientalism, several have travelled to the extremities of the old 'Celestial Empire', hoping to enter there a distant past in which an authentic, untrammelled, original cultural spirit unsullied by either the Chinese literary heritage or the literary modes of Western modernity would reveal itself.

In search of the raw and potent rejuvenating power of ancient, liminal cultural monuments and prehistoric spaces, the Han Chinese poet Yang Lian, an early and major practitioner of 'unofficial' lyric practice, stands in Tibet before the ruins of the Gandan Monastery partially destroyed by the agents of the Chinese Communist state, which are also the forces of Chinese colonialism, and writes:

> The sun unfolds, on an emptiness scrawled with the
> calligraphy of ruin

Breakers of rubble disintegrating hate and sorrow
Dusk, packs of dogs poke wet noses into history
Sniffing out the broken images beneath the earth
(Yesterday never passes, it is enfolded in today
The stars revolve, a single glance and primordial terror
Tumbles out of the darkness
All things complete at the same point of departure)[46]

While perhaps consciously acknowledging the role of the
Han Chinese in destroying the traditional material culture of
monasteries in Tibet ('broken images beneath the earth'), and
paying homage to the mysterious forces ('primordial terror')
of this peripheral – to the Chinese centre – and 'timeless' culture ('Yesterday never passes, it is enfolded in today'), the
Han Chinese 'unofficial' poet, writing in Chinese, also reinforces Han Chinese hegemony and reinscribes Tibet,
recuperating its history and its tradition into China.

This is not to invalidate the well-intentioned components
of the lyric production of contemporary Chinese literature
which reveals or illuminates not merely the ideology of official
society, but also feudalistic, patriarchal and chauvinistic
'common sense' ideology, whether or not appropriated by the
official and, till recently, dominant ideology. Yet this lyric
discourse does not just innocently subject this ideology to
critique, it is also informed by that very ideology. Here the
use of the concept of 'ideology' is similar to that developed
by Jorge Larrain, who in discussing cultural identity in the
Third World widens its referential frame to conclude that
'ideology conceals not merely class antagonisms but also
forms of gender, racial and colonial domination which
affect women, ethnic minorities and Third World peoples.'[47]
Also of use in understanding the complex ideologies of both
Chinese authority and its critics is Larrain's observation that
since 'the relationships between all these dimensions are not

[46] Geremie Barmé and John Minford, *Seeds of Fire* (New York: Noonday, 1989)
434.

[47] Jorge Larrain, *Ideology and Cultural Identity: Modernity and the Third World Presence*
(Cambridge: Polity Press) 15.

always articulated, it is possible to find theories which are unmasking and critical in one dimension and ideological in another dimension'. Much of the critique directed at Chinese authority during the 1980s by theorists and by cultural producers is best understood in the light of Larrain's expanded concept of ideology and its complications and contradictions. This necessarily demands a modification of the perception of 'unofficial' lyric practice in contemporary China as marginal. Poetry may be 'unofficial', as the frequent arrests of poets over the last decade have demonstrated, but to the extent that poets have experienced together with the rest of society a process of re-socialisation and an ideological shift, poetry cannot be determined as ideologically marginal. Nonetheless, 'unofficial' poetry has undoubtedly become minor in terms of its consumption. For a brief moment in the late 1970s and early 1980s, the dissident literary production of the 'unofficial' writers may have been widely consumed by the urban ex-Red Guard generation that had spent up to ten years in the countryside or the construction site, thus displacing 'official' cultural practices. That generation is now middle-aged. The urban youth in the succeeding generation were the consumers of the new, often underground popular music. Nowadays for all generations there is television, both official Chinese production and, for those with video machines or illegal satellite dishes, foreign products too. In a brief period of two decades, cultural expectations and patterns of consumption have developed rapidly.

The 'marginality' of unofficial lyric production is also misleading insofar as it is seen as a unitary monolithic discourse ranged against 'official ideology'. It is not so. Rather, what is ranged against official ideology is a constellation of practices and ideas which have been totalised as 'misty poetry', and more recently 'post-misty poetry'. The number of poets subscribing to or elaborating upon their adherence to 'mistiness', a term originally coined by official critics to denigrate what they represented as an anti-populist and incomprehensible élitist practice, was initially small. But the myth of the poet-as-patriot and popular tribune in Chinese history, and the image of Western and East European traditions of poet as anti-authoritarian subject, were seductive to both poet and reader. 'Unofficial' poets had an image of themselves as poets, marked off from the official producers of so-called proletarian and eulogistic lyrics of the Cultural Revolution era, positioned outside mainstream society yet meditating on history, social life and the natural world. The critical role of the Western modernist poet, infused with a form of romantic anti-capitalism or anti-bureaucratism, overlaps with the traditional Chinese role of poet-critic as spokesperson for the people.

In the mid-1970s when many unofficial practitioners of poetry were still, or had until recently been, exposed to the social and economic realities of ordinary people's lifestyles either in the countryside or in the urban environment of factories and construction sites, there was a real sense in which poets were functioning as voices of the people. The new poetic discourse gave voice to the collective torment of tens of millions of people. Poetic production had a twofold function: to write out the poet's and his or her social class's and generation's nightmare; and, consciously or not, to speak for and about 'the people'.

The poet Duoduo does this clearly and repeatedly in his 1970s poems. The following poem, foregrounding the fear and awe inspired by Mao Zedong, draws on the experience of the author's generation and class. It was an experience which, as a result of the Maoist policy of re-educating urban youth, included exposure to rural China and peasant lifestyles, leading Duoduo and his peers to first-hand knowledge of the materiality of peasant life. The unintended result is a reading of rural, and thus national, reality at odds with the narrative that constituted the Maoist myth:

UNTITLED

All over the befuddled land,
the coarse faces of the people and their groaning hands
before the people, an endless expanse of hardship
storm lanterns sway in the wind

the night sleeps soundly, but eyes are open wide
you can hear the great snoring emperor with his rotting
    teeth.
1973[48]

The allusion to Mao's decrepitude in the last line of the poem
stands in contrast to the euphoric and idyllic representation in
the contemporary officially produced poems which sang of a
joyous nation under the benign tutelage of Mao firmly controlled by China and by history:

> Cheers, the thousands of mountains and rivers
>   all liberated now,
> Unfurl the glowing red flag with five gold stars.
> Chairman Mao waves his hand at Tiananmen;
> In an instant, history has rolled away so many centuries.[49]

Duoduo's poem, which tells a different story, is from a series
of short verses written in the early 1970s and grouped together
under the title 'Thoughts and Recollections'. At that time they
were unpublished even in *samizdat* form. These poems draw
attention to the fascination of cultural producers of his generation with rural China, prefiguring the cinematic representation of the life of China's peasantry and their exploitation
by the party in the film *Yellow Earth*, directed by Chen Kaige;
a representation in which, as Rey Chow describes it, 'the
peasant's naïvety, poverty, deprivation, and hopelessness become tools of Party propaganda and the backbone of Party
power.'[50] Poetic reverie and inwardness are woven into images
of the awesomeness of rural existence which also heighten the
inner angst that feeds these poems:

AUSPICIOUS DAY

> As if it were not already over,
> as if the sacrificial wine were not already finished,
> outside the prison the first light of day breaks through

---

[48] Duoduo, *Looking Out From Death: From the Cultural Revolution to Tiananmen
Square*, trans. Gregory Lee and John Cayley (London: Bloomsbury, 1989) 25.
[49] Cited in Kai-yu Hsu, *The Chinese Literary Scene* (New York: Vintage, 1975) 259.
[50] Rey Chow, *Discourse* 12, 2 (1990) 92.

and the branch clumsily blossoms.
The shame of a lifetime already redeemed,
dream, although memory is still fresh, resounds like a bugle:

Wind, cannot blow away the desires of early years.
On harvested land under the shining sun
those wretched, idle villages.
As usual thoughts revive,
as usual putting the life of freedom out to pasture –
1973[51]

The brevity of the following short poem, written during the same historical moment, reinforces the isolation and emptiness of a time and space inscribed with repetitive and repeated incantations devoid of significance, except the significance born of religious repetition:

WAR

The afternoon sun lay charitably on the tombstone.
A deep low voice slowly narrates.
Tall, thin people take off army caps,
a distant life, a village full of relatives.
1972[52]

Although informed by the life of the masses and the experience of those plunged into that life and for all their familiarity with the rural ambience, these are still poems written beyond the life of the masses, inscribed into non-mass culture. They are at best the partial view of the observer-participant. The poetic voice nevertheless is opposed to a dehumanised social existence followed by senseless death. But at times during this early period of poetic production it is society as a whole, separated from and striving to dominate over a restorative and transhistorical Nature, that is constructed as guilty:

SEA

The sea retreats towards nightfall
carrying off history, and carrying off sadness.

[51] Duoduo 23.
[52] *Ibid.* 39.

The sea is silent,
not wishing to pardon man again, nor
hear man's praise again.

1973[53]

In 1976, the year of Mao's death and the fall of the so-called
Gang of Four, Duoduo wrote 'Instruction', which could be
read as an account of the experience of tens of thousands who
engaged, many enthusiastically, in the Cultural Revolution.
But the penultimate stanza complicates such an explanation of
the poem's narrative sense: 'They are not comrades.' 'They'
are perhaps those who have sought to usurp the voice of those
they cannot represent, and whose 'language through reification is as divorced from them as all are from each other; because
the present form of the collective is in itself speechless':[54]

INSTRUCTION

Just in the space of a night the wound broke open
even the books on shelves forsook them.

....

Misery has become their life's duty.

Who says that the theme of their early life
was bright and cheerful? Even now, they think.
It's a pernicious saying.
In an evening with a totally artless plot
the lamplight has its source in illusion.
All they see is only, is merely
a monotonous rope that appears in the winter snow.
They can only go and play tirelessly,
struggle with elusive things, and
live together with immemorable things,
if the earliest yearnings are revived,
emptiness is already the blemish of their whole life.

Their misfortune comes from idealistic misfortune,
but their suffering is brought on by themselves.

---

[53] *Ibid.* 40. Revised translation.
[54] Adorno, *Minima Moralia* 220.

It is awareness that sharpens their thinking
and through awareness blood is lost.
But they can't grant traditional reconciliation.
Although before their birth
the world had existed uncleanly for ages
they still want to find
the first culprit to discover 'truth'
and how long they must wait for
the destruction of the world.

Given the nooses around their necks,
their only madness
is to pull them tighter.
Their scattered destructive strength
still remote, has not seized the attention of society
and they are reduced to wrongdoers in the mind
merely because: They misused parables.

But at the very end they pray in the classroom of thought
and, when they see clearly their own writings, are comatose:
They haven't lived in the Lord's arranged time.
They are people who have missed life,
    stopped in a place where life is misunderstood.
Everything they have gone through is a mere tragedy of
    birth.[55]

In this poem there is a complex subject, or rather a confusion of subjects. This recalls Adorno's 'poetic subject, which
always stands for a far more general collective subject'.[56] 'We'
may read 'they' as a generation of idealists, or as a more general
'they', but in any case 'they' disturbingly hints at the complicity of 'I'. Moreover, given a political context in which
involvement was global, for the immediate (and perhaps also
the not so immediate) readership of the poem, 'they' may be
read as inclusive of 'you'.

Lyric production of the high culture type still faces the charges
of 'internationalisation', of failing to match the lyric glory of

[55] Duoduo 58 (revised translation).
[56] Adorno, *Notes* 46.

the Tradition, of failing to convey Chineseness. If the premises of such criticisms were accepted, where might the solutions lie? – in seeking to 'nationalise' and implant some *ersatz* Chineseness, in plundering the periphery for ur-culture, in reinscribing language with 'classicisms'? The answer, not to the 'problem' but to the politics of the academic and cultural environment that produces such critique, is simply to reject such regressive and often neo-colonial judgements. The main concern of lyric producers might rather be their relations with society. The lyric's future might also lie in disavowing hierarchies of difference, such as those attaching to region, language (including register and dialect), ethnicity, gender and sexual orientation. Equally important is the dismantling of the authoritarian structures of high and low, popular and élite. Beyond that, by rejecting the ideological concepts of nationalism and patriotism which have long manipulated Chinese lyricists, including its pop lyricists, by abandoning the monolithic national project – the 'burden' of reconstructing a national lyric language as a sort of modernisation project – poetic practice may perhaps reconnect with its sources: the production in society of stories and myths and new language. For if a literature is to 'emerge' it must ultimately emerge from a community. And now various forms of lyric production are continuing to emerge and grow in divergent ways.

There is, for instance, the production of exiled lyricists cut off from their community. Consider this poem by Duoduo written very shortly after the shock of the realisation of exile from China, and the awareness of the dislocation of existence in the centre of the European Other. In it, through and despite the production of modernist imagery, there is a relentless movement towards the evocation of the irretrievable homeland, which is ultimately as dislocated as the 'I' of the poem itself:

THE RIVERS OF AMSTERDAM

November as the city enters night
here are only the rivers of Amsterdam

suddenly

the mandarins on the tree at home
quiver in the autumn breeze
I shut the window, yet to no avail
the rivers flow backwards, yet to no avail
that sun all inlaid with pearls, has risen
yet to no avail

doves like iron filings scatter and fall
a road devoid of boys suddenly looks vast and empty

after the passing of the autumn rain
that roof crawling with snails
– my motherland

on Amsterdam's rivers, slowly sailing by.

1989[57]

Another poem, 'In England', traces a line through initial
culture shock to what seems like a negative critique of the
country of refuge. Here it is ultimately the trauma of separation
from the society which has contained the entirety of one's
lived experience, even for this most modernist, most 'internationalised' of poets, which is dominant in the poem:

From the mud hidden in the cracks of my nails, I
Recognize my homeland – mother
stuffed into a parcel, and posted faraway.[58]

Duoduo's poetry, in a way similar to yet more nuanced than
Bei Dao's early verse, speaks not from outside but from amidst
ordinary Chinese people, out of and to fellow victims – their
generation of urban youth. Suddenly they were, and still are,
exiled abroad, distanced from the 'motherland' and isolated
from both poetic and linguistic community.

Meanwhile, in China the popular lyricist Cui Jian had
continued to taunt the authorities with his 'New Long March
of Rock and Roll', and communities of poets have continued

---

[57] *Manhattan Review*, 6, 2 (Fall 1992).

[58] *Ibid.* 6, 1 (Fall 1991).

to experiment with language and to produce broadsheets and *samizdat* journals. Perhaps ultimately it is these latter who will now shape and develop China's still emerging modern lyric genre. For will it be possible for those engaged in poetic practice abroad to resist the duplicity of those engaged in the Sinological project who on the one hand use the new to foreground the 'glory' of the past, while still hoping to exploit the new modern Chinese poetic discourse to revive a dying project? Indeed, is it not in truth the continuance of the Sinological dominance of Chinese literature, a Sinologised culture, that is at issue? To this question let us answer tentatively: if the modern Chinese lyric discourse resists the tendency to assist in the substitution of the current nationalist and nationalising state ideology by providing a new, totalising, patriotic, 'democratic' version of that ideology, and remains a discourse which is – however problematically – 'deeply grounded in society' (that is unofficial society), even while 'it does not chime in with society', then yes, modern Chinese lyrics can and will remain a vital part of modern China's emergent literature. And yes, the modern Chinese lyric for all its 'anachronism', indeed by exploiting that 'anachronism', has something to say beyond the 'globalised' lyric, does indeed have an identity distinct from 'world poetry'. Where there is an historically specific modernity, there will be an historically specific cultural response, despite outward and seemingly 'outmoded' formal appearances.

5

EXILE AND THE POTENTIAL
OF MODERNISM

'No: there is only one terror, from which all others derive. For most
people it is the fear of losing the last illusion separating them from
themselves, the panic of having to create their own lives.'

—Raoul Vaneigem[1]

'Exile is strangely compelling to think about but terrible to experience.
It is the unhealable rift forced between a human being and a native
place, between the self and its true home: its essential sadness can never
be surmounted. And while it is true that literature and history contain
heroic, romantic, glorious, even triumphant episodes in an exile's life,
these are no more than efforts meant to overcome the crippling sorrow
of estrangement. The achievements of exile are permanently undermined by the loss of something left behind for ever.'

—Edward Said[2]

Edward Said's words, quoted above, may aptly be appropriated to describe the condition of those Chinese poets in
exile whom I have known. But the poet Duoduo, on whom
we focus here, was in a sense already an exile before he ever
left his native soil; he was estranged and alienated from official
society, as were most of his generation and social class, by the
violence and arbitrariness of what they had believed to be an
egalitarian and utopian project, the Cultural Revolution of
1966-76.[3] To no other twentieth-century 'revolution' are

---

[1] *The Movement of the Free Spirit: General Considerations and Firsthand Testimony
Concerning Some Brief Flowering of Life in the Middle Ages, the Renaissance and,
Incidentally, Our Own Time* (New York: Zone Books, 1994) 21.

[2] 'Reflections on Exile' in Russell Ferguson, Martha Gever, Trinh T. Minh-ha,
Cornel West (eds), *Out There: Marginalization and Contemporary Cultures* (New
York: New Museum of Contemporary Art, 1990) 357.

[3] Duoduo was born in 1951, two years after the founding of the People's Republic

these words of Vaneigem more appropriate: 'What started as a revolution against misery turned into a miserably failed revolution'.[4]

Even before exposure to the mythical universe of foreign modernist poetry, Baudelaire, Dylan Thomas, Plath, Tsvetaeva and their negotiation of alienation, the brutality and despair of Chinese social life are foregrounded by fanciful travels in a foreign poetic West of the mind, as in this poem written, without hope of publication, towards the end of the Cultural Revolution when Duoduo was twenty-two years old:

BLESSINGS

When society has difficulty giving birth
that thin, black widow ties magic words on a bamboo rod
which she waves at the rising moon
a blood-soaked streamer emits an endless stench
making evil dogs everywhere howl the whole night long

From that superstitious time on
the motherland, was led by another father
wandering in the parks of London and the streets of Michigan
staring with orphan's eyes at hurried steps that come and go
and again and again stuttering out old hopes and humiliations.
1973[5]

For this Chinese neo-modernist exotic reverie is the fabric of an engagement with modernism which had a deeply serious purpose. Modernism supplied the means both to negotiate and to engage reality; 'engage' since escapism alone might provide a means of negotiating reality, and Duoduo, much less ostentatiously but often more effectively than many of his contem-

---

of China, in Peking. His mother had trained as an opera singer and his father was an academic economist. After high school, the universities being closed, Duoduo, like many of his contemporaries, roamed the country and saw at first hand the material realities of New China.

[4] Vaneigem, *Movement of the Free Spirit* 22.

[5] Revised version of the present author's translation of the poem in Duoduo, *Looking Out From Death: From the Cultural Revolution to Tiananmen Square*, trans. Gregory Lee and John Cayley (London: Bloomsbury, 1989) 22.

poraries, very seriously engages and probes reality, furnishing a caustic critique of contemporary existence.[6]

The poet Duoduo and many of his exiled contemporaries may be categorized within a constellation of literary modernism. Modernism – or as it has been described above, irrealism or post-realism – in the Chinese context is essential to any discussion of exile and, it is argued here, to a discussion of a future for Chinese writing.

The metropolis is crucial to the growth of modernism, and in pre-Communist modern China that metropolis was the Shanghai of the 1920s and 1930s. As the late Raymond Williams told us:

it is not the general themes of response to the city and its modernity which compose anything that can properly be called Modernism. It is rather the new and specific location of the artists and intellectuals of this movement within the changing cultural milieu of the metropolis.[7]

Williams also describes a scenario which with very little modification and exercise of the imagination could be Deng Xiaoping's capital, the Beijing of the 1980s:

The metropolis housed the great traditional academies and museums and their orthodoxies; their very proximity and powers of control were both a standard and a challenge. But also, within a new kind of open, complex and mobile society, small groups in any form of divergence or dissent could find some kind of foothold, in ways that could not have been possible if the artists and thinkers composing them had been scattered in more traditional, closed societies.[8]

As Williams notes, there is a 'radical difference' between such 'struggling innovators' and the 'modernist establishment' which consolidates their achievement.[9] Of course, China has

[6] The recent acceleration of China's integration into the world market and of the economy's total conversion to market capitalism renders such ideological critique even more necessary. Indeed, social conditions in China are now such that it cannot be long before a more forceful social critique becomes the staple of Chinese cultural production.

[7] Raymond Williams, *The Politics of Modernism* (New York: Verso, 1989) 44.

[8] *Ibid.* 45.

[9] *Ibid.*

not had and does not have a modernist establishment as such. *Pace* Jameson, the 'modernism' pursued at the end of 1980s by such as the novelist, exploiter of modernist techniques and then Minister of Culture, Wang Meng, was not of the same order and was not grounded in the same experience as the modernism of 'unofficial' writing.[10] However, what Williams describes as the 'key cultural factor', the character of the metropolis, most decisively 'its direct effect on form', is applicable to Chinese conditions at several moments in the twentieth century. Certainly it could be said of urban China in the post-Mao era that 'encountering. . . a novel and dynamic common environment from which many older forms were obviously distant, the artists and writers and thinkers of this phase found the only community available to them: a community of the medium; of their own practices.'[11]

This community and its practices can also be seen as oppositional and resistant to the dominant ideology, and this is so all the way from the Democracy Wall period of the late 1970s to 4 June 1989 and beyond. But was the new cultural impulse fuelled by what Williams would call 'negative energy', what Lukács called 'empty dynamism'? In other words, is a phenomenon such as the new poetry of the 1970s and 1980s capable of more than a critique of the bankrupt but tenacious ideology of the state? Williams and others have often seen the ideological critique brought to bear by Western bourgeois society's avant-garde as incapable of going further. Throughout the twentieth century Chinese cultural producers have vacillated between various positions that either offer no meaningful critique of society, or provide a critique which points

---

[10] Fredric Jameson, 'Literary Innovation and Modes of Production: A Commentary', *Modern Chinese Literature* 1, 1 (Spring 1985) 77. It might also be recalled that it was during Wang Meng's tenure at the Ministry of Culture before the Tiananmen massacre that avant-garde art exhibitions in the capital were forcibly closed by the authorities.

For a detailed critique of Jameson's ideas on Third World literature, see Aijaz Ahmad, *In Theory: Classes, Nations, Literatures* (London and New York: Verso, 1992).

[11] Williams 45.

to no particular alternative, or give a critique which embraces modernisation under Chinese control. The majority of modern Chinese writers and artists have consistently felt the obligation to engage in critique.[12] But the question that arose in the 1930s, and again in the post-Mao era, was: what then? what comes next?

The lack of an attempt by progressive writers and artists to arrive at a formulation of what might have 'come next' left literary culture vulnerable to the deadening effects of socialist realism, revolutionary romanticism and a so-called proletarian literature authorised and authored by the Chinese Communist Party; literary modes which may have served a certain propagandistic purpose but which left most concerned, progressive producers of culture silent or confused. As V.G. Kiernan wrote in the 1973 postscript to his essay 'Wordsworth and the People':

> the Cultural Revolution has sought to unite thinking individual and mass mind in a newer, more organic fashion, and this accounts for much of its appeal to the West, particularly to the student movement it helped to generate. Whatever the political value of that grand upheaval, however, it would not seem to have had much value for the arts, or 'culture' in any traditional sense; rather it seems to have called on artists and intellectuals to become good Chinese by ceasing to care about being themselves.[13]

But what came next after the Cultural Revolution was the claim of a number of the Democracy Wall generation, in their mid-twenties in the late 1970s, to be in pursuit of 'pure literature' and to be apolitical in their art. As will be clear by this point, the very act of their writing both in China and in

---

[12] Leo Ou-fan Lee in *Voices from the Iron House: A Study of Lu Xun* (Bloomington: Indiana University Press, 1987) refers to Lu Xun's 'devastating critique of politicians': what I would call a conscious ideological critique of the dominant order and its ideology (135). But, as Lu Xun himself observed, this literature which engaged in ideological critique of society, what he called in his April 1927 address to the Whampoa military academy the 'literature of discontent', 'did not necessarily contribute to the outbreak of revolution'. Indeed, as Lee notes Lu Xun at this juncture basically denied 'the validity of "revolutionary literature" in a pre-revolutionary setting' (136).

[13] V.G. Kiernan, *Poets, Politics and the People* (New York: Verso, 1989) 118.

exile makes that act political. The entrenchment of the exiles' conviction that a genuine apolitical position was possible was demonstrated by the apparently genuine, surprised response on the part of some of them, who at that moment even shunned the label 'exile', when the Chinese Communist authorities in 1991 declared the Stockholm-based, relaunched Peking Spring literary magazine, *Today*, a 'reactionary publication'. A similar response met the party's notification of certain cultural figures' 'work units', editorial offices and so on, that they were now *personae non gratae* and were not to be allowed to take up their posts again should they return to China. The naïve yet prevalent wisdom seemed to be that if politics as such was avoided and the designation 'exile' avoided, no political action would be taken against them.

The real situation is that exiled writers, who are by and large modernists, do indeed occupy a political and ideological position. As Tony Pinkney in his introduction to *The Politics of Modernism* puts it, glossing Williams, ' "In a sobering second stage [in other words after the resistance and oppositionism of modernism]. . . what we want to become, rather than what we do not now want to be" becomes a crucial issue.'[14] Certainly the alternative to such cultural producers defining and determining their own identity will be having their identity determined by the Western modernist establishment, concerned with commodification and packaging of the writer/artist, and the whole commercial circus that surrounds literary activity which reaches its whirligig crescendo when sanctioned, and sanitised, by the Nobel Prize for Literature.

It is very difficult for Chinese cultural producers in exile, and particularly for poets, to avoid having their work classed as merely Chinese 'works of radical estrangement'.[15] However, Chinese writers and artists in exile do seem to have saved one another from mutual isolation – as their colleagues in China have done. Moreover, despite the arguments of

[14] Williams 22; Pinkney is citing Williams's 'Afterword' to *Modern Tragedy* (London: Chatto and Windus, revised edition with afterword, 1979).
[15] Williams 35.

'politicality' and 'pure' literature, it is my contention that much of the neo-modernist post-Mao lyric production itself implies what might 'come next'. This, if anything, constitutes the potential of modernism.

In thinking about that modernist potential, it is the humanising possibilities that are of interest; in particular, the capacity of modernist practitioners to reconfigure reality, as some contemporary Chinese poetry and fiction has done, the better to engage, challenge and interrogate humanity's dominative relation to Nature. There is an attempt in many of the contemporary poet Duoduo's texts to interrogate the contradiction between Nature and our domination of it. The interrogation frequently ends in a reaffirmation of separation, in an assertion of Nature's arbitrary power. Imbricated in the foregrounding of invincible Nature is a critique of the project of life-sapping modern society bent on the transformation of Nature. The result, which is unstoppable, is increasing alienation:

> In weather such as this
> no meaning at all is to be had from weather
>
> rejected by a dreamed-out dream
> stuffed into a shoebox
> controlled by a sort of lack of means of denouncing
> in the time an insect takes to walk by
> those fearful of death increase their dependence on fear
>
> In weather such as this
> You are an interval in the weather
>
> whatever you stare at, you are stared at by it
> inhaling what it exhales, it bores into your smell
> staring upon the change before day-break
> you find the opportunity to turn into grass
> passing by trees grown by people
> you forget everything
>
> In weather such as this
> you won't stand by weather's side
>
> nor will you stand by faith, only by the side of fabrication
> when horses' hooves no longer fabricate dictionaries
> ask your tongue to fabricate hornets no more

when wheat in fabrication matures, afterwards rots away
would you eat up that last plum in the nightingale's song
eat it up, afterwards leave the sound of winter on the branch

In weather such as this
only fabrication advances[16]

In this poem by Duoduo, the response to society's fabrication of falsehood, the attempt to traverse the divide, is a recourse to oneiric fabrication. Within the space and moment constructed by this poetic text, Nature's element, 'weather', offers none of the usual clues and guidelines. The habitual means of orientation are effaced; 'land has no boundary, railroad tracks no direction.' What directs 'you' now is the absence of power to resist, 'to denounce'. The fear is the ultimate fear, that of death. It is the most poignant reminder of Nature's dominance. 'You' are a space cleaved into weather, an 'interval', in which the cleft between the subject, 'you', and Nature is deferred, as Nature penetrates, 'bores' into 'you'. Standing within manifestations of Nature there is the fantasy of becoming one with Nature, turning 'into grass', and yet even at that moment the 'trees planted by people' recall the reality of modern civilisation's attempted dominance. So 'you' retire into a space where language ('dictionaries', 'tongue') is in apparent contradiction with natural objects and phenomena. But this altered reality affords the possibility of asking if even 'in weather such as this', when there is only the fabricated poetic spectacle, 'the plum in the nightingale's song', the only accommodation possible with Nature is consumption. Even in the production of resistance to reification made by this poem, by its 'fabrication' of images that defy easy comprehension, there is also produced, fabricated, the possibility of the poem itself being consumed as commodity.

In Europe and North America, modernism has often been perceived as *dis*engaged from reality; what Alex Callinicos calls 'the aesthetic withdrawal from reality'.[17] Writing of moder-

---

[16] *Manhattan Review* 6, 2 (Fall 1992).

[17] Alex Callinicos, *Against Postmodernism: A Marxist Critique* (New York: St Martin's Press, 1990) 49.

nism in the European context, another Trotskyist critic, Chris
Nineham, has noted 'the contradictory nature of all modernism' which may appear as a 'retreat from society'.[18] 'But the
search for new artistic method, and the corresponding self-
consciousness about the role of the artist in society, could lead
to a critique of society itself.'[19] Despite art's self-referentiality
that has facilitated its 'drift into harmless obscurity', Nineham
predicts that 'new artists will want to learn' from earlier
modernist artists' 'efforts to break down the barriers between
art and life'.[20] Raymond Williams towards the end of his life
also reassessed modernism and its possibilities. Tony Pinkney's
reading of him establishes that Williams had discerned in
modernism a potential force situated between, or perhaps
beyond, capitalism on the one hand and on the other a Leninist
philosophy so 'divorced from experience' that it threatened to
reproduce 'within socialism the "dominative" relation to Nature and other characteristics of capitalism'.[21] As Pinkney
indicates:

> Modernism had already been a resource of sorts against such domination:
> Ibsen has shown both the actual impossibility and the disastrous human
> consequences of the abstract will, evincing [a]. . . sense of the organic
> textures of 'community' that must be defended against the predations
> of the 'planning' from above.[22]

Similarly in the visual arts the British modernist painter David
Bomberg (1890-1957), the teacher of Frank Auerbach and
Leon Kossoff (all of whose marginalised work – there is one
Kossoff in New York's Metropolitan Museum – is now coming to be seen as among the most socially meaningful of
post-Second World War British art), was convinced that
'humanity could only be saved by countering the threat of
uncontrolled technological advance', a conviction which led

[18] Chris Nineham, 'The Two Faces of Modernism' in *International Socialism*
(Autumn 1994) 135.
[19] *Ibid.* 136.
[20] *Ibid.* 139.
[21] Williams 26.
[22] *Ibid.*

Bomberg to declare that 'with the approach of scientific mechanization and the submerging of individuals we have urgent need of the affirmation of [the human being's] spiritual significance and... individuality.'[23] He summed up his own approach in the terse statement that 'our search is towards the spirit in the mass'.[24]

Bomberg and his followers were exceptional. Those artists who subscribed to the dominant avant-garde trends in the post-Second World War West

> may have begun in the belief that their art could be a haven from a hostile world, but some of them quickly discovered it could provide them with a passport to privilege in the post-war boom.... After the war 'avant-garde' abstract painting became the officially sanctioned culture of corporate America. The paintings of Jackson Pollock and Theodore Roethke looked impressive, seemed meaningful and had absolutely no connection with any aspiration to change the world.[25]

Raymond Williams ascribed the reason for post-1950 avant-garde introspection to 'what can be seen as a failure in that most extreme political tendency – the Bolshevik variant of socialism – which had attached itself to the ideas and projects of the working class.'[26] But was not Bolshevism rather a 'variant' of capitalism? Writing in 1967, Vaneigem commented that the 'planned Chinese economy, in refusing to permit to federated groups the autonomous organization of their labour, is condemning itself to attaining that perfected form of capitalism, called socialism.'[27]

Like Cuba's, China's revolution was more nationalist than it was socialist and relied heavily on the discourse and ideology of nationalism, very much capable, at least for a time, of

---

[23] David Bomberg, foreword, *Exhibition of Drawings and Paintings by the Borough Bottega and L. Marr and D. Scott*, catalogue of exhibition held at the Berkeley Galleries, London, November-December 1953, cited in Richard Cork, *David Bomberg* (London: Tate Gallery, 1988) 40.

[24] *Ibid.*

[25] Nineham 138.

[26] Williams 26-7.

[27] Raoul Vaneigem, *Traité de savoir-vivre à l'usage des jeunes générations* (Paris: Gallimard, Collection Folio/Actuel, 1967, 1992) 72.

convincing people to 'submit themselves to the draconian discipline involved in the primitive accumulation of socialist capital'.[28] Today the urban classes of China are no longer convinced of the Chinese Communist Party's patriotic credentials and the mantle and ideology of nationalism have been eagerly seized by those who have gathered around the banner of the failed political revolution of Tiananmen 1989. But such nationalism, whether appropriated by Communist or anti-Communist, never was, and still is not, sufficient as a politically ameliorative ideology.[29] It does not deliver autonomy, it does not challenge hierarchical control of people's time and labour. In speaking of the Western context, Williams allows to modernism the possibility of 'the alternative directions in which a continuing bourgeois dissidence might go'.[30] If we rephrase the proposition for post-Maoist dissidence which refutes 'the Bolshevik variant of socialism', it can be suggested that there are still in China alternative directions in which such dissent might go. The possibility of alternative directions has been demonstrated in Europe by modernists like Bomberg. The dehumanising, mechanising, industrialising, and militarising of the world by capitalism and by bureaucratic socialism – the supremacy of modernity, *not* modernism – was seen to despoil and destroy, and so Bomberg stressed individuality and difference, just as Chinese poets like Bei Dao and Duoduo would be seen to do in post-Cultural Revolution China. Of course, despite all their protestations to the contrary, there *was* an ideology and political purpose underlying the avowed apoliticalness of contemporary Chinese dissident or 'unofficial' writing. Neither Bei Dao's nor Duoduo's work is ultimately

---

[28] Terry Eagleton, foreword to Kristin Ross, *The Emergence of Social Space; Rimbaud and the Paris Commune* (Minneapolis: University of Minnesota Press, 1988) xiv.

[29] Or as Eagleton puts it, 'no political revolution, whatever libidinal attractions it offers, to contemporary Western critics, will ever succeed unless it manages to penetrate to the very heart of capital, and overthrow its long-superseded sway'; Ross xiv.

[30] Williams 27.

apolitical, nor is there a lack of critique of society and its dominators.

If there is anything positive about the experience of exile, it is perhaps the insight afforded by the externality of the exilic situation. According to Bakhtin:

In order to understand, it is immensely important for the person who understands to be located outside the object of his or her creative understanding – in time, in space, in culture. For one cannot really see one's own exterior and comprehend it as a whole, and no mirrors or photographs can help; our real exterior can be seen and understood only by other people, because they are located outside us in space and because they are others'.[31]

Here we return to a poem written by Duoduo shortly after arriving in Europe. The poem, 'In England', juxtaposes fragments of perceptions of the country as a place of exile:

> After the spires, and the city chimneys sink beneath the horizon
> England's sky, is darker than lovers' whispers
> Two blind accordion players, heads bowed pass by
>
> There are no farmers, so there are no vespers
> There are no tombstones, so there are no declaimers
> Two rows of newly planted apple trees, stab my heart
>
> It was my wings that brought me fame, it was England
> Made me reach the place where I was lost
> Memories, but no longer leaving furrows
>
> Shame, that's my address
> The whole of England, does not possess a woman who cannot kiss
> The whole of England, cannot contain my pride
>
> From the mud hidden in the cracks of my nails, I
> Recognize my homeland – mother
> Stuffed into a parcel, and posted faraway
> 1989-90 [32]

This poem ultimately is about home, about not England but mother China. The poem also exudes that common exile

---

[31] M.M. Bakhtin, *Speech Genres and Other Essays*, ed. Caryl Emerson and Michael Holquist, transl. Vern V. McGee (Austin: University of Texas Press, 1986) 7.

[32] *Manhattan Review* 6, 1 (Fall 1991).

sentiment, guilt: 'Shame, that's my address.' The 'exile leaves
on an impulse to escape, not to enjoy travel' and in conse-
quence his or her focus is on home, not the exotic.[33]

But can exile alienate the person exiled to the extent that
he or she is able to Otherize his or her own culture? Bakhtin
asserts that 'entry as a living being into a foreign culture. . . is
a necessary part of the process of understanding it', which
might rather lead the exile to insights into the *host* culture
unavailable to the culturally indigenous. But Bakhtin also
emphasises that 'creative understanding does not renounce
itself, its own place in time, its own culture; it forgets nothing',
which would seem to point to the exile always being an Other
and thus affording her or him reflective insight into home.[34]
Seamus Heaney, writing on a related topic, recalls Stephen
Dedalus's 'enigmatic declaration that the shortest way to Tara
[the legendary seat of ancient Irish kings] was via Holyhead [a
Welsh ferry port], implying that departure from Ireland and
inspection of the country from the outside was the surest way
of getting to the core of Irish experience.'[35]

Another later poem by Duoduo locates the poetic voice
squarely in the Other's West, but only as a site of exilic
reflection on what might be read as the tragedy of China's
politicised youth. Yet as the title of the poem 'They' (or
'Them') emphasises, *they* appear to be very much the non-*I*;
they are others to the subject, the 'I' and the 'We' of the I's
generation:

> Fingers stuck into pants pockets jingling coins and genitals
> they're playing at another way of growing up
>
> between the striptease artist's elevated buttocks
> there is a tiny church, starting to walk on three white horse legs

[33] Andrew Gurr, *Writers in Exile* (Atlantic Highlands, NJ: Humanities Press, 1981)
25.

[34] Bakhtin 7.

[35] Seamus Heaney, *The Government of the Tongue: The 1986 T.S. Eliot Memorial
Lectures and other Critical Writings* (London: Faber and Faber, 1988) 40.

they use noses to see it
and their fingernails will sprout in the May soil

the yellow earth of May is mound upon mound of flat explosives
imitated by death, and the reason for death is also

in the very last jolt to the soil of the ironware in heat
they will become a part of the sacrificed wilderness

the silence of the long dead dead before dying
makes all they understood immutable

the way they stubbornly thought, they acted
they gave away their childhood

made death preserve intact
their hackneyed use of our experience.
1991[36]

On reflection, is not the final historical complicity of the I's generation with 'them' reached in the final couplet, with the repetition of the same old mistake, 'their hackneyed use of our experience'?

What of Duoduo more than five years into exile?[37] Obviously he is disconnected from the once vital source of his poetry. He appears to have found it relatively easy to write self-reflective pieces and short stories inspired by his new exilic experiences. He has suffered separation from family and friends; the death of his mother since he left China was a tragic blow. As Said tells us, the 'achievements of exile are permanently undermined by the loss of something left behind for ever'.[38] It is not simply land and culture, but people that get left behind.

Now Duoduo literally wanders from country to country in search of a livelihood. In China, I saw him as often lonely, frustrated, enraged even, by the isolation which marked his existence in Beijing. Tormented, like others, by boredom and

[36] *Manhattan Review* 6, 1 (Fall 1991).

[37] These comments are based on the present author's acquaintance and conversations with Duoduo during 1986 in China and over the years since 4 June 1989.

[38] Said 357.

everyday existence, by the tedium of work on a state newspaper, he sought to fight through the mire of mere survival, 'the requirements of soulless routine', in order to live.[39] Obliged to do a hack writing job by day which sapped his energies – he was a reporter on the *Peasant's Daily*, having to cycle an hour each way down Beijing's Chang'an Avenue to work and back –his strength lay in his defiant difference, his life in poetry. Daytime was constituted by work, habit, routine; night-time by moments of autonomy, by the sparks of creativity which shine 'all the more brightly in the night of nihilism which at present envelops us'.[40] His struggle for life over survival was waged through the making of poetry. In the year or two before 4 June 1989 he was beginning to be accepted and published by the 'liberalising' literary establishment and by the literary anti-establishment too. In 1989 he was invited to Holland and Britain to read his poems. By a twist of fate he was due to leave on 4 June. Having spent the night of 3-4 June at Tiananmen Square, having witnessed the People's Army mowing down the people, Duoduo made his way to the airport and took his seat on a British Airways flight to London. Suddenly, but briefly, he was the European media's favourite 'dissident poet'. The directness of political expression he had long shunned was suddenly thrust upon him as he was devoured in an orgy of rapacious consumption by the media and culture industry. As his translator I witnessed it all, powerless to do anything but deflect the worst excesses of marketing managers, and point out the exploitation of which the poet was in any case aware. All this media attention allowed him at least moments of solidarity with the dead and with those left behind to survive. When media interest in Tiananmen and China waned, he found himself as isolated and alienated as ever, except now commodified. In exile his 'dissidence' was packaged; a dissidence always so simplistically projected by the Western media establishment as anti-Communist and pro-capitalist, as

[39] Vaneigem, *Revolution of Everyday Life* 191.
[40] *Ibid.* 193.

the desire for the Western liberal notion of freedom. A Soviet exilic predecessor, the poet Igor Pomarantsev, in 1987 described the phenomenon thus:

The key to my recognition. . . is otherness, my foreign birth and language. But. . . it happens to be the case that [this culture of the West] only accepts those. . . poets who have had their finger nails pulled out at home. The vulnerability of finger nails, or their absence, is – like it or not – somehow connected with poetry. The possibility cannot be excluded that the reader, in order to justify his own creative passivity, will recognize talent only in those poets who have paid for their celebrity with finger nails. . . . Fate, pain, finger nails, like music, do not need translation. You believe them.[41]

But even fingernails can be forgotten. The news media's commodification, even festishisation, of shock and revulsion and compassion is transferred, in a flash, to the next 'sexy' story. For Duoduo, isolation and alienation, the desire to live and not just survive, impelled him to write, but suddenly for a brief media moment it was not his poetry as such – the complex recorded representation of and reflection on his and society's reality, a series of negotiations of thought, life and language spanning a decade or more – but rather his poetic act, his 'miraculous' appearance in London and his ardent denunciation of the butchery of Tiananmen Square that counted. His written poetry was a sign of anti-Communist 'dissidence' that the Western media could read as facilely as they read Soviet and East European dissidents/dissidence.

In China, his poetry critiqued a humdrum social existence and a rebarbative culture of work maintained by the 'revolutionary' authority. It was this regnant authority, sustained by an ideological mystique of power, responsible for the misdirection of the destructive and poetic revolutionary potential of youth, that the creativity and cultural production of a handful of young poets partially unmasked. And then, upon arrival in Europe, Duoduo found himself confronted by the ideologies of the capitalist West, literary production con-

---

[41] Igor Pomarantsev, 'Lost in a Strange City', *Times Literary Supplement*, 26 June 1987, 695.

trolled and creativity restrained not by bureaucrats but by commodification. In China it was the Communist Party and its organs of literary control which suffocated literary creativity; in the West it was the commercial exploitation and needs of the culture industry which attempted to consume him and his production. Exiles like Duoduo may also be smothered by the kindness of well-intentioned Western hosts: 'The whole of England does not possess a woman who cannot kiss'.

Duoduo continues to craft a poetry that addresses his actual and original community's past and present to produce a critique of modernity that speaks to and about us all. Foregrounded is the isolation that the poetry's 'I' has yet to overcome. Take, for example, the poem 'I've Always Delighted in a Shaft of Light in the Depth of Night':

I've always delighted in a shaft of light in the depth of night
midst the sound of wind and bells I await that light
in that morning asleep until noon
the last leaf hangs as if dreaming
many leaves have entered winter
leaves falling from all sides hem in the trees
trees, from the rim of the sloping town gather winds of four
   seasons –

Why is the wind always misread as the center of being lost
why do I intently listen to trees hinder the wind once more
force the wind to be the harvest season's five prized-open fingers
the wind's shadow grows new leaves from the hands of the dead
finger nails pulled out, by hand. By tools in hands
clenched, the spitting image of a human, yet spat on by humans,
like the shadow of a human, walked over by humans
there it is, driving the last glint of light from the face of the dead
yet honing ever brighter the light that slices into the forest!

Against the light of spring I enter the light of before dawn
I recognize the only tree that hates me and has remembered me
Under the tree, under that apple tree
the table in my memory turns green
the splendors of May, bones by wings startled awake, unfold
   towards me
I turn around, fresh grass has grown over my back
I'm awake, and the sky has already moved
death inscribed on the face has entered words

illuminated by stars accustomed to death
death, projects into light
making the solitary church the last pole to measure starlight
making the left out, left over.
1991[42]

Duoduo has always written out of a time and space determined by great social and political manoeuvres and their
consequences for everyday existence, and so his poetry surely
is not limited to a critique of a society constrained and
moulded by China's particular matrix of feudal, authoritarian
and capitalist ideologies, but extends to a critique of the
modernity which dominates us all. As in China, so in exile the
'creative spark, which is the spark of true life' continues to
flash brightly in the universal gloom that enshrouds us as the
midnight of the century draws near.[43]

While the wind and the forces of Nature have been symbolic of political forces in Chinese poetry, for Duoduo Nature
(trees, the wind) represents a source of power unrestrained by
humanity, a power fundamentally hostile to modern human
projects. In this sense, surely Nature is the ally of the poet in
his critique of society and of himself. Death has long been a
motif of Duoduo's poetry, from the youthful poems composed
in the early 1970s during the Cultural Revolution, down to
his post-Tiananmen lyric production. The deaths of compatriots over the last few decades may be one of this poem's
concerns. But it may also be a negotiation of private grief, a
contemplation of the death, a year into the poet's exile, of his
mother in Peking, and of his brother several years previously.
Beyond this, there is also a more general meditation on death,
and thus on life itself. 'Light', traditionally associated with life
and goodness, is here implicated with 'death'; 'death, projects
into light', stars are 'accustomed to death'. Despite the light of
spring and dawn, the 'I' of the poem is forgotten by the trees,
except for one which hates him. He is isolated like the 'solitary
church', dead or as good as dead, an observer alienated in and

---

[42] *Manhattan Review* 6, 2 (Fall 1992).

[43] Vaneigem, *Revolution of Everyday Life* 193.

by the forest, who is unaided by the ultimately unenlightening 'shaft of light'. But the constant reiteration of 'death' only causes discomfort in those who survive without living. Extinction after survival is surely terrible. Yet the 'absolutism of death on the installment plan' can be vanquished by the 'individual will to live', which stands as a 'guide to the emancipation of all'.[44]

Does the 'freedom' of exile sever the poet from the 'freedom' to participate in the revolution of everyday life? Certainly, according to Joseph Brodsky it deprives the writer of immediate social significance:

Because of his previous incarnation, he [the exile poet] is capable of appreciating the social and material advantages of democracy far more intensely than its natives are. Yet for precisely the same reason (whose main byproduct is the linguistic barrier) he finds himself totally unable to play any meaningful role in his new society. The democracy into which he has arrived provides him with physical safety but renders him socially insignificant. And the lack of significance is what no writer, exile or not, can take.[45]

It is just such a significance that Chinese exile writers and intellectuals have been at pains to deny, as the arguments about so-called *chun wenxue* (pure literature) illustrate. When a writer says in the Chinese context, 'I just want freedom to write', she or he is being either naïve or disingenuous, for what does it mean 'to write' in China, or for that matter about China? Internal exile in China, exile of the mind, alienation, ostracisation, exclusion from official literary arenas gave rise to a sense of communion with the canonised modernist poetic heroes, whether Western or East European. But being physically in the West opens up a Pandora's box in which the exile starts to see the ideologies and imaginaries of the capitalist world, of Western civilisation, unveiled.

[44] Vaneigem, *Movement of the Free Spirit* 235.
[45] Joseph Brodsky, 'The Condition We Call Exile', *New York Review of Books* (21 January 1988) 16, 18, 20.

Modernism in China fulfilled a need, it challenged the non-revolution of the Chinese Communist Party; it may continue to do so. Even exiled modernists can continue to do so, if they can resist commodification and exploitation. Just as in the West, in earlier stages, modernism challenged dominant bourgeois values, so in China it has challenged the supposedly 'revolutionary', supposedly 'collective' image of society projected by the state; an ultimately false and hypocritical image. Innovative modernism breaks away from restrictions, flouts rules, in short is rebellious and revelatory. Its attraction is obvious, and yet the same modernist impulses have in European and American cultures long since been trivialised, recuperated into the orthodox fabric of commodity culture; have lost the power to shock, to challenge. So can this recent Chinese manifestation persist into what Raymond Williams calls the 'second stage'? Can it go on to contribute 'to a modern future in which community, but without uniformity, may be imagined again'?[46] In exile, can the isolated, individual artist resist being coopted by the commodifying impulse of Western society? Can the fragile Chinese modernist challenge to conservatism, statism and economism survive in the capitalist world which has tamed and institutionalised the modernism that bourgeois Europe and America once produced? Moreover, how will Chinese modernism negotiate the emerging globalised capitalism of which consumerist China of the late twentieth century is now a part?

This would require overcoming the risk of being subsumed under the totalising, collectivising, modernising and – most difficult to withstand – patriotic project that Chinese writers and artists have subscribed to, often to their peril, for the last hundred years. It would mean trying to establish trans-individual relations which avoid the rule of pseudo-collective identities such as the twentieth century, not least in China, has witnessed. It would mean not that creative 'individuality' should be denied or its importance diminished, but that

---

[46] Williams 35.

individualist careerism and opportunism should be mini-malised. Cliques and *guanxi* (the unfair exploitation of relation-ships and connections) would need to be resisted. Is there a likelihood of such an initiative? As it is, Bei Dao and Chen Maiping's Scandinavia-based *Today* magazine has provided a potential site, or at least focus, for such a free association of writers for whom not conformity but a human and humanising culture for China would be the aim; not that the majority of its contributors necessarily subscribe to the kind of utopian vision I describe. But can such magazines – for surely there is a need for more than one, and inside China too – and group-ings survive the vicissitudes of the cultural market place, and competing ideologies of those who demand a *chun wenxue* (pure literature) and those who seek a more pragmatic ap-proach to the use of writing? Finally, can it be expected that from those in exile and from those who struggle in China there could come a real cultural invigoration to inspire and rejuvenate not a monolithic but a diversified project or projects which would be tolerant and supportive of difference, and allow the realisation of the socially transformative and humanising potential of poetic action? History would be against it, but why should we take seriously the inevitability of history? We can at least hope for the final exorcism of the Chinese cultural producer's 'obsession' with China. For in this last decade of the twentieth century when the planet has been uniformly covered by a 'tide of destruction, pollution and falsification', then it is surely the case that one 'cannot go into exile in a unified world'.[47]

[47] Guy Debord, *Panegyric*, trans. James Brook (London: Verso, 1991) 47.

6

CHINESE TRUMPETERS, FRENCH TROUBADOURS: NATIONALIST IDEOLOGY AND THE CULTURE OF POPULAR MUSIC

'Whoever controls music has the world spinning on the palm of his hand.'

—Maxine Hong Kingston[1]

'As if the theatre, the music hall, the public dance, or the book were not, had not always been, cultural techniques, as if technology started with television and the microchip.'

—Régis Debray[2]

'Dream me a song
Sing me a song
about blue skies.'

—Elaine Okoro[3]

Popular music as a modern medium, recorded and transmitted by mechanical and electronic means, has developed and expanded throughout the twentieth century, and phonographic, tape and compact disc recordings have had almost as much of an impact in Asia as they have in the West and in other societies where the technology of recording and diffusion has been

---

[1] *Tripmaster Monkey* (New York: Vintage, 1989) 53.

[2] *Cours de médiologie générale* (Paris: Gallimard, NRF, Bibliothèque des Idées, 1991) 66-7.

[3] 'Dream Me', in *Once I was a Washing Machine: An Anthology of Poetry and Prose*, introduction by Ken Worpole (Brighton: Federation of Worker Writers and Community Publishers/Queen Spark Books, 1989) 43.

available. Already in 1930s semi-colonial China there was a burgeoning recorded popular music industry. Now at the end of the twentieth century, as the West's music industry falters together with the rest of the capitalist manufacturing industries in the face of continuing Western capitalist decline, the hopes and fortunes of the recording business are invested in the continued expansion of the market for popular music and music videos in Asia, especially in East Asia, for 'except in the Asia-Pacific Region, the rest of the world's music market is declining'.[4]

Some of the questions I hope to raise here include: can music have different functions in Asia or will it be used in ways similar to those in the West? For instance, will there be, in the production and consumption of popular music in capitalist China, space for the kind of critique that other popular music traditions have afforded? Will the practices of Chinese popular music be able to recuperate and develop 'nativist' elements and will such developments in any case render popular music any more progressive or critical? What might be the nature of alternative voices or, even more ambitiously, strategies within the discourse of popular music?

Since I am also attempting to address questions of nationalist ideologies and their discontents, as well as the notion of hybridity, I have elected to analyse aspects of modern popular music traditions in France, an advanced consumer society, in addition to those in China, now embarking on a capitalist spree of consumption and already one of the ten largest economies in the world and set to be the largest early in the next century. I use France not simply because the French popular music industry displays the global attributes typical of that industry, but also because certain practitioners have shown ambivalent, sometimes antagonistic, attitudes towards the

[4] Record industry executive Cheung Man-sun in *South China Morning Post Weekly* 1, 33 (5-6 December 1992), p. 6. By 1989, according to a report in the *New York Times* (16 April 1989, p. 27), more than 200 commercial record companies were issuing pop and rock cassettes and LPs in China. By 1995 the United States and China were on the brink of a trade war over the issue of the pirating of American music compact discs and computer software.

domination of Anglo-American popular music; both the original product and the imitation of its sound and style in French pop culture. In addition, as in China, localised practices which contest the metropolitan hold on cultural production have developed, and there have been consistent and repeated moves to resist homogeneous, national music.[5]

Whether or not popular music has a future as a truly popular, or rather people's music, recuperated and produced by those who are now consumers, as Jacques Attali somewhat idealistically foresees in the 'Composition' section of his work *Bruits* (Noises), it may still be too early to say. But the question of whether popular music is as irredeemable as Adorno (in his perceptive, enlightening, yet ultimately élitist essay 'On Popular Music', now fifty years old) would have us believe, can now be addressed.[6]

There are, of course, different kinds of popular music, even within that which seeks to be 'hit' music. There is, for example, the consciously political: songs, music and performance (visually recorded for distribution or not) which have a clear political agenda and message(s). In the Chinese (in its widest sense) context, there are, for instance, the lyrics of the Taiwanese, Hong Kong-based Luo Dayou which contain important messages in themselves. The popular and commer-

---

[5] One might also have chosen to work comparatively with certain Latin American popular or folk music practices, or with competing practices in Japan where the popular music industry of the centre is contested by, for instance, the peripheral culture of modern folk and popular music in Okinawa where songs are sung in patois. Similarly one could have examined Louisiana's Cajun and Zydeco music, its use in the preservation of a Cajun sub-national identity and its successful resistance to the general American popular music industry after a century of white Anglo attempts to stamp out the French language and the culturally different traditions that resulted from it in south-western Louisiana.

[6] With the assistance of George Simpson, in *Studies in Philosophy and Social Science*, IX,1, 17-48, published by the Institute of Social Research, New York City. The chapter on popular or 'light' music in the later *Sociology of Music* is substantially similar to the article written with Simpson and relies on the same research; in other words both refer to the production and consumption of popular music in the USA of the late 1930s. (Theodor W. Adorno, *Introduction to the Sociology of Music* (New York, Continuum, 1989); transl. by E.B. Ashton of *Einleitung in die Musiksoziologie* (Frankfurt-am-Main: Suhrkamp, 1962).

cially successful mainland singer Cui Jian's message is conveyed not merely by sound, but also by a subversive and ironically deployed semiotics of visual image (the now celebrated red blindfold and People's Liberation Army [PLA] green jacket). But even the enunciation of the lyrics (characterised by a coarseness and self-conscious use of street-wise accent), and the near grammatically incoherent words themselves, challenge the tame lyrical practices of official Chinese popular music production and join the music in the production of a kind of emotion that, 'beyond words', disrupts the official order.[7] In France the socially conscious pro-Communist singer Jean Ferrat has relied on straightforward lyrical expression to convey his politics, while his music and performance style are almost indistinguishable from those of the run-of-the-mill hit song performer; indeed Ferrat, 'in singing very polished pieces (following the line of the French Communist Party), marks the limit of a genre'.[8] Others, like the Fabulous Trobadors, a southern French, Occitan, regionally based duo with an agenda of radical political change which aims to make the peripheral Toulouse region an alternative progressive and autonomous cultural space, rely on both their lyrics and the appropriation of styles of music to produce a hybrid, alternative creation which thus seeks to foreground and impress upon the consumer/listener the difference of their music and the difference it hopes to make. The seemingly utopian ideology of this group and its music embraces the cultural forms of the Other, particularly of the colonised North African, and welcomes the Other to join their project. Their position is that the metropolis has dominated the regions with its nationalising, and thus colonising, cultural project just as it has colonised those beyond the hexagon of metropolitan

[7] Rey Chow, 'Listening Otherwise, Music: A Different Type of Question about Revolution', *Discourse* 13, 1 (Fall–Winter 1990-1), 135.

[8] According to the compilers (Chantal Brunschwig, Louis-Jean Calvet and Jean-Claude Klein) of *Cent ans de chanson française* (Paris: Seuil, 1981) 158, while Jean Ferrat may be the archetypal *chanteur engagé*, the commitment shown in his songs is 'only literary, it is seen in the text but not in its form, in the music or interpretation, which remain very traditional'.

France. The question with which they, and others who attempt to reach us via recorded music, face is whether by participating in a discursive practice controlled by a centralised profit-making industry one can hope to disintegrate that discourse. My own immediate response is that in principle any technology or practice can be appropriated and employed in an emancipatory way despite, and even against, those who dominate them.

Not all songs and performers have such explicit agendas. Some songs might minimally be expressions of protest often relevant to an immediate issue; for instance, there was a burst of pacifist and anti-war songs in the 1950s and 1960s in France, just as there was in America. Nevertheless, such songs naturally have an ideological impact beyond their immediate concern; you cannot challenge a government's war without questioning *in toto* the legitimacy of the regnant authority waging that war.

Then there is what could be called the unconsciously political. The majority of hit songs are those promoted by the music industry purely and simply as commodities; which is not to say that the category of 'political' songs/music and singers/musicians may not be so promoted. Yet this second category of popular music can also effect, or retard, political change by either bringing about changes in the ideological environment or maintaining an ideological stasis.

We shall first deal with seemingly 'unpolitical' commercial hit music, and focus on a rather benign account of contemporary hit-songs: Antoine Hennion's reading of French popular music, which would include both French rock and roll and *chansons* or *variétés* (solo singer ballads). Hennion articulates the view that there exists a sort of post-modern democracy of the music market place with a music industry which tries to literally play to and understand the desires of consumers. He also holds that through 'the history of popular music one can glimpse the history of those who have no words, just as feelings that cannot be expressed otherwise find their way into music.'[9]

[9] Antoine Hennion, 'The Production of Success', *Popular Music* 3 (1983) 161.

This is redolent of Adorno's somewhat imperious comment on lyrical expression, that all have the right 'to grope for the sounds in which sufferings and dreams are welded'.[10] While many critics, from differing ideological positions, see popular music as almost uniformly negative in its social effects, engineered with the sole purpose of keeping or putting in place an obnoxious ideological apparatus, in certain specific circumstances even this supposedly 'unpolitical' political function of popular 'hit' music can, according to Hennion, have a positive function, not in a formally critical way but in catering to a social life of people which is neglected by official society. As he puts it:

[W]hen this [social] reality is projected onto the screen of popular music, the picture one gets is reversed, as though one were seeing a negative on which were printed the hidden side of social life. In a rather unreal way, we catch a glimpse of all that official history, always written in terms of the power structure: hopes that are disappointed almost before they are formulated, a bitterness that nobody cares about, useless emotions. Producers are the representatives of a kind of imaginary democracy established by popular music; they do not manipulate the public so much as feel its pulse.[11]

Professional music producers, according to Hennion, are engaged in a 'permanent and organized quest' for what the 'public' wants, 'for what holds meaning for the public'. This meaning is defined as the 'socio-sentimental', a meaning 'found "down below" in those areas which carry the public imagination, its secret desires and hidden passions'. Hennion's macro-category, the 'socio-sentimental', includes

key phrases, sounds, images, attitudes, gestures and signs, infra-linguistic categories which are all the more difficult to pin down insofar as they escape definition by the official language, and are not autonomous but inseparable from the social context within which a given group attributes a special significance to them.[12]

The craving for lyrics and song to alleviate the pain of

---

[10] Theodor W. Adorno, *Notes to Literature*, vol. 1 (New York: Columbia University Press, 1991) 45.
[11] Hennion 191.
[12] *Ibid.* 160.

everyday survival with a dream of the unreal, which is the
hope for the pleasure of real living, is articulated in a poem
entitled 'Dream Me' by a black British poet, Elaine Okoro,
who lives in Manchester in northern England:

> Dream me a song
> Sing me a song
> about blue skies
>
> ....
>
> Dream me, dream me a song about you and I
> Love pie high in the sky
> Shepherd delight sunsets
> Romantic untouched love.
>
> Dream me, dream me
> Something so unreal,
> so everlasting
> That it takes me away
> from all I feel.[13]

There is no question that 'a given group attributes special
significance' to certain phenomena, but what informs this 'public
imagination', how is it formed? How much is ideology, how
much 'authentically' expressive of social resistance and autonomy?
Surely the 'socio-sentimental' itself is also a product of Western
capitalist consumer culture, and consumers are in fact display-
ing the shared responses and conventions of a collective
imaginary in part reproduced by the popular music industry.
However, Hennion is doubtless right to indicate that record
producers provide a release for popular dissatisfaction and
disaffection, rather than bringing to bear on society a critique
which can effect or help to effect change. Hennion himself
believes the ultimate use of these hit-songs that address the side
of social life neglected by society is equivocal, since the 'underlying mythic themes are ambivalent, lending themselves equally
well to submission or revolt, desire or hostility'.[14]

---

[13] *Once I was a Washing Machine* 43; Elaine Okoro describes herself as a 'black writer
born in Britain, African in heart and mind'.

[14] Hennion 176.

To help us understand the function that the music producers perform, it may help to invoke the concept of bardic television developed by Fiske and Hartley, who propose that the social function of television is akin to the mediating function of the bards, a distinct and separate institution in Celtic societes.[15] Like the bards, television channels stand between the ruling class, who pay for and license them, and the rest of society, whose speech and events are processed by them into a 'specialized rhetorical language' which is then played back to them.[16] This mediating role is active and implies that neither the ideology of the owners/rulers nor the experience of viewers/consumers is merely *reflected*; theirs is a mediated, processed 'reality', an artificial construct, arrived at by the investment of much ideological labour. It might, of course, be argued that these are distinct discursive practices: while much television production is meant to 'make sense' of the world, lyrics constitute a discourse of distraction. Yet something of this mediating, bardic function is discernible in the practices of popular music, as one would expect of a music industry so firmly and increasingly enmeshed in the electronic and broadcast media.

It is a sort of bardic function that Hennion describes when he writes of popular music producers' seeking and reproducing 'infra-linguistic categories', the 'socio-sentimental'. For, as with the television message, we are 'at once celebrated and implicated' in the message of the popular hit-songs, in the ideologically structured 'socio-sentimental' (re)produced by the bardic music producers.[17] Hennion, however, emphatically subscribes to the view that the industry is simply responsive to the consumers' wants: 'Pop songs do not create their public, they discover it.'[18] Furthermore, he is critical of the position that points to 'the arbitrary imposition of meanings by producers

[15] John Fiske and John Hartley, *Reading Television* (London: Methuen, 1978).

[16] Tim O'Sullivan, John Hartley, Danny Saunders and John Fiske, *Key Concepts in Communication* (London and New York: Routledge, 1983, 1992) 18.

[17] *Ibid.* 19.

[18] Hennion 191.

and sellers' on a public seen as 'passive, ready to absorb whatever it is presented with'; a vision that, according to Hennion, 'overlooks the active use to which people put popular music, the imaginary existence they lead through it, which is not reducible to the official social hierarchies.'[19]

But again surely the consumption of music resembles more the uni-directional nature of media flow, whether domestic and locally controlled, or that of satellite television such as Hong Kong-based Star Television.[20] To what extent can even the consumer 'choice' provided by MTV pretend to reverse the one-directional nature of such broadcasting? Moreover, in the case of Asian MTV and its successor Channel V, which transmits some locally produced music but also substantially the same European-American MTV product as in the Anglophone West, the hegemony of this uni-directional flow is reinforced.

In the early 1990s the classic Maoist revolutionary songs dating back to the Yan'an guerrilla base days of the 1930s and 1940s made a comeback in China. Such consumption perhaps is in part due to a certain popular nostalgia for simpler, pre-consumerist and more idealistic times, parallel to the display of Mao badges and posters by bus drivers and others as good luck charms. But that same nostalgia had been previously deployed by subversive rock stars such as Cui Jian, and the irony of the capitalist Western musical interpretation of Maoist songs perhaps reached its height with the R & B and reggae cover versions of Beijing Reggae, a group put together by an American producer, Jeffrey Cheen.

Official Chinese producers have been quick to exploit the trend for profit, perhaps in the hope of extracting political capital from it. So on the street stalls in China's cities one finds disco and other re-styled versions of Maoist classics. On the bookstalls, right next to a song book featuring Madonna is a book cover showing Mao Zedong encircled by an array of his

[19] *Ibid.*
[20] Strictly speaking: direct broadcasting by satellite (DBS) directly to the point of consumption, the household.

heavily made-up contemporary television variety show inter-
preters clad in white tuxedos and sequined ballroom gowns.
On the street stalls selling music cassettes and compact discs
Mao is on sale alongside a subversively dressed rock star, Cui
Jian. In late twentieth-century capitalist China, the market has
established a consumerist and mythic equivalency between
Mao and Madonna and Cui Jian.

Adorno, in his essay on 'free time', concluded that what
'the culture industry presents people with in their free time,.
. . is indeed consumed and accepted, but with a kind of
reservation.'[21] To a degree, Hennion's critique makes a similar
point in rebutting the idea that the consumer is totally passive.
For instance, many more songs are produced than ever make
it into the hit-parade, and moreover if all the consumers, all
the time, were satisfied with what the industry gave them, then
new styles of music would not emerge and the industry would
not have to invest in appropriating them. New styles like punk
and reggae and rap are, of course, very quickly recuperated
into the mainstream discourse; so as to satisfy the desires of the
public for novelty perhaps, but also surely so as to maintain
the music industry's profits by commodifying a music which
initially threatens resistance against official society and its
capitalist priorities.

The 'use to which people put popular music', then, according to Hennion, is akin to taking a palliative. That an 'imaginary existence' is considered to be authentic resistance to
'official social hierarchies' is surely precisely the kind of musical
function that official society desires. As Hennion has observed:
'Pop songs often end. . . by fading out the sound on a repeated
"loop": one cannot end a dream, "full-stop", just like that.'[22]

Hennion's narrative of the relationship between the consumer and the music industry looks to the social use of music
and its role in aiding people to 'get through the day'. But apart
from making profits for the music industry, is this not exactly

---

[21] Theodor W. Adorno, *The Culture Industry: Selected Essays on Mass Culture*
(London: Routledge, 1991) 170.
[22] Hennion 170.

what official society wants? If popular music can provide additional tools of suppression, over and above economic mechanisms, by culturally reproducing existent social formations and thus neutralising or appropriating eventual discursive practices of society so as to perpetuate existing power relations, then the industry provides additional value in sustaining dominant interests. The Chinese regnant authority's licensing of Hong Kong popular music distribution and performance in China, and its own distribution of revolutionary songs refashioned as popular music, are just such attempts to exploit popular culture by naturalising and legitimating the social authority of dominant, and in this context distinct but not necessarily conflicting, interests.[23]

While producers may be providing a dream, are they really 'feeling the pulse', as Hennion's bodily metaphor has it, benevolently to provide what the audience desires? Are they not rather, as Jacques Attali has suggested, concerned with the production not of the product but of 'demand'? For 'everywhere music is present, there also is money'.[24]

As to the other uses that a regnant authority has for music, Attali has identified three: '*Faire Oublier, Faire Croire, Faire Taire*'. And in all three cases – making people forget, making people believe and silencing people – music is 'a tool of power: ritual, in the case of having people forget fear and violence; representative, in the case of having them believe in order and harmony; bureaucratic, in the case of silencing those who contest.'[25] The dream world constructed out of popular music which is described by Hennion resembles Attali's category of 'making forget', if not in this context 'making believe' and 'making silent'.

Attali's discussion of the use and power of music is particularly pertinent to totalitarian states, to the Chinese context

[23] O'Sullivan 64.

[24] Jacques Attali, *Bruits. Essai sur l'économie politique de la musique* (Paris: Presses Universitaires de France, 1977) 12.

[25] *Ibid* 36.

and to the East German, Chilean, Brazilian or South African contexts over the last half-century:

> [The theoreticians of totalitarianism] have all, without distinction, explained that it was necessary to forbid subversive noise, because they announce demands of cultural autonomy, claims of differences or of marginality: the anxiety of maintaining tonalism, the primacy of melody, distrust of new languages, codes, and instruments, the refusal of the abnormal is found in all these regimes. These are explicit translations of the political importance of cultural repression and control of noise. For Zhdanov. . . music, as an instrument of political pressure, had to be quiet, reassuring, calm.[26]

It had to be reassuring and calm, because 'noise', Attali tells us, 'is violence: it disturbs.' But the fact that noise disturbs means that it can disrupt the dominant order; its subversive potential is thus ever present. 'To make noise, is to interrupt a transmission, unplug, kill. It is a substitute for murder.'[27] In ancient China the violent and terrifying power of noise was understood and deployed by feudal generals, as we read in *The Story of Hua Guan Suo*: 'His eight thousand troops scattered amid the sounds of the songs of Chu.'[28] More recent extreme examples of the use of musical noise as a simulacrum for violence would be the deployment of classical music as a weapon in the filmic representation of the war in Vietnam, *Apocalypse Now*, and the 'real life' invasion of Panama in 1989, during which Manuel Noriega's presidential residence was blasted by US forces with heavy metal music. The bombardment with noise of the besieged sect in Waco, Texas, in 1993 also vividly illustrates how the authorities have grasped very directly the disruptive effect of broadcast noise.

'Totalitarian' or otherwise, no matter which mode of production a state deploys in its project of modernisation, dominant classes and opposition movements have used music

---

[26] *Ibid.* 17–18. Zhdanov was a notorious controller of Soviet cultural life.

[27] Attali 47.

[28] *The Story of Hua Guan Suo*, trans. with an introduction by Gail Oman King (Tucson: Arizona State University Center for Asian Studies, 1989) 33. I am grateful to Alexa Olesen for bringing this quote to my attention.

to sell nationalist sentiment and likewise have used nationalist sentiment to sell music.[29]

The exploitation of patriotic sentiment occurs in various guises and for seemingly different ends; for example, to promote a certain political project, or to extract profit from people's nationalist ideology: sometimes both at once. Recently, some cultural producers in China have indulged in what seems like an ironic redeployment of nationalist rhetoric and semiotics. The Chinese group Hei Bao (Panther), a Hong Kong-Taiwan managed and marketed group, did this in song and through music video for profit and career advancement; while Cui Jian's recuperation of party-state signifiers (red kerchiefs, PLA uniforms, revolutionary lyrics), both ironically and perhaps also in an attempt to recover a lost idealism, is part of a political project: his 'New Long March of Rock and Roll'. But even the group Hei Bao, with an ambition seemingly limited to professional advancement and profit-making, nevertheless defy official society and occupy national space in a subversive way. Their critique may seem more superficial than Cui Jian's, and yet in its moment is no less damaging to the regnant authority. Hei Bao's violence is not solely, perhaps not mainly, channelled through their music and lyrics, but rather into their video image. Their video pictures show the group (self-as-commodity) in Beijing against settings such as the Great Wall, Chang'an Avenue, the Forbidden City: all almost sacred spaces in the national(ised) collective imaginary. Defiance of authority is illustrated by the appropriation of a traffic podium at a major Beijing intersection; elsewhere there is an altercation with a policeman. Such acts of defiance against the patriarchal regnant authority and its central spaces is similar to the message

[29] Alain Touraine, in *Critique de la modernité* (Paris: Fayard, 1992), observes that 'nothing authorises the identification of modernity with a particular mode of modernisation, the capitalist model, which defines itself by this extreme autonomy of economic action. From France to Germany and from Japan or Italy to Turkey, to Brazil or to India, historical experience has shown, on the contrary, the almost universal role of the State in modernisation. . . . Outside a few centres of the capitalist system, modernisation has been carried out in a more coordinated and authoritarian manner'(237).

inscribed into the early 1980s British MTV videos analysed by E. Ann Kaplan, 'anti-parental, anti-authority videos, revealing adolescent disillusionment with, and distaste for, parental, work-related, or state authority'.[30]

Then there is mimicry of Western popular music lore, most notably in the band's re-enactment of the scene depicted on the Beatles' *Abbey Road* album cover in which the Beatles walk in synchronised fashion across a pedestrian zebra crossing. This is surely a form of allusion which will be understood neither by the bureaucrats of official society nor by the majority of the Chinese popular audience. So for whom and for what are these visual references to Western popular music mythology? When *Abbey Road* hit the Western music charts, mainland Chinese people were chanting Maoist slogans in Tiananmen Square. It is true, of course, that the video was made mainly for consumption beyond the mainland, in Hong Kong, Taiwan and so on, but nevertheless it will, like many other MTV videos, have been seen in mainland China too.

It is the recuperation of national symbols and spaces which is of interest here. These symbols, ideological and mythical constructs – whether the Great Wall or the Long March – are imbricated not just in the construction of the nation but also with the Chinese Communist Party. The recuperation of these symbols also entails recovering or challenging the idealism of nationalist Communism; and that is precisely what Cui Jian's 'New Long March' does. There is irony, yet also a recuperation of an originary, popular nationalism which not only grips high cultural intellectuals but popular cultural heroes too. Cui Jian's naïve nationalism is illustrative of the entire twentieth-century project, dominated hitherto by writers and intellectuals, to 'save the nation'. His trumpet is emblematic of the party-state's dilemma in condemning that which is 'polluted' by the West. When sanctioned by the state, the instrument itself becomes 'official'; Cui Jian as a boy played the trumpet in a state-run orchestra. When the instrument is played

[30] E. Ann Kaplan, *Rocking around the Clock: Music Television, Postmodernism and Consumer Culture* (New York: Routledge, 1987) 67.

'officially', it is legitimised, authentic and Chinese; used for the state it becomes an instrument of the state. But when it is used against the state, when Cui Jian extracts from it tortured and defiant notes in his subversive performances, it is constructed as decadent, outlawed and Western (once more). Cui Jian's use of the trumpet is at once an appropriation of an 'official' and so 'Chinese' instrument, and a reappropriation of a Western instrument.

Also exploiting the national heritage is a group whose very name lays claim to the Chinese tradition: Tang Dynasty. A recent made-for-MTV video makes use of a sort of Orientalist dream sequence of an abandoned (perhaps Tang) temple, the Buddha and even earlier ruins situated somewhere on the periphery of China. As in the Hei Bao videos, the band itself is seen performing both in the studio (in typical masculinist heavy metal poses) and on location. While the past supplies the props, the video production technique is standard for the 'post-modern' modernist video: 'We never know why certain things happen, or even precisely what *is* happening. We are forced to exist in a non-rational, haphazard universe where we cannot expect any "closure" of the ordinary kind.'[31] Another technique this video adopts is also typical of 1980s heavy metal videos, in which bands are depicted in the studio exuding a hectic vitality. Thus we cut between the known and knowable heavy metal band in classic pose, and an incoherent narrative 'undercut by pastiche' in which 'signifying is undercut by images that do not line up in a coherent chain'.[32] But this video cannot resist having some of its imagery communicate an almost clear 'signified'. There are a number of large red flags displayed falling to the ground throughout the video, and at the end of it five large red flags (perhaps representative of the five stars of the Chinese state emblem) hang limply on poles in a dimly lit interior, thus connecting

[31] *Ibid.* 63.
[32] *Ibid.*

the crumbling traditional signs of the past to the fading signs of the official present.

In China, as in France, there is a tradition of producing patriotic lyrics. Patriotic sentiment has been exploited in popular lyrics both to bolster nationalist ideology itself and to further the aims of particular political parties and groups. However, when the organs of the only remaining significant Communist state, China, not only passively acquiesce in but actively engage in the marketing of so-called new feeling, new style, new rhythm disco-karaoke remixes of revolutionary era songs, are we witnessing a last-ditch attempt to reinvigorate a state ideology that has rapidly lost credibility, or is this merely a response from Chinese cultural units to the centre's new capitalist edicts to make money? Or is it simply a desperate attempt to do both in the would-be 'hybridity' of 'socialism with Chinese characteristics' which is no more than late twentieth-century Chinese capitalism?

But ought this state-sponsored marketing of the party-state heritage (Mao memorabilia, Maoist disco-beat musical eulogies and so on) be so surprising? Is it not the logical outcome of a state-managed socio-economy in the process of modernisation? Nationalism is invested in this modernisation like all other resources; like poetry, like pop lyrics. Alain Touraine has described nationalism as the 'mobilization' of the past and of tradition in the service of the future and of modernity, and the function of the nation not as 'the political face of *modernity*', but rather as 'the principal actor of *modernisation*, which is to say it is the non-modern actor which creates a modernity in which it will try to maintain control at the same time as accepting its partial loss to the benefit of internationalised production and consumption'.[33]

In China Cui Jian speaks from within a patriotic discourse which, in its modern manifestation, dates back to the end of the nineteenth century when poet, intellectual and political actor were constructed as a unitary subject. It was a discourse

[33] Touraine 162.

reinvented and reinvigorated by the patriotic intellectual and cultural movement of 1919 known as the May Fourth Movement and, with its dual appeal of modernisation and national (re)assertion, it has proven an indispensable discourse of power ever since. While he engages in a critique of capitalist consumption and state control and looks to an ideal which is somehow more spiritual, Cui Jian's idealism seems still to be constructed in terms of some sort of overhauled nationalism.

In a different context, that of 1950s France, singer-songwriter, novelist and jazz musician Boris Vian produced songs that were both anti-militaristic and thus 'unpatriotic' ('Le Déserteur' – The deserter) and anti-authoritarian ('On n'est pas là pour se faire engueuler' – We didn't come to be yelled at); and anti-consumerist ('La Complainte du progrès' – Ballad of progress). As a popular entertainer, Boris Vian wrote and performed many songs in his short life, not all of them as obviously and topically 'political' as 'Le Déserteur'. But the critique of consumerist, Fordist capitalist development in songs such as 'La Complainte du progrès' tends to be overlooked, as does the ludic irony of Vian's *chansons rock*, which at once appropriate and satirise the contemporary French popularity of the American rock and roll hit-song. These songs are both an appropriation and a contestation of American popular culture, a sort of critical negotiation and mediation of an intrusive and imperialistic culture. While Vian exploited and made light of American 1950s popular songs, he celebrated and identified with the music of oppressed black America; in the 1940s and 1950s he was on good terms with many black American blues and jazz artists, including Miles Davis, Charlie Parker, Tommy Potter and Kenny Dorham. Vian had no time for narrow-minded and xenophobic French nationalism and notions of cultural purity. Another oppositional singer-songwriter who gained popularity in 1960s and 1970s France was Jacques Brel, a Belgian. Averse to petty-minded nationalism, he criticised his fellow-citizens' inclination to 'piss in two languages'.

As we have seen, resistance to Fascism and foreign

militarism during the Second World War had been framed in extremely nationalistic terms. France's recovery from the national 'humiliation' of German Nazi occupation and the collaboration of significant sectors of the population, including much of the political élite, involved the attempt to re-establish domination in former French colonies and the consequent bloody wars in Vietnam and Algeria which lent to the country a reputation far removed from the ideal of 'Douce France' (Gentle or Sweet France). This extremely popular, much-adored, morale-boosting song, written and sung by Charles Trénet, came out just after the Second World War. It was a song that reinvigorated the national body for a population reoccupying space and institutions in a land which had been administratively and politically divided and fragmented. Its music was redeployed in a slick post-modernist video commercial in the 1988 campaign to re-elect François Mitterrand, at a time when the President needed to put together a rainbow coalition which emphasised not a social democratic vision but a pluralist, racially harmonious, 'republican' vision of a modern, tolerant France. The modernised version of the music lent to the colourful, montage-type advertisement just the right amount and sort of nationalist sentiment ('good' Frenchness, wholesome patriotic feelings; not for the state but for the people and the nation) that Mitterrand needed to attain his narrow electoral victory. Doubtless the seductive qualities of the colourful cinematic visual imagery were important and reinforced the 'music's power over the psyche'.[34] It was a propaganda commercial which perhaps met the multiple desires of the viewer/elector: that of seeing a vision of a beautiful, colourful and tolerant France, a modern France mindful of its traditions; and the nostalgic wish − fuelled by Trénet's 'Douce France' with its reverberations of a halcyon, post-war period when the nation was reborn and reunified − for a mythic stability. Of course, this was a false and incomplete picture, as the prime function in the 1940s of Trénet's song

[34] Anne Hollander, *Moving Pictures* (Cambridge, MA: Harvard University Press, 1991) 9.

was to make people forget their misery and guilt and to dream of better times ahead.

Such totalising, nationalising strategies in which music is employed were and are frequently challenged by a minority discourse of popular music, such as Vian's and Brel's and more recently by the Fabulous Trobadors, who promote the idea of a racially and culturally diverse society, a society tolerant of difference. Their music, like Hong Kong Cantopop for a brief moment in the late 1980s and early 1990s and that of Hong Kong-based producers like the Music Factory, is subversive of the centre's culture and language.[35] The Trobadors often sing in southern dialect and introduce English and Arabic and other linguistic accents at will, thus challenging the hegemony of the northern metropolis and its music industry.

The Fabulous Trobadors challenge the listener to act, but also provide enjoyment through word-play and the pleasure derived from their critique of 'official' France. Just as Hennion reads hit-songs as providing a dream world for 'the French' consumer, so the Trobadors project a dream of autonomy for the Toulousains and tolerance for others on the periphery (the Arab, the African). These are not fanatical political independentists, regionalists or sub-nationalists. They sing mainly in standard French rather than in the Occitan language. The group identifies itself by a hybrid English-Occitan name, the Fabulous Trobadors, the second part of which draws on the tradition of the original troubadours who of course composed and sang in southern French Provençal, rather than the *langue*

---

[35] 'Cantopop' may be defined as a sort of pop ballad sung in Cantonese which drew on the late 1980s wave of nostalgia for a disappearing Hong Kong cultural identity. During the 1980s and, in particular after the Tiananmen massacre of 1989, it seemed to be a vehicle of popular, everyday 'resistance' to the northern, Mandarin-speaking authoritarianism of Beijing. Recently, however, the Chinese state, more receptive to solo ballads than to rock and heavy metal, has sought, seemingly successfully, to woo a Cantopop industry ever-ready to enhance its primary function, the accumulation of profits. On 18 April 1993 sixteen Cantopop superstars performed to an audience that included leading Politburo members. Ethnic unity and patriotism were foregrounded during the event, not least by the prolonged television shot of the state seal of the People's Republic of China. See Willy Wo-lap Lam, *SCMP Weekly* 2, 1 (24–5 April 1993), 11.

d'oïl or northern French of their later imitators the *trouvères* (the most legendary of whom was Richard the Lionheart's minstrel Blondel).[36] The Fabulous Trobadors attempt to promote a southern cultural autonomy, a sort of cultural anti-centralism based on the diverse dialects and practices that constitute Occitan culture, while trying to avoid the narrowly chauvinistic. The Trobadors also find common cause with those who are different and marginalised, such as the North African immigrants. Some of their melodies and rhythms allude to Arab music.[37] Their rap is analogous to American rap. They draw on north-east Brazilian music, in which they perceive, via Portugal which was very much a part of the medieval troubadour space, a troubadour heritage.

Are the Fabulous Trobadors practising a globalised culture, or are they resisting it? Perhaps rather they are mediating different cultural practices into a synthesis, a hybridity, a reaction to northern French cultural centralising colonialism, which draws on the music of other marginalised peoples, as well as on the mass culture of North America towards which Parisian purists have been so traditionally hostile while ignoring their own 'cultural imperialism' – in Africa in particular, but also in metropolitan France itself.[38] The Trobadors, who record their café performances live and have toured the

[36] *Trobador*, troubadour; *trobar*, to find, compose verses.

[37] This appropriation is quite likely a reappropriation: 'the categories of thought and the artistic techniques that the [original] troubadours introduced so swiftly' could only have come from a more precocious civilisation; 'it could only be Islam' and the 'imagination of the poets of Baghdad'. Henri-Irénée Marrou, *Les Troubadours* (Paris: du Seuil, 1971) 113.

[38] Witness, for instance, the French culture industry's manoeuvres to secure a 'cultural exception' in the 1993 GATT negotiations on open markets, and the pressure the French state brought to bear on the 47 delegations at the fifth 'summit' of Francophone nations in 1993 to support its campaign. Between 45% and 50% of broadcast programmes in Senegal are imported from France, and between 23% and 30% in Cameroon. The Cameroon journalist Michel Lobe Ewane has written of the exercise of a 'French cultural imperialism', the subtlety of whose ideology lies in 'making Africans believe that they belong to the same cultural mould as France because of a shared language and that it is in their interest to defend French language and culture'. Cited in *L'État de la France. Édition 94-95* (Paris: Éditions La Découverte, 1994) 165.

countryside and towns in their multicoloured van, have largely eschewed complicated instrumentation and extensive use of synthesizers and electronically created sound. They also pursue alternative means of distribution (selling tapes and compact discs in the streets), but inevitably are implicated in the dominant discourse of popular music for profit and its means of distribution. However, is it justifiable to argue, as one French reviewer did, that they 'simultaneously condemn the prostitution of commercialisation, and make a living at it'? Is it true to say that the Fabulous Trobadors are indulging '*une idéologie politique simpliste*' (a simplistic, political ideology) when they promote '*démocratie à fond* ' (grassroots democracy)?[39] Or is this again the voice of the metropolis, the centre, refusing to recognize the efforts towards autonomy at the periphery?

What is certain is that the musical noise of the late twentieth century, popular lyrics, in particular rock songs, can disturb the state. That the state attempts to stifle, subvert or otherwise control the noise of popular music is understandable. What seems perverse, however, is that the state continues to be disturbed by the producers of poetry to the extent that they are harassed and imprisoned, a reaction out of all proportion to their contemporary influence. But, then, every state 'which has a monopoly of ideas, fears the written word'.[40] Historical attitudes to the lyric in China also render the over-reaction against marginalised poetry less surprising; for since the orality of popular song was appropriated by the state and made literary in the *Shijing* or *Book of Songs* over 2,000 years ago, lyrics have consistently been interpreted politically, and authority has always been aware of their subversive potential.

Earlier, I discussed Hélène Cixous's reading of poetic discourse as critically and subversively effective. In her discussion of Marina Tsvetaeva she claims that while history 'simply smothers and squashes', there are some lyrical works that

---

[39] *L'Immature: Littérature* 4 (September–November 1992) 68–9.

[40] Tariq Ali, 'Literature and Market Realism', *New Left Review* 199 (May–June 1993) 143.

demonstrate that 'one can remain poetic in the very midst of history'.[41] Cixous, however, might balk at an 'intersection' between popular music and history, which we evidently have seen in Hong Kong and China in the last decade, since it is in the 'slowness. . . thought and silence' of poetry that she seeks to evade the 'noise machines' of modernity. 'Noise machines' for Cixous are imbricated in a life 'oriented by speculation, money, and profit', which would pass as an appropriate description of contemporary Chinese society.[42] But what we have witnessed in the recent Chinese context, in addition to the undoubted 'speculation, money, and profit' associated with the 'noise machines' (video and karaoke machines) of the music industry, has been a resistance to the prospect of mere survival illuminated by the materialist consumption of capitalist modernity. Now in China, as elsewhere, poetry, which was for so long song, has been given back its sonorous voice; it is once again loud noise. That the state in China has increasing difficulty in controlling the broadcasting and dis-tribution of unlicensed cultural products becomes daily more obvious, and the poetry of the contemporary technological world empowered by noise insists on being heard. Houston Baker claims:

if the state keeps itself in line. . . through the linear, empty space of homogeneity, then poetry worries this place or time with heterogeneous performance. If the state is a place of reading the lines correctly, then poetry is the site of audition, of embodied sounding on state wrongs.[43]

---

[41] Hélène Cixous, *Readings: The Poetics of Blanchot, Joyce, Kafka, Kleist, Lispector, and Tsvetayeva,* transl. and ed. Verena Conley (Minneapolis: University of Minnesota Press, 1991) 111.

[42] Cixous continues: 'In the milieu of the media, people are entirely governed by the obligation to create scandals. Scandal is what sells. In place of the word, reflection or thought, we need noise. The public has to be satisfied. The public is not stupid, the institutional powers are. But the media spirit has even infiltrated the halls of the university' (*ibid.* 111-12).

[43] Houston A. Baker Jr., 'Hybridity, the Rap Race, and Pedagogy for the 1990s', *Technoculture,* ed. Constance Penley and Andrew Ross (for the Social Text Collective), Cultural Politics, vol. 3 (Minneapolis: University of Minnesota Press, 1991) 205.

In this supposedly 'post-poetry' world, Baker easily elides distinctions between poetry lyrics and popular lyrics, talking of American idols like Chuck Berry as 'people's poets'.[44] Unlike Cixous, Baker finds that loud noise, the loudness of popular music, fits easily into his reading of lyrical discourse; a reading which accommodates both poetry and rap alike. Learning from Stallybrass and Bhabha that 'nationalist and postrevolutionary discourse is always a discourse of the split subject', Baker concludes that in order to 'construct the nation, it is necessary to preserve a homogeneity of remembrance (such as anthems, waving flags, and unifying slogans) in conjunction with an amnesia of heterogeneity.'[45] He thus sees poetry again 'like rap, as an audible or sounding space of opposition'.[46] Ultimately, he is not so very far from Cixous.

Chinese rock star Cui Jian turns the tropes and signs of remembrance back on the state, to recall what it wants to forget, but he also redeploys them in his own patriotic project which aims to save China from the new materialism through the consumerist culture of popular music that he calls the 'Long March of Rock and Roll'. The question becomes: is the deconstruction of one totalising practice not bound to lead to another? The Fabulous Trobadors construct, and appeal for, a renewed, revived cultural nation of the south: a local 'patriotism' which nevertheless eschews traditional chauvinistic and militaristic nationalism, stresses tolerance and constructs its claim to self-determination and difference by appropriating black rap and Arab North African rhythms, thus reaching back to a time when heterogeneity was a reality of a multi-ethnic Mediterranean, a site of inter-cultural negotiation between the civilisations of Africa, Asia and Europe which produced a common hybridised culture for much of the region.

Historical hybridised cultural traditions are necessarily hidden and suppressed by the modern state; its traditions have to

[44] *Ibid.*
[45] *Ibid.* 206.
[46] *Ibid.*

be mono-cultural. But can any culture based on a *patrie* – however marginalised, however worthy – be tolerant and lacking in totalising ambition?

While Hobsbawm clearly accepts that French as a national language was foisted on the inhabitants of the space called 'France' by the regnant authority, he nevertheless still sees the 'nation' as a serviceable vehicle on the road to a more progressive society.[47] Alain Touraine conversely sees a correspondence between 'modernity and the nation, either in its colonial form, or in its nationalist form, which has destructive effects', whilst the dissociation of economic modernity and national consciousness seems to Touraine to be 'one of the important aspects of the fragmentation of the classic idea of modernity and of conceptions of modernisation which consider industrialisation, democratisation and the formation of national states as three interdependent aspects of the same general process', an idea which ought to be 'more and more forcefully rejected'.[48]

Is there then, as the Fabulous Trobadors claim, a space for a 'cultural nation' resulting from 'cultural decentralisation', a dissociation of cultural national consciousness from the destructive potential of nationalist state power?[49] Can there be a sense of belonging, of cultural identity, which will not become a 'nationalism' deployed as an 'instrument in the service of the modernising, authoritarian and nationalist state which in calling on the artifically reconstructed idea of a *Volk*' in the worst case creates 'a totalitarian power in the name of *Ein Volk, Ein Reich, Ein Führer*';[50] an instrumentality which as we have seen again recently in former Yugoslavia is not restricted to large states. Touraine would certainly see the

---

[47] E.J. Hobsbawm, *Nations and Nationalism since 1870: Programme, Myth, Reality* (Cambridge University Press, 1991). Yet Hobsbawm does insist that 'no serious historian of nations and nationalism can be a committed political nationalist' since nationalism 'requires too much belief in what is patently not so' (12).

[48] Touraine 165.

[49] The Fabulous Trobadors. Jacket notes. *Era Pas de faire*, Ròker Promocion/Indépendance, HD CD 9245, Distribution Danceteria D 700, 1991.

[50] Touraine 165.

possibility of such a dissociation in the 'fragmentation of classic modernity': 'It is. . . the increasing separation of the supposed attributes of rationalisation, itself identified with modernity, which best corresponds to today's world.'[51]

We now turn to the effectiveness of music as a tool of subversion. In the Chinese context, is there cause for those who constitute the regnant authority to be concerned by the subversive potential of mechanically and electronically reproduced music? It may well be that the creator and producer of Beijing Reggae takes pleasure in bringing Afro-Caribbean musical expression into electronically reproduced Chinese popular music. He may believe he is doing something novel, even progressive, but he does it with the full and open cooperation of Chinese Communist officials in charge of the music industry. Moreover, the product again is intended mainly for Hong Kong and overseas distribution and consumption. In producing reggae and rhythm and blues cover versions of revolutionary classics, is he not negating the ironic and subversive potential at what should be the very moment of subversion?

Occasionally Cui Jian's concerts have been banned, while Hong Kong performers are allowed to perform in the People's Republic. While their popularity rests on a mild critique of Chinese Communist Party-dominated society, there is a sense that they will not push that too far for fear of losing access and, of course, profits. Cui Jian and other musicians and lyricists with similar mentalities are still the minority in the music business and they are after all subject to the constraints of that business. Moreover, concerts of all types are nevertheless comparatively few, while what Attali terms 'the individualised use of order' (for instance, the Walkman, and increasingly the karaoke machine) is widespread and continuously available.[52]

---

[51] *Ibid.* Given Touraine's deft critique, his turn to the right is regrettable.

[52] Attali 100. Anne Hollander (9) has also observed how the advent of the Walkman has enabled art museums to provide 'canned audible captions to go along with the pictures, furnishing continuous commentary on tape with earphones, a moving track of sound that speaks personally to each visitor and turns the whole gallery into a movie house'. See also Rey Chow, 'Listening Otherwise, Music Miniaturized', in which she discusses in detail the difference that the Walkman

But although both Western and Chinese popular music may initially appear, and even be, subversive and run counter to the official musical order of the Maoist period, ultimately the availability, facilitated by consumer capitalism, of stockpiled sociality itself may lead to the repression of people.[53] As Williams and Hirschop have it in their critique of Attali, 'a medium established to cement sociality now provides desires, interests and a sense of identity at such a deep level that public occasions' (such as pop concerts, but one might also include 'official' music concerts, live or recorded, of 'revolutionary' or officially sanctioned music) 'are no longer necessary to "cement" anything'. Or as they add, glossing Attali, 'once conformist personal desires can be manufactured, repression becomes unnecessary as people repress themselves.'[54]

According to this logic, even the remarketed, remixed and repopularised Maoist revolutionary songs are unnecessary to effect the desired repression, in which case the function of the marketing of such music would be simply the making of profit and the fulfilment of pre-existent desires.

This is a somewhat totalised view of the consumption of popular music, akin to the belief in the total efficacy of a dominant ideology. In fact the 'significant effects' of an ideology may, as British sociologists Abercrombie, Hill and Turner have argued, be 'primarily on the dominant rather than the subordinate class. What has been important for the stability of capitalism is the coherence of the dominant class itself, and ideology has played a major role in securing this.'[55] Such a claim may well have some validity for China, where the ruling

---

has made to music consumption, and Iain Chambers, 'A Miniature History of the Walkman', *New Formations* 11 (summer 1990) 1-4.

[53] Alastair Williams and Ken Hirschop, review of Jacques Attali, *Noise* (Minneapolis: Minnesota University Press/Manchester University Press, 1985), a transl. of *Bruits*, in *Textual Practice* 3, 3 (winter 1989) 469.

[54] *Ibid.* 469.

[55] Stephen Hill, 'Britain: The Dominant Ideology Thesis after a Decade', in Nicholas Abercrombie, Stephen Hill and Bryan S. Turner (eds), *Dominant Ideologies*, (London: Unwin Hyman, 1990) 2.

authority's domination of society is secured by a variety of means; namely economic imperatives, the threat or use of force, and only partially the success of ideological control. The periodic campaigns for the reassertion of Communist Party ideological purity would indeed seem to suggest that the dominant class is convinced by its own ideological positions. Witness the criticism levelled at what is perceived as Western-style, popular culture by the Chinese Communist Party ideological purists, the 'conservatives' in the leadership, who focus on its capacity to (re)produce 'bourgeois individualism'. They want a modernised national economy without the development of individualist mentalities. On the other hand, those elements in the CCP who support the promotion of consumer capitalism have understood that capitalism can flourish without any parallel expansion of rights and liberties. As Abercrombie, Hill and Turner have claimed, 'individualism and capitalism have no necessary or enduring relation: any linkage is entirely contingent'. They continue:

Individualism did give capitalism a particular shape in America and Britain, notably in the early capitalist period, and capitalism in turn shaped individualism by emphasizing its positive features. However, oriental capitalism and late capitalism in the West bear no particular relation to individualism; indeed they flourish best in the absence of an individualistic culture. While collectivism may be an appropriate cultural milieu for capitalism, individualism now degenerates into the culture of individuality, which has little economic effect. We conclude that the capitalist form of economic organization has no need of the bourgeois cultural form of individualism. Indeed, on theoretical grounds, we find that capitalism has no necessary ideological requirements at all.[56]

We should not, therefore, impatiently await the collapse of the Communist-nationalist Chinese state simply because new cultural forms and phenomena have appeared in the public sphere. The prevalent ideological discourse, a Cold War legacy, reproduced by government mouthpieces throughout the Western world and designed to have us believe that

[56] *Ibid* . 5.

market capitalism, a loosening of economic controls and the opening up to the world (markets) will somehow naturally lead to a more 'democratic' society with enforceable human rights – in other words that amelioration will come about in non-material as well as material conditions – is surely now becoming increasingly transparent. Yet this mentality is still dominant both in non-Chinese and Chinese analyses of China's socio-economy; it is, for instance, the ideology that permeates the narrative of the then controversial mid-1980s television series *River Elegy*. Yet surely it must become clear to all at the end of the twentieth century that there is no organic link between capitalism and democracy. Whether or not individual interests 'are better served by individual rather than collective strategies', it is the lack of any obvious nexus between materialist progress and a more altruistic vision for society that emerges strongly in Cui Jian's discourse.[57]

But while the linkage between individualism and capitalism may not be essential to profit-making, surely the marketing of the dream of individualism is essential to the extension of the music industry. In any case, although the 'individual' may believe that while engaged in solitary consumption of music he or she is either indulging a private or personal taste, or participating in some larger collective or network of use, whether or not the music is resistant to official society and its dominant values or engaged in active critique, the result is an effective and necessarily unperceived alienation.

This chapter has tended to privilege the subversive potential of the periphery against the centre. There is, however, a danger in privileging the marginalised, the periphery, of abandoning the centre and the centre-controlled; a centre whose regnant authority still dominates the lives of many who, while in a sense marginalised, are hierarchically, vertically dominated in

[57] *Ibid.* 26. See Cui Jian's statements in 'China Rocks: The Long March of Cui Jian', Rhythms of the World, Penumbra, BBC 2, 16 February 1991. BBC TV interview *passim*.

a more traditionally conceived way. As Hill has put it, 'while instrumentalism is an important dimension of values, there is also a strand of altruism and principled commitment in popular culture'.[58] This is why it is difficult to discount comprehensively the songs of Ferrat, which work within a more traditional discursive framework yet address capitalist society's hierarchical inequalities which have not gone away simply because there are more attractive and often less complex issues to work with.

Similarly the marginality of the 'lost cause' of Hong Kong difference render Luo Dayou and his Music Factory's project of subversion and critique more attractive than Cui Jian's naïve patriotic and anti-materialist sentiments. Nevertheless, his sound-challenge at least maintains an oppositional discourse on the mainland that other voices may yet develop. The noises of opposition (whether in colonial and soon-to-be recolonised Hong Kong, or on the Chinese mainland; whether in Toulouse, or in France as a whole) remain essential, for noise 'enables a social occupation of space, and the political establishment of forces within a demarcated area'.[59]

There is naturally no reason to suppose that popular music in the late capitalist era will not continue to function, in a bardic manner, to maintain relations of dominance around the globe, whether in China, France or elsewhere. But that bardic function of 'official' media will not prevent the voices of subversive, trouble-making troubadours from disturbing the dominant order of official noise and urging that we *passer à l'action* (turn to action).

> Make no concessions
> Make no concessions
>
> ....
>
> Throw yourselves into discussions

---

[58] Hill 25; drawing on J. Rentoul in *Me and Mine: The Triumph of the New Individualism?* (London: Unwin Hyman, 1989).

[59] Thomas Docherty, *After Theory: Postmodernism/Postmarxism* (London: Routledge, 1990) 11.

You've got to yak, got to yap,
Got to toast, got to rap,
Got to talk, got to sing
For the truth to come out!

Don't listen to the news
They're a bunch of liars
Birds of misfortune
They're doleful, fateful, all that ends in '-ful'
You're better off on your own.

....

SINGERS FOR THE COUNTRY
SINGERS FOR THE CITY
WE WANT ALL THE COUNTRY
TO SAY NO TO FATALISM

It's a very beautiful song
It's me who wrote it
It's ready and I'd like it
To enter your head
And follow you around.
Got to turn to action
Go into the streets

....

Be genial, original,
Put yourselves in capitals.

Power is achieved through unity
Unite, talk
Conceive, project
Imagine, agitate
Don't surrender your ideas!

Be careful of regressions
Take issue with what is provincial
Do away with false debates
Above all don't give up
In the face of all their blahblahblah. . . [60]

---

[60] The Fabulous Trobadors, 'Ne faites pas de concessions', *Era Pas de Faire*. My thanks to Claude Sicre and Ange B. for their kind permission to cite this song. See also the group's 1995 CD *Ma ville est le plus beau park*, Philips, 526 916-2.

7

FEAR OF DROWNING:
PURE NATIONS, HYBRID BODIES,
EXCLUDED CULTURES

'Shame to mankind! but shame to Britons most,
Who all the sweets of Liberty can boast;
Yet, deaf to every human claim, deny
That bliss to others which themselves enjoy;....'
—William Roscoe[1]

'*N* is the Navy
We keep at Spithead
It's a sight that makes foreigners
Wish they were dead.'
—*ABC for Baby Patriots*[2]

'Four hundred African immigrants fled a farming town in southern Italy
to evade racist attacks of which they were the victims, Italian public
television announced on 17 August. Employed as seasonal workers at
Stornara. . . they were pursued after an eighty-year-old man died as a
result of his house being broken into last weekend. For certain of the
inhabitants there was no doubt that the burglars were immigrant
workers. The police emphasised that there was no evidence at all to
that effect.'
—*Le Monde*, 19 August 1993

In 1993 the economies of Europe went into recession. The
resulting unemployment fuelled a racism that is ever waiting
to rear up in the modern world. All over Europe racism against

---

[1] 'Mount Pleasant' (1771) cited in *Liverpool and Slavery: An Historical Account of the
Liverpool-African Slave Trade by a Genuine 'Dicky Sam'* (Liverpool: A. Bowker and
Son, 1884; reprinted by Scouse Press, 1985) 57. Roscoe was a poet, historian,
philanthropist and celebrated Liverpool abolitionist.
[2] Reproduced in Liz Curtis, *Nothing but the Same Old Story: The Roots of Anti-Irish
Racism* (London: Information on Ireland, 1985, 1991) 66.

non-whites continues to rise. During 1993 hundreds of incidents occurred in Germany, where Turkish immigrants have been burnt out of their houses and killed. In Italy there have been numerous examples of the racism illustrated by the story from *Le Monde* quoted above. In France the new government instituted weekly deportation trains from the Gare de Lyon in Paris to transport unwanted non-white, mainly Arab, foreigners to the border, often after the authorities had arbitrarily decided to expel them. One Algerian academic who had been in France for ten years was about to complete his doctorate at the University of Paris when his residence permit was withheld. So as to remain within the law he stopped working at his part-time job. His wife kept working legally and was able to support him and their French-born child. He was subsequently deported to a country where he no longer had any ties and where thousands of intellectuals have been assassinated by fundamentalists. The reason for the deportation was that he did not have enough funds to support himself, even though the authorities had been the cause of his giving up his job. In England, in August 1993 a black Jamaican women was suffocated to death by an over-zealous deportation squad. In February 1995 a black member of a French rap band, Ibrahim Ali, was shot in the back and killed by members of the extreme right-wing and racist French *Front National* who were billsticking for the presidential campaign of Jean-Marie Le Pen; in May skinheads drowned a Moroccan in the Seine.

Racism is nothing new to modern societies, and unfortunately seems to be as vigorous and as exploitable as ever. It is one of the scourges of modernity. This chapter focuses on how racism has been constructed, how it has been represented and how it has been experienced. Since literary skills are not merely deployed in the production of élite culture, but in diverse written discursive practices too, the chapter does not only examine various kinds of lyricism, but also popular fiction and the daily newspapers. In the instance of nineteenth-century anti-Chinese racism in America, mass-circulation newspapers were, indeed, the primary instrument for the production and propagation of this particular racism and legislative institutionalisation.

   The previous chapters in this book have been mainly concerned with the lyrics of the oppressed, or of those who would represent them, and yet lyricists do not always side with the oppressed. In Europe and America popular lyricists have also given voice to the xenophobic, self-congratulatory and crudely patriotic sentiments so central to ethnocentric racist discourse. In 1899 it was Kipling who famously articulated the 'rights' and responsibilities of white supremacist and imperialist ideology in these lines of counsel based on the British imperialist experience, and addressed to the United States as it embarked on its new, external, imperialist project in the Pacific:

THE WHITE MAN'S BURDEN
1899
(*The United States and the Philippine Islands*)

> Take up the White Man's burden –
> Send forth the best ye breed –
> Go bind your sons to exile
> To serve your captives' need
> To wait in heavy harness
> On fluttered folk and wild –
> Your new-caught sullen peoples,
> Half-devil and half-child.
>
> ....
>
> And when your goal is nearest,
> The end for others sought,
> Watch sloth and heathen Folly
> Bring all your hope to nought.[3]

These lines allude to many of the ideological tenets of a colonialist racism which translated smoothly into the racist discourse of the imperial metropolises: the innate savagery of 'wild' natives; the 'sullen' ingratitude of the colonised; the

---

[3] *A Choice of Kipling's Verse made by T.S. Eliot* (London: Faber and Faber, 1941, 1963) 136.

infantile and perverse mentalities of the 'half-devil and half-child' foreigner; and the laziness and immorality, the 'sloth and heathen Folly', of the non-white. A century later this refrain from the song 'U.S.A. Today' on American country singer Hank Williams Jr's *Lone Wolf* album (Warner Bros CD 26090) reproduced similar anti-'foreign' sentiments, while reiterating the American ideology's 'patriotic' conviction of the U.S.A.'s supremacy:

> It's true we got our problems, Lord knows we make mistakes,
> And every time we solve one, ten others take its place,
> But you won't see those refugees headin' the other way.
> Welcome to the U.S.A. today.

What I focus on in this chapter is how, in literary discourse, racial hatred can be generated and produced from human phobia: the fear of contamination; the fear of the Other's penetrating 'our' body (the nation, the race), bodies (the alienated individual) and 'our' culture ('Civilization'). We start with the Chinese in America.

China in/out of America

> 'Ignorant of what we hold as the best, the highest, most sacred, and of most importance to our liberty and civilization, John may prove a more troublesome and dangerous creature than any we have yet taken on board our ship.'
> — Charles Nordhoff [4]

The story of the Chinese in America really begins in the mid-nineteenth century, when American capital was in need of cheap labour, to dig, construct and cultivate. From that moment on, and against the interests of capital, there was constructed an ideological and institutional anti-Chinese racism that would be the norm in the United States for over a century. This story of exclusion calls into question romanticised histories of class solidarity, of inter-ethnic fraternity, of cooperation between oppressed races.

[4] *Nordhoff's West Coast* (1874; London: KPI, 1987) 91.

After the final suppression of the Native American in the second half of the nineteenth century, the American ideology's need to construct another Other against which to invent its self-image of civilisation, democracy and republicanism seems to have been even more pressing than the needs of capitalism. The Chinese provided that Other.

In the middle of the last century there were a few thousand Chinese who came to supply labour to California. The project to exclude Chinese people from America, from citizenship, from being American started around 1850, was partly accomplished by 1870, with the Naturalisation Act which denied the right to naturalisation to Chinese, and nominally concluded with the Exclusion Act of 1882. The campaign was not restricted to or solely generated by California, but rather was nation-wide and transcended class and ethnic boundaries. Legislatively the project continued with anti-miscegenation laws, ideologically with the discourse of the 'Yellow Peril'. Legal exclusion was prepared over two or three decades by the transmitters and negotiators of America's social imaginary and dominant ideologies: the then mass media, the press.

The West Coast has long been demonised as the engine of the movement to exclude the Chinese from America, but it was in fact the influential *East* Coast newspapers of the nineteenth century which vociferously led the exclusion campaign. The exclusion of the Chinese was advocated initially by reason of their 'depraved nature'. Their habits, lack of religious faith, supposedly 'feminised' qualities, general 'baseness' and cultural dissimilarity were cited as reasons to exclude these Chinese, who were deemed incapable of 'assimilation'.

A *New York Daily Tribune* editorial of Friday, 29 September 1854 alerts the East Coast reader to the 'fears' of white Californians: 'Any of the Christian races . . . are welcome. . . [in California], or any of the white races. They all assimilate with Americans. . . and are gradually all fused together in one homogeneous mass.'[5] If only, the editorial laments, California

---

[5] *New York Daily Tribune* 29 September 1854, p. 4.

could be settled by 'hardy educated Americans, it would be the greatest blessing she could enjoy'.[6] But the narrative of 'hardy' white American males colonising a female–gendered California was not to be. Only a people 'like the Chinese' – and that 'like' is invested with deep, derogatory significance: *not* like 'us', not white – is available, and the editorialist expresses 'grave doubts' about admitting a people 'like the Chinese':

Take a look at Chinamen in San Francisco. . . . Some of these are Christians; and with the aid of the liberal men of San Francisco have erected a fine brick chapel. . . and we are told that John [i.e. John Chinaman] in his devotions shows quite as much religious feeling as any white man. But their number is very small; a mere drop in the bucket.[7]

The editorial then shifts to a carefully constructed enumeration of racial and national 'characteristics'. Some are specific to the Chinese, the unknowable Oriental. Others are more general racist slurs. They have formed, for much of the last 140 years, the basis for American and European dominant perceptions of the Chinese and the 'Oriental':

They are for the most part an industrious people, forbearing and patient of injury, quiet and peaceable in their habits: say this, and you have said all the good that can be said of them. They are uncivilized, unclean, filthy beyond all conception, without any of the higher domestic or social relations; lustful and sensual in their dispositions; *every* [this is italicized in the original newspaper text] female is a prostitute, and of the basest order; the first words of English they learn are terms of obscenity or profanity, and beyond this they care to learn no more. Clannish in nature, they will not associate except with their own people. . . the Chinese quarter of the city is a by-word for filth and sin. Pagan in religion they know not the virtues of honesty, integrity or good faith; and in Court they never scruple to commit the most flagrant perjury.[8]

There is here an especially extreme position taken towards women, who to the racist eugenicist present not only the danger of reproduction of the inferior race, but of contamina-

---

[6] *Ibid.*

[7] *Ibid.*

[8] *Ibid.*

tion of the superior race. The psychosocial nexus between the menstrual flow and contamination by an unclean race is imbricated in this particular racist notion. Klaus Theweleit in his book *Male Fantasies* traces this connection between metaphors of fluidity and the fear of contamination. 'The flood' in German early twentieth-century texts 'seems to flow from the inside of those from whom the constraint of the old order has been removed. Something comes to light that has hitherto been forbidden, buried beneath the surface'.[9]

Also woven into the narrative of the *Tribune* text are those mythical characteristics so different from the 'American' norm, inimical to American values – the supposedly introspective, untrustworthy, furtive and secretive traits of the Chinese race which render its members impervious to the rule of law: 'They have secret societies among themselves. . . by whose edicts they are governed, and whom they dare not testify against for fear of secret death: thus rendering our very laws powerless'.[10]

Notable in the passage cited is the construction of racism by imputing to the Chinese, the discriminated group, 'a strong identity, a capacity to mobilise more or less hidden resources, an ability to call on more or less mysterious networks, to identify with a unifying principle of itself malevolent'.[11] Further, what is represented here is a fundamental kind of racism based on the 'absolute negation of difference'.[12] This is what Albert Memmi describes as a 'variant', characterised by an ideology based on biology, of 'heterophobia', the rejection of others on the basis of any difference whatsoever.[13] In other

[9] Klaus Theweleit, *Male Fantasies* (Minneapolis: University of Minnesota Press, 1987) 1, 231.

[10] *New York Daily Tribune*, 29 September 1854, p. 4.

[11] Michel Wieviorka, 'L'Expansion du racisme populaire' in Pierre-André Taguieff (ed.), *Face au racisme*, vol. 2 (Paris: Éditions La Découverte, 1991, 1993) 77. In the twentieth century such racial 'traits' would be discerned in the 'international Jewish conspiracy' and 'Islamic fanaticism'.

[12] Pierre-André Taguieff, *La force du préjugé. Essai sur le racisme et ses doubles* (Paris: Éditions La Découverte [Gallimard/Tel], 1987) 29.

[13] Albert Memmi, *Le racisme* (Paris: Gallimard, Collection 'Idées', 1982) 118. Cited in Taguieff, *La force du préjugé* 29.

words, heterophobia 'presupposes a negative evaluation of all difference' and implies an ideal, explicit or not, of 'homogeneity'.[14] In our example, 'any of the white races' are preferable to the Chinese immigrant, since they 'all assimilate. . . and are gradually all fused together in one homogeneous mass.'[15]

Heterophobia, or the fear of difference, as Taguieff has argued, is a confused idea, for its embraces the fact of the relationship of difference between Self and the Other, and the attribute of difference of the Other. In the former the phobia entails a desire to 'abolish the difference between Us and Them' by either assimilation or extermination – just as all but occurred with the Native American – of all the representatives of Them. In the second case, heterophobia seeks to erase the characteristic of difference by eugenic or educational means, or 'efface the existence of the Other (render the Other invisible or blind oneself to his existence) by rigorous separation of an *apartheid* type' – such as putting the 'Indian' on a reservation.[16]

The argument that was being constructed in mid-nineteenth century America was that the Chinese were too different and too numerous to be assimilated. In other words to prevent the Chinese becoming like the 'Negro' and the 'Indian', an internal Other in the United States, deportation and exclusion formed the only remedy.

To justify the thesis that the Chinese would be numerically overwhelming, statistics were misrepresented. But primarily, literary metaphors were invoked to represent the size of the potential group of Others. The major trope employed is what may be called the trope of inundation. Unwanted immigrants of colour everywhere have frequently been described as 'pouring in', 'swamping', 'flooding in', as coming in 'tides' and 'waves'.[17] In the *Tribune* editorial, the phobia of death by

---

[14] *Ibid.* 29-30.

[15] *New York Daily Tribune* 29 September 1854, p. 4.

[16] Taguieff, *La force du préjugé* 30.

[17] I recall when I was a young child seeing an elaborate racist, anti-black ditty which intimated that black people were coming to England to scrounge on the white people's welfare state. I can recall one line clearly: 'They come here and wash in

drowning in an alien and unclean fluid is invoked. The metaphor alludes to an allied and recurrent image typical of this racist discourse, that of the fear of contamination, the terror of being made unclean by the filthy and sick.

In Theweleit's study of the construction of the Fascist, racist narrative which would come to fruition in Germany's Nazism in the 1930s and 1940s, when 'the flood' was the red flood of Bolshevism, 'a kind of ocean that surges on in waves, inundating and engulfing', he isolates the power of the inundation metaphor in a discourse of hate which was, of course, quintessentially racist.[18] One of the examples Theweleit gives, a text by Edwin Erich Dwinger, describes Germany's First World War defeat thus:

The whole world poured out over Germany: Americans and New Zealanders, Australians and Englishmen, Portuguese and French. The bitterest pill to swallow was the stationing of blacks everywhere by the French: Moroccans and Senegalese negroes, Indochinese and Turks.[19]

Tide.' There was a play on the word, since 'Tide' was, and still is, a popular brand of laundry detergent. There was the implication not only that the Other was entering the country illicitly at the country's seaboard, and thus uncontrolled and in great numbers, but also that he was ignorant of the ways of British society, unused to washing and uninformed of the difference between toilet soap and clothes washing detergent, and thus ultimately inassimilable. Allusions to immigrants flooding into dominantly white societies are still currently employed by those who seek to invoke fears. Jean-Marie Le Pen, perhaps the most notorious of Europe's racist ideologues, repeatedly deploys the inundation trope: in his *La France est de retour* (Paris: Carrère/Lafon, 1985) he claims that 'we' are being 'pushed out by a veritable human tide' (p. 52; cited in Taguieff, *Face au racisme* 1, 130); more recently that there 'is no more integration possible. There is only resistance possible, or sooner or later submersion by invasion' (*Présent* 13-14 November 1989; Taguieff, *Face au racisme* 1, 132); and again in his book *L'Espoir* (Paris: Albatros, 1989) which holds out the prospect of a dwindling European population to be 'rapidly replaced and submerged by foreign populations' (p.14; Taguieff, *Face au racisme* 1, 133). However, racist deployment of the trope of inundation is not restricted to the far right. The 'respectable' and very bourgeois French Premier Edouard Balladur at the first public meeting of his presidential campaign (16 February 1995) claimed, as one of the successes of his two-year premiership, that 'immigrant floods were receding'; cited in *Charlie Hebdo*, 22 February 1995, 7.

[18] Theweleit 1, 230.

[19] Edwin Erich Dwinger, 'Die Armee hinter Stacheldraht' in *Deutsches Schicksal*, vol. 1 (Jena, 1929) 76. Cited in Theweleit 231.

The non-white Other in racist discourse is often constructed as 'dirty'. Adrian Forty defines dirt as 'matter out of
place: dirt is the label we attach to what we perceive as
disorder, a state that is often regarded as threatening'.[20] In the
late nineteenth and early twentieth centuries 'people in
Europe and America began to find dirt more alarming and to
be increasingly anxious about cleanliness.'[21] In Britain, as Forty
demonstrates, this enabled the Victorian middle classes to
categorise the working classes as 'dirty' and thus marked by
difference, a difference the Victorians were at pains to emphasise in their design and dress. In America the Chinese
immigrants, who were poor and who worked, were the
objects of this fascination with and aversion to 'dirt'.

Christian Enzensberger defines dirt as 'anything that impinges. . . on the person's anxiously guarded autonomy'; to the
fear of dirt, he finds allied people's fear of decay. 'They turn
away in fright when something at the bottom moves toward
the top. . . also when a structure dissolves (or the reverse)'.
After the dirt of decay, there is the 'dirt of the mass' and the
hatred of 'anything that throngs or sprawls, any mass in which
they might become caught up and irretrievably lost'.[22] Taguieff
in his study of racism has noted the recurrence of the image
of the rising tide ('*le flot*') of 'inferior elements (degenerate,
mentally deficient: the biosocial "waste")' which 'threatens to
submerge all of society'.[23] This kind of imagery is frequent in
the racist imaginary, especially in the phobia of miscegenation,
of 'mixed blood'.

Seeking to invoke such fears of dirt and contamination, the
New York Daily Tribune depicts a youthful, promising California facing the yellow contagion of 'Asiatic hordes' of a

---

[20] Adrian Forty, *Objects of Desire: Design and Society since 1750* (London and New
York: Thames and Hudson, 1986, 1992) 157.

[21] *Ibid.*

[22] Christian Enzensberger, *Grösserer Versuch über den Schmutz* (Expanded Essay on
Dirt) (Munich, 1968) 23ff; cited in Theweleit 1, 385.

[23] Taguieff, *La force du préjugé* 351.

decadent, decaying, degenerate Celestial Empire just across the sea:

The youngest of Young America next door to the oldest of nations ... [with] the densest population on the globe. They are *pouring in* upon California. Their great companies are shipping them to that region by thousands as coolies... Already there are 40,000 there, and the cry is still they come. If the *tide* continues they must yet outnumber whites on the Pacific; and they are not like the European immigration to the Atlantic States, for they have no sympathy with Americans, whether in religion, habits or language. [emphasis added][24]

That such people, who are so different from Americans should be 'free' in America is unthinkable to the author of the editorial, for

[if] free, then we have living in the Pacific Empire a people, living in daily violation of the laws of our land. . . . [No] two people with distinctly marked and uncongenial characteristics can occupy the same territory at the same time on terms of equality. Either there must be sympathy enough between them to produce fusion, or the one will be virtually if not nominally the master of the other.

They would, then, necessarily have to be slaves, but the prospect of the 'horrors of the Africans slave-trade. . . renewed on the shores of California' is also unthinkable. In other words, the Chinese are far too different to be dealt with by the strategy of assimilation, too inferior to be treated as equals.[25]

The only option, then, is 'rigorous separation'. In answer to the rhetorical question 'whether a stop shall be put to this sort of immigration, or whether the state shall be overwhelmed by this flood of ignorant, filthy idolaters', the editorial responds optimistically that the 'prospect seems to be that the exclusive policy will be adopted'. Those who instigated and produced

[24] *New York Daily Tribune*, 29 September 1854, p. 4.
[25] The shifting sands, and altered targets, of racist theories are indicated by the relative acceptance of Chinese and South-East Asians in America and most European countries today. In France, for instance, the relative ease with which immigrants from former French Indochina (usually beneficiaries of a good education and often belonging to the middle classes) assimilate is frequently compared to the 'incapacity' or 'unwillingness' of Arabs and Africans to assimilate. On the other hand, it is heartening to see today French judges of Vietnamese parentage refusing to issue deportation orders against African immigrants.

this editorial – those same people who voiced white liberal, abolitionist sentiment, yet who also constituted the voice of racism – did indeed succeed in having their wish granted, but not until a barrage of similar ideology-forming texts had done its work.

Eleven years after the *Tribune* article, and after the military end of the Civil War, the *New York Times* of Sunday, 3 September 1865 editorialised, with a by-now naturalised vocabulary, that while the 'tide of Chinese emigration to America' might be 'profitable to the dominant race', nevertheless 'we are utterly opposed to. . . any extensive emigration of Chinamen or other Asiatics to any part of the United States.'[26] Furthermore, the *Times* opined, there were 'other points of national well-being to be considered beside the sudden development of material wealth', in particular 'the moral welfare of the country'. This nationalist–racist ideological stance is continued:

> The security of free institutions is more important than the enlargement of its population. The maintenance of an elevated national character is of higher value than mere growth in physical power. . . with Oriental thoughts will necessarily come Oriental social habits.[27]

One habit that was of concern to *The Times* was 'the establishment of. . . polygamy on a large scale'. Moreover, America had enough problems of that sort:

> The free institutions and Christian virtues of America have a sufficiency of adverse elements to contend with already. . . We have four millions of degraded negroes in the South. . . and if, in addition. . . there were to be a *flood-tide* of Chinese population – a population befouled with all the social vices. . . with heathenish souls and heathenish propensities, whose character, and habits, and modes of thought are firmly fixed by the consolidating influence of ages upon ages [then] – we should be prepared to bid farewell to republicanism and democracy.[28]

Clearly, the racist ideologues were in the dominant position over those who advocated capitalist development through the

[26] *New York Times*, 3 September 1865, p. 1.
[27] *Ibid.*
[28] *Ibid.* Present author's emphasis.

'importation' of cheap Chinese labour; metaphors of newspaper discourse were more sonorous than the pragmatism of a minority of American capitalists. Over the next century, similar 'arguments' against using Chinese labour to develop American capitalism would become entrenched in national policy. Indeed, American racist exclusionism became a model for other nations' anti-Chinese exclusion policies. In 1906 Theodore Roosevelt delivered to Congress a message justifying his adamant refusal to allow Hawaii to be developed by Chinese labour. It was subsequently cited as a precedent by the incumbent British Prime Minister, Sir Henry Campbell-Bannerman, in a speech made during the 1906 British general election campaign.[29] The issue of the use of Chinese labour in the gold mines of the British dominion of South Africa loomed large in the campaign, and was even extended to the menace of Chinese labour in Britain itself. The Prime Minister quoted the American President as saying:

That territory [Hawaii] has serious commercial and industrial problems to reckon with, but no measure of relief can be considered which looks to legislation admitting Chinese... A status of servility can never again be tolerated on American soil. Hawaii shall never become a territory in which a governing class of rich planters exists by means of coolie labor, even if the rate of growth in the territory is thereby rendered slower. That growth must only take place by the admission of immigrants fit in the end to assume the duties and burdens of full American citizenship.[30]

Multiple issues vie for critical attention in this text, not least the irony of Hawaii being an American colony whose indigenous people had already been dispossessed and enslaved without American qualms. The argument here is restricted to the professed aversion — expressed so as to invoke the collective memory of the Civil War — to a sort of slavery, 'a status of servility'. The spectre of slavery is deployed as a moral excuse *not* to admit Chinese immigrants at all and to restrict immigration to the undifferent, to those 'fit' to be Americans.

[29] *Liverpool Daily Post and Mercury*, 11 January 1906, p. 8.
[30] *Ibid.*

The 'morality' in question lies in the immorality of possessing slaves. However, it seems to have been considered quite moral to exclude a whole race from the class of 'citizen' because of their racial origins.

Similarly, it was the 'taint of servitude' at which the British Prime Minister claimed to baulk. Emanating from the head of an imperial government that had enslaved millions of people of colour in dozens of societies around the world, it seems to have been nothing less than hypocrisy and political opportunism when he said, 'I recall the sentiments of President Roosevelt. . . nothing of the sort can be tolerated in the Dominions of the King (loud cheers).'[31] Thus political expediency, pandering to a racist labour union agenda so as to win an election, was privileged over capitalist economic priorities.

The production of this naturalising, racist discourse, the arrival at a way of talking about the Chinese that made it seem normal to consider them as unfit 'to assume the duties and burdens of full American citizenship', as unequal to the white, depended to a large extent upon the construction of an exoticised China, whose contemporary inferiority stood in contrast to its past glory. China was often portrayed by the press as a barbarous, left-over object of curiosity to be deciphered; the Chinese a heathen people to be civilised and Christianised. Americans claimed that through the application of superior, modern scientific methods they could *read* China, and dismantle the barriers which kept it pagan and thus uncivilised.

The contemporary Orientalising and Otherising of the China across the ocean was important to the racist construction of the Chinese in America and to the success of the project of Chinese exclusion. It was the narrative of total otherness, of total difference, of total inferiority, that supplied to Americans, as it did to the British and other imperialist powers, the ideological rationale for subjecting China to economic,

[31] *Ibid.*

cultural and territorial colonialism, and in the American case provided the means to pursue the exclusion of Chinese people from America until into the 1960s and beyond.

In 1844 the United States became the first nation to demand and obtain extra-territorial rights for its citizens in China, which meant they were immune from Chinese law. Americans thus removed themselves from Chinese jurisdiction. Juridically Americans when in China were in America. By the same token, the Chinese were excluded in their own country. By the turn of the century so naturalised and legitimate had this system of extra-territoriality become that Congress, in 1906, established the United States District Court for China.[32]

In 1855, eleven years after America had institutionalised extra-territoriality for its citizens, an alleged brief encounter between an American, H.B. Dorrance, MD, and an unnamed Chinese official was the subject of a *Graham's Magazine* article. The piece is entitled *A Chinese Gentleman*. The mandarin is depicted as exotic, refined, feminine; the country he represents portrayed as overrun with helpless starving masses; the life of ordinary Chinese people depicted as cheap and expendable. No epithet of sympathy is extended.

According to Dorrance, the mandarin came on board his clipper and engaged in conversation, adumbrating in statistical detail the ruined condition of his country, which Dorrance reports to the reader with apparent relish:

Misery and starvation were everywhere abroad in the land. Ingenuity was taxed to its utmost to devise comfortable modes of suicide, thousands sacrificing themselves daily, and in ways hardly conceivable. In this kind of chat, an hour slipped away very pleasantly.[33]

In contrast to the baseness of these supposedly lemming-like

---

[32] There also existed a 'US Postal Agency Shanghai China' which issued stamps surcharged at double the original value of the stamps and sold in local currency. The stamps were valid for mail dispatched to the United States. According to the *U.S.P.O. Bulletin*, the Shanghai office of the United States Post Office was closed in December 1922. My thanks to Mr Henry D. Blumberg for providing this information.

[33] H.B. Dorrance, MD, *Graham's Magazine* 1854, IV, 204.

masses, the upper-class mandarin is fetishised and feminised, his ultimately ineffectual nature foregrounded: 'I could not help noticing the beautiful shape of his hands, so small and delicate, the fingers tapering so daintily to the longest possible and most pearly white nails.'[34]

In the same 1854 edition of the *New York Daily Tribune* which warned of the danger of the 'flood of ignorant, filthy idolaters' is a review of a book by an American philologist, Stephen Pearl Andrews, entitled *Discoveries in China: On the Symbolism of the Primitive Character of the Chinese System of Writing*. The work, described as dealing with the 'Etymology. . . of the written characters of that curious language', is destined to gain its author 'an eminent rank among explorers in this branch of Philology'. Andrews is credited with the 'solution of the mystery of Chinese writing'.[35]

The 'discourse of grammars, the discourse of philology', writes Henri Meschonnic, 'demonstrates that no discourse on. . . languages, even when it presents itself as scientific, and even if it is, escapes from its historicity, from its ideological position.'[36] The discourse which talks of 'discoveries' in China, 'curious language', 'explorers' solving the 'mystery of Chinese writing', is indeed embedded in an ideological position, that of cultural colonialism. It is also a discourse born of modernity, and thus necessarily imbricated with the project of capitalism. Indeed, the reviewer of *Discoveries in China* informs the reader of the 'value [of the book's discoveries] to the commercial. . . world'.

The Chinese language itself is reified, made into an object of wonder, of 'mystery', represented as concealed, and thus discoverable, decipherable by a white American scholar, solved like a Chinese puzzle or a board game: 'The composition of the characters offers a sort of a puzzle and a charm equal

---

[34] *Ibid.*

[35] *New York Daily Tribune*, 29 September 1854, p. 3.

[36] Henri Meschonnic, *Critique du rythme. Anthropologie historique du langage* (Lagrasse: Verdier, 1982, 1990).

to a game or a child's riddle book, so that the work cannot fail to attract many readers as an object of amusement.'[37]

Henri Meschonnic has pointed to the ambivalence of the relationship between the Self's and the Other's language, how languages are constructed as aesthetically pleasing or amusing. Language is at times constructed as a 'lost, paradise-like, distant otherness', an 'image of the union between words and things'; at others it is imagined as close, intimate; and at yet others as 'what one owns exclusively, and in which one revels with all the means of fantasy'. At such times, when it is seen as embodying a native, national essence, language acquires a 'maternal beauty, incestuous, that the Other will never be able to attain nor even understand, the incomprehensible strange'.[38] Because of its written characteristics, the Chinese language has been deployed as the archetypal linguistic bearer of otherness: 'When China was Europe's subconscious, characters, supposed to contain in their little pictures a natural relation with things, had a metaliteral beauty that the letter of the Western alphabet did not, and would never have.'[39]

But the main attribute of *Discoveries in China* for the *Tribune's* nineteenth-century reviewer is its deployment as a practical instrument. The book is useful to missionaries as a linguistic tool, as an aid in the task of teaching English, the aim of which is 'breaking down the wall of separation between the Chinese and European and American mind'.

In fact, nineteenth-century academic Orientalism, rudimentary Sinology and the cult of Chinoiserie (which seems to have continued until this day) functioned to devalorise contemporary China, by privileging the ancient. It foregrounded the splendour that *was* China, at the expense of the modern and unpleasant reality for which Western imperialist and capitalist designs were greatly responsible.

Walter Benjamin in a 1938 essay on 'Chinese Paintings' observed that connoisseurs in the West had condemned *in toto*

---

[37] *New York Daily Tribune*, 29 September 1854, 3.

[38] Henri Meschonnic, *La rime et la vie* (Lagrasse: Verdier, 1989) 41-2.

[39] *Ibid.*

the cultural production of the Ming and the Qing dynasties, that is artistic production from 1644 to 1911. This 'recent' tradition of painting was stigmatised as decadent and without value. Only the cultures that preceded the Ming, that of the Tang (618-907), the Song (960-1279) and the Yuan (1271–1368), were authentic and valorised. Indeed, I was once told by a British colleague specialising in the study of material culture that there was nothing worth studying after the Han. That dynasty ended over 1,700 years ago.

The discourse of racism in America was not only dominant in the organs of the élite. The *Irish Citizen*, a publication devoted to another marginalised immigrant community, was also concerned with the Chinese question. Specifically, the journal espoused the promotion of Irish immigration and advocated the protection of Irish labour. On 9 July 1870, resorting to the myth of Chinese inferiority and immorality, it demanded racial rather than ethnic discrimination as the foundation of United States immigration policy: 'We want white people to enrich the country, not Mongolians to degrade and disgrace it.'[40]

The term 'Mongolians' was frequently used well into the twentieth century as a synonym for Chinese, and encompassed on occasion other East Asians and South-East Asians. The *Irish Citizen*'s recommendation with regard to 'Mongolians' would be echoed in the official policy of the American state five days later. On 14 July the 1870 Naturalization Act was passed, excluding Chinese from naturalisation as US citizens. It was the same act that technically allowed to Americans of African descent the legal right to citizenship. One excluded class was thus juridically replaced by another, the function of one Other displaced on to another Other. While the material and, despite constitutional changes, the legal reality of the exclusion suffered by African Americans remained, their institutional

---

[40] *Irish Citizen* 9 July 1870. Cited in Stuart Creighton Miller, *The Unwelcome Immigrant: The American Image of the Chinese 1785-1882* (Berkeley: University of California Press, 1969, 1974) 199.

degradation was reinscribed on to the body of the 'Celestial' Other. This act of substitution, this institutionalising of racist ideology, re-empowered the Chinese exclusion movement which was subscribed to by liberal and conservative, capital and labour, Anglo and non-Anglo-American, alike.

The supposedly liberal Catholic historian, James Gilmary Shea, wrote in the *Americans Catholic Quarterly Review* of 1879 an article entitled 'The Rapid Increase of the Dangerous Classes in the United States', demanding that along with 'paupers, lechers, Mormons, and utopian socialists' the Chinese be ejected from the United States. For while Shea admitted that crime and vice existed among the Irish community, he contended that this was due entirely to poverty, since by nature the Irishman was 'pure, virtuous and healthy'; but as for the Chinaman, his faults were 'hereditary'.[41]

Academia made its contribution in the person of Andrew D. White, president of Cornell University, who wrote lending his support to Senator Sargent, the prime mover of the exclusionist campaign in Congress. The august educator is cited, in the 1877 congressional record, as admitting to a 'deep-seated dread of this influx of Asiatics of a type which it seems to me can never form any hopeful element in this nation'.

In 1882 the House of Representatives passed the Chinese Exclusion Act with 201 yeas and 37 nays, making it virtually impossible for new Chinese immigrants to enter the country. After this almost every state in the union went on to pass anti-miscegenation laws. Despite scientific assertions in the first decade of this century that the idea of racial mono-hematism, the 'blood myth', should be abandoned since it was founded on 'a primordial identification' between 'race' and 'blood', the blood-race myth, 'a variant of the myth of the pure and the impure', continued to be ideologically useful to advocates of mono-racial nation states.[42] In 1919 the mixo-

---

[41] *American Catholic Quarterly Review* 1879, IV, 240-68.
[42] Taguieff, *La force du préjugé* 343.

phobic racist-eugenicist Charles Richet would call for 'universal and rigid laws preventing mixed marriages'.[43] But even sixty years later, as the discourse analysis of the social psychologists Wetherell and Potter has recently illustrated, both 'popular biology' and 'lay psychological analyses through which identity is construed and narrated in "post-modern" consumer cultures' continue to be prominent among the discursive resources that racism 'plunders'.[44]

The Chinese Exclusion Act was not finally repealed until 1943. Japanese Americans had been interned in concentration camps, and furnished the necessary Oriental Other. Moreover, China was now a Second World War ally of the USA. It would have been diplomatically embarrassing, and out of kilter with the new anti-Japanese, pro-Chinese narrative, not to make the gesture of repeal. The new congressional act allowed the naturalisation of Chinese and permitted a quota of 105 immigrants per year. However, at the end of the war thirty-one states in America still had anti-miscegenation laws on the statute books. It was not until 1948 that the State Supreme Court of California declared the ban on inter-racial marriage unconstitutional, and not until 1967 that the US Supreme Court ruled anti-miscegenation laws unconstitutional.

Such anti-miscegenation laws were never passed in Britain, nor did that country have immigration laws targeted explicitly at Chinese; although the 1905 and 1914 Aliens Acts and the Aliens Restriction Act of 1919 effectively limited any increase in the numbers of the Chinese in Britain. The country was also the metropolitan centre of a 'family' of colonies and dominions that constituted the empire. Millions around the globe were subjects of the British crown, but they were not, of course, 'English'. If you did not look English, you were

---

[43] Charles Richet, *La sélection humaine* (Paris: F. Alcan, 1919), 89; cited in Taguieff, *La force du préjugé* 342.

[44] Margaret Wetherell and Jonathan Potter, *Mapping the Language of Race: Discourse and the Legitimation of Exploitation* (New York: Columbia University Press, 1992) 4.

not. Even today you may be black and British, but you are
not 'English'.

The plight of the hybrid

' "God created the white man and God created the black man, but the
devil created the mulatto." Therein lies a well-known problem. In
reality, we are in total ignorance of the moral and intellectual qualities
of the *métis*. It would be absurd to expect of the union of a European
hooligan with a black woman of the same moral level children marching
at the forefront of humanity.'

—F. von Luschan[45]

'We are confronted by a myth of purity/impurity, purity being found
in distinct and recognisable racial types, impurity being imputed exclusively to the mixed type, or rather to this typologically neutral,
out-of-play, being, the *métis*.'

—Taguieff[46]

'to be of mixed race
was a form of disgrace,
in the hostile climes
of post war England.

Adolescence –
brought growing pain,
and a desperate need
to feel whole again,
one personality
split into three,
in the hostile climes
of post war England.'

—T.Wildebeest[47]

[45] F. von Luschan, 'La race au point de vue anthropologique' in Universal Races
Congress, *Mémoires sur le contact des races. Communiqués au premier congrès universel des
races tenu à l'Université de Londres au 29 Juillet 1911* (London: P.S. King and Son,
1911) 26-7.
[46] Taguieff, *La force du préjugé* 348.
[47] 'Whiteness' in *Once I was a Washing Machine: An Anthology of Poetry and Prose*,
introduction by Ken Worpole (Brighton: Federation of Worker Writers &
Community Publishers/Queen Spark Books, 1989) 148. T. Wildebeest is a
member of the Manchester-based writing group, Commonword.

'You think I'm Chinese. While you think I'm English.
But I have the upper hand.
I know what you're both thinking.'

—Big Prawn[48]

In the 1890s a Mr Chan, an orphan in southern China, took the money his Catholic Chinese aunt gave him to buy and light candles for her and bought books instead. He studied for the Chinese Imperial Examinations. But in 1905 they were abolished. So he learnt English, learnt the principles of banking, went to Hong Kong, took and passed the relevant examinations and attempted to gain employment in a British bank. He was refused. Such posts were for the white colonial clerical class. He left China in 1909. On the ocean liners he acquired another finance-related skill as he sailed from one port of the British Empire to another. He learnt to gamble. It was a capacity that would over his long life afford him moments of relative prosperity, but leave him most of the time simply poor and at times almost destitute. He would die penniless.

In 1911, the year the last Chinese imperial dynasty fell, he arrived in the seaport of Liverpool, England. In that year the *London Magazine* reported that compared to San Francisco, Liverpool's Chinatown seemed 'tame and commonplace'. But such an impression was deemed deceptive, since 'beneath its calm and dingy exterior there stir the same dark passions, instincts and racial tendencies which cause this mystic yellow people to be so misunderstood, feared and hated.'[49]

At about the same time a young Englishwoman, a Miss Ward whose stepfather, a Greek ship's carpenter, had recently died, settled in Liverpool with her mother and sister and two

---

[48] Michelle Lacy, Lili Man and Jessie Lim (eds), *Exploring our Chinese Identity* (London: Lambeth Chinese Community Association, 1992), 39.

[49] Herman Scheffauer, 'The Chinese in England: A Growing National Problem', *London Magazine* (June 1911) 466, preserved in Public Record Office, Kew, England (ref. HO 45/11843 5009). Also cited in Maria Lin Wong, *Chinese Liverpudlians* (Birkenhead: Liver Press, 1989) 65.

brothers. Their travels, for the whole family had travelled the Mediterranean for years, had come to an abrupt halt. She took employment in a tobacconist's near Chinatown. It was frequented by Mr Chan.

They had five children, three boys and two girls. One day Mr Chan had a big gambling win in Chinatown. He rushed home and scooped up his two-year-old daughter and took her out to the candy store. It was a bitterly cold day. She contracted pneumonia and a week later died. The surviving daughter was this author's mother.

The Chinese community in Liverpool is perhaps the oldest in Europe and at one time was the largest. Many would-be emigrants to America from other parts of Europe, especially from Ireland, got no further than Liverpool's docks and settled in the city. There were also economic migrants from Scotland and Wales. There were many seamen, from Scandinavians to Africans, who came and went. Some stayed. England does not see itself as a hybrid nation, but Liverpool, like many ports, is an undeniably hybrid city. It has always been a marginalised community, a troublesome town and, during every British Conservative Party administration, seemingly rebellious and punished. And yet one would not want to romanticise this city whose bourgeoisie was responsible for mounting the African slave trade, establishing the 'slave triangle' and thereby amassing enormous fortunes. By the time the trade was abolished Liverpool was established as an important international port, serving the Americas and the Empire. The patchwork working class of Liverpool also has an unusual history, totally dissimilar to the radical and legendary prowess of, say, the South Wales coalfields. Irish politics was more important in the city than English until well into the mid-twentieth century.[50]

---

[50] 'Any neat formula that reduces political aspiration and affiliation to class alone, especially in the context of a working class that encompasses many ethnic groups, should be rejected. One quarter of Liverpool's population was Irish or of Irish

Around the middle of the nineteenth century a Chinese community developed in Liverpool. Many of the Chinese residents were seafarers and their numbers varied from decade to decade. During the 1940s the city was the home of the Chinese Merchant Seamen's Pool. Thousands died at sea to keep the Allied nations fed and armed. The Japanese occupation of China's major ports during the Second World War prevented many of them from returning home, and so many were literally trapped in Liverpool. Despite their contribution to the 'war effort', Chinese sailors were maltreated and severely underpaid by British shipping companies:

Approximately 5,000 Chinese seamen were employed on British-registered ships, most of them by. . . Blue Funnel, Ben Line and Shell. . . [a number which] doubled after the Japanese occupation of Hong Kong, early in 1942. . . . Like Indian seamen, the Chinese also had to resort to strikes to secure wage increases that were awarded to Europeans without a struggle. The Chinese, however, were in a far stronger position than the Indians because soon after Japan's entry into the war the ports from which Chinese had been recruited – Hong Kong, Singapore and Shanghai –were closed and it was no longer possible to send dissidents home.[51]

Many Chinese refused to serve, but were marshalled into service by the British and American authorities. As Tony Lane has written in his study of the wartime merchant seamen, contrary to the British government-propagated myth of class and colonial solidarity:

social relations in Britain were in general no more harmonious than they had been before, and. . . the longer the war continued, the more divided Britain became. The same divisions applied on ships crewed by Indians and Chinese. Without suggesting that the strikes and mass desertions on these ships can be construed as vanguards of nationalist

---

descent and had considered Irish independence and self-determination to be a decisive political issue. Appeals to class solidarity and class allegiance had no meaning unless "class" meant something other than the concerns of the English working class. . . . Indeed, until 1929 the North End of the city elected an Irish Nationalist as their member of parliament'. Sam Davies, Pete Gill, Linda Grant, Martyn Nightingale, Ron Noon and Andy Shallice, *Genuinely Seeking Work: Mass Unemployment on Merseyside in the 1930s* (Birkenhead: Liver Press, 1992) 148-50.

[51] Tony Lane, *The Merchant Seamen's War* (Liverpool: Bluecoat Press, 1990) 162.

movements, there was certainly no indication of the filial loyalty so often prominent in imperial rhetoric.[52]

Apart from the war years, the Chinese community remained small and rarely moved above three figures until the 1950s. There were few Chinese women. Thus Chinese men found themselves in a situation similar to their compatriots in California, except that in Britain there were no anti-miscegenation laws. Thus the interesting feature of the Chinatown community was that from the beginning it was racially mixed: Chinese men married local white women.

British anti-Chinese, racist discourse followed a similar pattern to America's from the 'Yellow Peril' propaganda of the mid-nineteenth century onwards. Again, the implications of cheap labour were seen as a menace to the white working class both 'at home' in Britain and in the Colonies and Dominions. And yet the dominant class of Britain, also the dominant class of the British Empire, was torn between a more pragmatic and economistic view, and a concern for the preservation and reproduction of English, and thus white, 'values'. In 1877, an editorial in *The Times* eulogized the benefits of cheap, Chinese labour, noting that 'when white men make exorbitant demands for wages, when they begin striking and giving trouble in a thousand ways, the employer of labour may be glad he is not absolutely dependent on them, and that he has at hand a more docile race of beings, who can be satisfied on more easy terms, and who will be less forgetful of the relation in which they stand to him. . .' However, the editorialist, who was in fact commenting on Australian state governmental initiatives to exclude Chinese labourers, in favour of English (white) workers, qualified his remarks with a refusal 'to believe that white labour is not, for the vast majority of purposes, superior to what is termed yellow labour, or that it would not in itself be very much preferred by the employer'.[53] But the overall tone of the editorial draws on a

[52] *Ibid.* 8-9.
[53] *The Times*, 25 August 1877, 9. Also cited in part in Wong 60.

now familiar anti-Chinese discourse and presages the White Australia policy. Capital's desire for the immediate benefits of cheap imported labour is ultimately subsumed under the long-term need to ensure the stability of the metropolitan capitalist state, and emergent capitalist states, by avoiding confrontation with the white majority workforce. To that end, the 'logic' of racial superiority is once again invoked:

In Australia and California alike it is thought not desirable that the country should be deluged with these questionable visitors, to the exclusion *pro tanto* of the superior races of men who are assumed to be its lords and masters. We value [the Australian Colonies]. . . as the homes of men our own race. . . and as likely in the distant future to grow up to a greatness equal to our own. . . . It would sadly interfere with this agreeable vision if Australia were really destined to be peopled, not with English, but with Chinese settlers, if the abominations of a Chinese quarter are to be found everywhere, and if white labour is to be driven out before the advancing steps of its rivals.[54]

In England itself, white organised labour once again revealed its parochialism, the bounds of its progressive pretensions, and the Eurocentric nature of its professed ideals of international working men's fraternity. In 1902 the annual assembly of the Trade Union Congress was told in emotive language that 'the Asiatic locust is dreaded in America, and is an evil in Canada'. Again, the pagan and thus 'uncivilised' nature of the Chinese, and the enormous proportions of the potential threat, are suggested by the use of the Biblical echoes of the 'horde of locusts'. The omnivorous 'horde' is named in the union leaders' attempt to convey the extent of the evil, an evil that could only be imagined by envisaging 'what it would mean to the workmen of this country to have a horde of Chinamen introduced to take their place'.[55] In addition to its Biblical connotations, the suitably 'Mongolian' connotations of the word horde made it a privileged item in the racist discourse which sought to inflate the real extent of immigrant numbers and emphasise their alterity.

[54] *Ibid.*

[55] *Report of the Proceedings at the 35th Annual Trades Union Congress*, 1902, 53-4; cited in Wong 60.

During the 1906 parliamentary general election campaign, the threat of cheap Chinese labour was again exploited. On this occasion, those seeking to profit from the 'menace' were adherents of the supposedly socialist British Labour Party; a party which was a creation of the union movement. Chinese labour had been brought to work in the Transvaal in British South Africa. The labour union leader, Labour Party candidate in Liverpool and local government councillor, James Sexton, was a particularly vehement anti-Chinese campaigner, who seems consciously to have deployed the discourse of racism to consolidate exclusively white working-class solidarity.[56] So as to create publicity and exploit the potential of unemployed workers' fears of unemployment, Sexton paraded through the streets of Liverpool fifty dockers dressed up as 'Chinamen'.[57] The Liverpool newspaper, the *Weekly Courier*, in December 1906 carried column after column of reports and rumours relating to the local 'Yellow Peril' and popular reaction to it. The headlines read:

A YELLOW PERIL
PUBLIC INDIGNATION INCREASING

The paper reported James Sexton at a Gasworks' Union meeting advising 'Liverpool workmen of all grades to commence to organise' to face a 'great crisis' which 'was stealing upon them like a thief in the night'. Sexton told the union

[56] Sexton was a Liverpool Irish docker who became secretary of the Liverpool Dockers (National Union of Dock Labourers), formed in 1889. Sexton had earlier been an Irish Nationalist, but became a founding member of the Independent Labour Party in 1893. See Henry Pelling, *The Origins of the Labour Party* (London and New York: Oxford University Press, 1965) 199. According to one chronicler of Labour Party history, Sexton was one of the pioneers who 'took up the fight, always putting before their audiences something that was more than just an economic creed – that was a new faith, a vision of a new world'. See Francis Williams, foreword by Clement Attlee, *Fifty Years March: The Rise of the Labour Party* (London: Odhams Press, n.d.) 104.

[57] *Report of the Proceedings at the 35th Annual Trades Union Congress*, 1902, 53-4; cited in Wong 60.

gathering that within the 'past five or ten years, while they had been asleep, a Chinese colony had been formed'. In the guise of a man who had seen the world, Sexton recalled seeing in his youth 'the horribly gruesome scenes enacted in San Francisco'. Seeking to dispel any suspected incongruity between his attitudes and his socialist, syndicalist beliefs, Sexton claimed that he 'did not wish to deny the brotherhood of men', but:

[T]he Chinese did not understand the brotherhood of men, they were strangers to it as in the sense of the word they were not men. (Hear, hear). A Chinaman's morals are beastly.... He comes here like an international octopus, spreading its tentacles everywhere, and he undermines and corrupts the morals, and pulls down the wages of the English people. (Shame).[58]

The head constable of Liverpool's police force in December 1906 had reported only 356 Chinese people in the city, 'of whom about 224 were resident and 132 transient'.[59] The numbers involved were always tiny. The *Weekly Courier* the previous week had noted the outraged reaction of Liverpool white laundry owners to news that the Immigration Board had allowed thirty-two Chinese to come to the city from the Port of London, and in the same edition produced an exoticised, and exoticising, racist editorial on the city's Chinatown:

Purple shadows blur the outlines of the old houses and veil the few sauntering figures.... Suddenly out of the dusk loom strange figures, moving with impassive eyes, set aslant in saffron, mask-like faces, at the incongruous surroundings... The street is part of Liverpool's Chinatown... and all around prowl and patrol the children of the mysterious East.[60]

This construction of exoticised Chinese 'difference' would

[58] *Weekly Courier*, 8 December 1906, p. 7.

[59] 'Report of the Commission Appointed by the City Council to Inquire into Chinese Settlements in Liverpool' in the *Proceedings of the Council*, 1906–7, p. 1748. The figure for March had been 337, as against 356 in December, which fact leads the report to conclude that the Chinese population had 'increased considerably during the nine months succeeding March'. Nevertheless, the report concedes: 'It is possible that some of the Chinamen may have been born in Hong Kong and so be British subjects.'

[60] *Weekly Courier* 1 December 1906, p. 3.

be easily redeployed in the more viciously negative and racist
'Yellow Peril' discourse produced in, and promoted by, mid-
dlebrow fiction. In 1913 Sax Rohmer published the first in a
series of novels focused on Dr Fu-Manchu, 'the most evil
genius of the Orient'.[61] In addition to the lucrative book
royalties, Rohmer would eventually sell the film, television
and radio rights to the stories for £1.5 million.[62] *The Mystery
of Dr Fu-Manchu* tells the story of the pursuit of the Chinese
'agent' by the very English Nayland Smith, 'a servant of the
British Government, lately stationed in Burma', and his Wat-
son-like amanuensis, Dr Petrie.[63]

Fu-Manchu is the undercover agent of a plot conceived by
an 'Eastern Power', China, to overrun the Western world.
Fu-Manchu has at his disposal 'all the resources of science past
and present'.[64] The 'past' naturally denotes Oriental
knowledge, the secrets of the ancient, mysterious East, while
the 'present' encompasses the techniques of Western modernity. The murderous Fu-Manchu is responsible for the deaths
of high functionaries of the French and British imperial
governments, men who know 'the secret of Tongking', 'the
truth about Mongolia', the importance of the Tibetan frontiers, which were also the frontiers of the British Raj.[65] These
men of vision, now assassinated, were to have alerted the West
to the menace posed by China's masses and their leaders.

The material and political situation in which semi-colonised
China found itself in 1913 should be recalled. The Chinese

[61] Sax Rohmer, *The Mystery of Dr Fu-Manchu* (first published 1913; Bath: Chivers
Press, 1992). The description of Fu-Manchu as 'evil genius of the Orient' is given
in the blurb on the dust jacket newly designed for the 1992 Black Dagger Crime
series reprint of the book published by Chivers Press in England. The blurb also
states that the book is not merely recommended by the Crime Writers' Association,
but that the Black Dagger Crime series is the result of a 'joint effort' by the publishers
and the Association to introduce 'outstanding examples of detective' fiction,
'classics that have been scarce for years. . . to a new generation who have not
previously had the chance to enjoy them'.

[62] Granville Wilson, preface, *The Mystery of Dr Fu-Manchu* (1992 edn) vi.

[63] Rohmer 18.

[64] *Ibid.* 18-19.

[65] *Ibid.* 19.

Revolution of 1911 had overthrown the Manchu imperial order, but the country and its government were weak and fragmented and under the economic and political domination of Western governments and corporations. Nevertheless, at a moment when China had never been more disempowered, let alone capable of posing a threat to the Western world, Rohmer constructs a racist discourse reliant on fear of the 'Oriental' and his furtive and cunning campaign to attain world dominance:

> Is there a man who would arouse the West to a sense of the awakening of the East, who would teach the deaf to hear, the blind to see, that the millions only await their leader? He will die. And this is only one phase of the devilish campaign. The others I can merely surmise.[66]

Fu-Manchu is a consciously constructed composite of the stereotypical traits generally reproduced in anti-Chinese racist discourse. The character has animal instincts, revealed in his 'feline' appearance and 'cat-green' eyes. His eyes are described as 'magnetic', the instrument of mysterious, unnatural, ancient powers, for Fu-Manchu is 'adept in certain obscure arts and sciences which *no* university of today can teach'. Fu-Manchu is not simply ungodly, with 'a face like Satan', he has been put on earth by the 'powers of evil'.[67] 'Oriental' cunning is a trait that the discourse of anti-Chinese racism always ascribes to Chinese people, and the 'perverted genius' of Dr Fu-Manchu is invested with 'the cruel cunning of an entire race'.[68] 'He is the advance agent of a movement so epoch-making than not one Britisher, and not one American, in fifty thousand has ever dreamed of it.'[69]

Since these agents of the British authorities 'are dealing with a Chinaman, with incarnate essence of Eastern subtlety', appropriate deviousness is required to catch Fu-Manchu: 'guile

---

[66] *Ibid.*
[67] *Ibid.* 19, 40.
[68] *Ibid.* 19.
[69] *Ibid.* 40.

against guile!'[70] A covert operation is organised; disguised as 'Dago' seamen, the British agents attempt to infiltrate Chinatown to uncover the 'Chinese devil hiding somewhere in London.'[71]

The sections of dialogue in the book are employed supposedly to mimic and expose the otherness of Chinatown's inhabitants. In Chapter 6, 'The Opium Den', Smith and Dr Petrie, disguised as seamen, enter a barber's shop which is the front for an 'opium den'. In describing the physical surroundings the standard allusions are made to dirt and decay (the 'dirty room', the 'grimy towel', 'decayed teeth') and to 'foreignness' by reference to language (a 'Yiddish' poster, establishing an association with another marginalised group in Europe, and Chinese writing, the quintessential barely decipherable sign of Chinese difference and 'mystery'). The Chinese man's speech is referred to as chattering, a clear reference to the racist notion that the Chinese resemble apes, and for good measure the adjective 'simian' (pertaining to anthropoid apes) is employed, while the Chinese man's hand is referred to as an animal-like 'yellow paw':

We stood in a bare and very dirty room, which could only claim kinship with a civilized shaving saloon by virtue of the grimy towel thrown across the back of the solitary chair. A Yiddish theatrical bill of some kind, illustrated, adorned one of the walls, and another bill, in what may have been Chinese, completed the decorations. From behind a curtain heavily brocaded with filth a little Chinaman appeared, dressed in a loose smock, black trousers and thick-soled slippers, and advancing, shook his head vigorously.

'No shavee – no shavee', he chattered, simian fashion, squinting from one to the other of us with his twinkling eyes. 'Too late! Shuttee shop!'

'Don't you come none of it wi' me!' roared Smith, in a voice of amazing gruffness, and shook an artificially dirtied fist under the Chinaman's nose. 'Get inside and gimme an' my mate a couple o'pipes. Smokee pipe, you yellow scum – savvy?'

My friend bent forward and glared into the other's eyes with a vindictiveness that amazed me, unfamiliar as I was with this form of gentle persuasion.

[70] *Ibid.* 37.
[71] *Ibid.*

'Kop 'old 'o that', he said, and thrust a coin into the Chinaman's yellow paw. . . .

'No habe got pipee –', began the other.

Smith raised his fist, and Yan [the Chinese barber] capitulated.

'Allee lightee', he said. 'Full up –no loom. You come see.'

He dived behind the dirty curtain, Smith and I following, and ran up a dark stair. . .

'No loom –samme tella you', said Shen Yan, complacently testing Smith's shilling with his yellow, decayed teeth.[72]

In both Rohmer's representation of Limehouse, London's Chinatown, and in the journalistic descriptions of Liverpool's, Pitt Street, in the the *Weekly Courier*, archetypal 'truths' of the discourse of racism are produced and reproduced. First, it is accepted as self-evident that 'people can be divided into biologically distinct types'. Secondly, it is a given that each 'race' possesses physical characteristics, and psychological and cultural traits 'which are also biologically transmitted', and thirdly, it is held that a hierarchy of races from more advanced to less advanced can be constructed.[73] These ideas occur repeatedly. In the British and American texts in which the anti-Chinese discourse of racism is produced, the lack of adherence to Christianity is particularly foregrounded as an attribute of difference and racial inferiority. Of course, it was not just the Chinese who were thus imagined. Other 'Orientals' were also constructed in similar terms. An entry in the 1910 *Encyclopaedia Britannica* describes the Arab as

the degenerate offspring of a race which only from its history and past records can claim any title to respect. Cringing, venal, avaricious, dishonest, the Arab combines all the faults of a vicious nature with those which a degraded religion inculcates or encourages.[74]

A further, and perhaps the most potent, fear discursively promoted and manipulated by racist ideology is mixophobia. The pages of the *Courier* of December 1906 propagate that

[72] *Ibid.* 42-3.

[73] Wetherell and Potter 16-17.

[74] *Encyclopaedia Britannica*, 11th edn 1910, vol. 3, 765.

distinctive discourse which foregrounds the mixophobia generated by the contemplation of the hybrid, the 'half-caste', the 'half-breed'. Again, economic concerns are secondary to those of maintaining the integrity of the national body, for while the presence of a few hundred Chinese in the third largest city in Britain meant for the *Courier* that the 'conditions of labour for our own people are made more difficult', 'yet graver' was the danger of the race 'becoming tainted with Chinese blood'. Under the heading 'TAINTING THE RACE' the reader is told:

Many Chinamen have married English women and more live with women without having passed through any ceremony. The result of such unions is found in the swarms of half-bred children to be seen in the district. This is the worst feature of Chinatown, and it is becoming everyday more prominent. It is not only degraded women who mate with these men.[75]

The allusion to impurity in this invective is common to racist discourse from the late nineteenth century onwards. As Taguieff discovered in his study of racist theories, in argumentation that emanates from racist eugenicists there is a combination of images; that of the 'stain' or 'taint', representing 'impurity, dirtiness, split identity'; and that of the 'defect' associated with 'inferiority, weakness, the subhuman'.[76] For Gustave Le Bon, who afforded the aura of respectable science to the deployment of such biological myths, the racially mixed 'constitutes a population very inferior to the products from which it is derived, and which is completely incapable of creating, or even continuing a civilisation', although 'crossbreeding can be a progressive element between superior races which are closely enough, as is the case with the English and the Germans in America.'[77]

It is the 'tainting' of blood, blood which is supposed to be of a specific quality and through which 'we' assure reproduc-

---

[75] *Weekly Courier* 8 December 1906, 7.

[76] Taguieff, *La force du préjugé* 351.

[77] Gustave Le Bon, *Lois psychologiques de l'évolution des peuples* (Paris: F. Alcan, 1894) 59; cited in Taguieff, *La force du préjugé* 341.

tion, that seems to inspire fear and hate. Those who advocated a prohibition on racial mixing believed that what was valuable in a race resided in the purity of its blood, and since different qualities of blood flowed in the veins of superior and inferior races racial mixing or crossbreeding necessarily resulted in a mixing of a blood. Procreation operated like a blood transfusion.

Procreation was the tangible embodiment of mixing that was latent in the mere presence of the Other, the foreign body on or indeed in the national body of the collective Self. Indeed, the corporeal metaphor was extended with the construction of the immigration of racially undesirable foreigners as a 'massive ethnic blood transfusion'.[78] Thus the articulation of the fear instilled by the hybrid individual is a lower order utterance belonging to a metalanguage of racism which determines the *influx* of immigration as a contamination of the purity of the 'indigenous' race's blood by the impure, the inferior. Worse still for the mixophobic racist, since each race is supposed to correspond to a human type presumed to be stable, racial mixing produces instability, which politically could lead to 'anarchic' behaviour and mentally to madness.[79]

Here Enzensberger's *Essay on Dirt* can be usefully invoked. Enzensberger observes that 'people regard anything that is only ambiguously part of themselves as unclean. By analogy, they are disgusted at the prospect of contamination, heterogeneity'. In the face of such contamination they become afraid of 'being harmed by a process of amalgamation, insertion, addition, extraction, seepage, or infiltration', which is why 'people so often name in between states when asked for examples of dirt. This is probably also the basis for the indelible connection between dirt and the primary type of commingling: sex.'[80]

While legally no steps were taken to ban mixed marriages in Britain, they were still ideologically constructed in written texts as an abhorrence, especially, just as in America, by the

[78] Taguieff, *ibid.*
[79] *Ibid.*
[80] Cited in Theweleit 1, 385.

agents of organised, establishment Christianity – which, in addition to the usual metaphors associated with racist discourse, refer to 'the primary type of commingling', sexual union between two races, as an 'evil'.

Echoing the sentiments of the *American Catholic Quarterly Review* of fifty-five years before, the Church of England's *Liverpool Diocesan Review* in the mid-1930s apparently welcomed scientific racist contributions. But this organ of the English church establishment, far from appealing for measures favouring the immigration of the Irish, called once again for their 'rigorous separation', on the grounds of insurmountable racial differences. In a series of three articles the academic G.R. Gair, FRAI, MSAS, 'editor of the Scottish Anthropological Society', addressed 'The Irish Immigration Question'.[81] Gair made the 'scientific' claim that while most of the inhabitants of the British Isles belonged to the 'tall, stolid, phlegmatic northern race', the 'Nordic race', in the 'western part of the British Isles we have a branch of the Mediterranean race'. Consequently, 'there is a marked distinction in mental outlook and culture'. As often occurs with such articles seeking to propagate racist ideology, the argument swiftly moves from a deployment of 'common sense' attitudes to extremist allegations of difference in terms of inferiority, criminality, the risk of contagion from a sickly people, and even the greater incidence of madness to be found in the race in question. In this instance, the Irish are said to 'possess a higher ratio of criminals than the natives'; 'possibly also owing to inherent racial reasons, it is also an ascertained fact that Irish are more subject to certain diseases than the Nordics'; while 'insanity, and other undesirable features, are greatest. . . in those classes in which the Irish form the greater section of the population.' Once again the immigration and segregation policies of the United States of America are held up as a model for emulation:

[81] *Liverpool Review* vol. IX, nos 1-3 (January-March 1934). FRAI: Fellow of the Royal Anthropological Institute; MSAS: Member of the Scottish Anthropological Society.

The United States, seeing her institutions likely to crumble before this menace, and with the glaring lesson of the deleterious effects of 'wops' 'dagoes' and Irish, in her lower orders, has with admirable courage, closed the doors and adopted a policy which aims at the maintenance of the Nordic race-type.[82]

Once more the ideologically racist roots of this discourse are demonstrated by an insistence on purely racist considerations coming before capitalist imperatives, for while unlike the United States Britain had 'made little or no attempt to maintain the purity of her racial type', what 'little legislation' that had been enacted was 'intended for economic rather than for eugenic or ethnic reasons'. So although economic arguments for exclusion are employed, for instance 'the aggravation of unemployment among our own people', of greater concern is the prospect of contamination of racial purity: 'the propagation of a strongly tainted blood stream'.

The results of penetration by this 'alien Mediterranean race' would be the 'total collapse of Britain as a world and imperial power: and perhaps with it, who knows? civilisation'. Moreover, it is claimed, this conclusion is based on scientific observation of the 'disastrous nature of this hybridization in our midst in Merseyside'.[83]

The writer recommends segregation as 'the only solution'. If the Nordic British were to have 'the courage and the clear-sightedness of the Americans and introduce some race legislation', then it might not be too late to save 'the heart of the one Empire that can be of real world-service for humanity free from a cancerous decay, which would otherwise shatter irretrievably its solidarity and virility.' Once more the Other, here the Irish, is represented as an alien and dangerous sickness, a cancer, which impinges upon the integrity and manliness of the national body.[84]

Such ideas were not confined to local magazines, but were held by most eminent scientists. R.M. Yerkes, Professor of

[82] Ibid.
[83] Ibid.
[84] Ibid.

Psychology at Harvard and president of the American Psychological Association, claimed: 'The possibility of racial admixture here in America. . .is infinitely worse than that faced by any European country for we are incorporating the Negro into our racial stock.'[85] Henry F. Osborne, president of the American Museum of Natural History and 'one of America's most eminent prestigious paleontologists', wrote that 'the northern races invaded the countries to the south. . . as contributors of strong moral and intellectual elements to a more or less decadent society. . . . Columbus, from his portraits and from busts, whether authentic or not, was clearly of Nordic ancestry.'[86] In 1935, the year following the publication of Gair's articles in Liverpool, the year in which the present author's own 'Eurasian' mother was eleven years old, the Reverend Bates, the local Church of England parish priest, wrote in the same *Liverpool Diocesan Review* of his concerns about 'half-caste' unions with whites.[87] Bates was the vicar of St Michael's Church and a 'specialist in ethnology', since his work brought him into 'daily contact with Chinese, Africans, Egyptians, Arabs, Spaniards, Germans and Portuguese'. Why should the anthropologist 'proceed to Polynesia for field work' when 'the Liverpool tram for one penny will take you' into the 'midst of a babel of tongues, where every other child has the curly hair of the negro, or the wide slanting eyes of the East'?

'Naturally the question of mixed marriages, and illicit unions is very much to the fore in a quarter like this.'[88] Of specific concern are the products of these 'unions', those who

---

[85] Cited in R.C. Lewontin, *The Doctrine of DNA: Biology as Ideology* (Harmondsworth: Penguin, 1993) 26. Professor Lewontin's excellent and accessible book thoroughly and meticulously demystifies past and present myths of biological determinism.

[86] Lewontin 26-7.

[87] *Liverpool Diocesan Review* (formerly *Liverpool Review*) vol. X, no. 8 (August 1935), 589.

[88] *Ibid.*

find themselves in what Enzensberger termed 'in between states'. The Reverend expressed this concern for the spiritual and mental state of the offspring in a prose grounded in racist and Orientalist ideologies:

The children. . . speak English, but their mode of thought is Eastern. Their real ego is wrapped in an impenetrable silence, and whilst lips speak, the face is a mask, so different from the spontaneous frankness so delightful in English children.[89]

The vicar reminds the diocesan readers that these masked, and thus unknowable, children are not *English* – although they were legally British – since their 'yellow masks' exclude them. 'Racial difficulties', the Reverend Bates continues, 'develop at the marriage age': ' "If only God had made me white" is the bitter cry of the half-caste girl in love with a decent white man.' The white man is necessarily decent, for he is white. The half-caste is only half-decent, in an in-between state. The reader of the official publication in which Bates was writing had the previous year already been instructed in the evils of hybridity:

It is a notorious fact that really hybrid peoples are incapable of stability. . . . The reason is not far to seek. Remember that this, after all, is a biological question, and one only capable of solution in accordance with the known laws of science. . . mix two races and there is bound to be a falling apart, a crumbling of the national edifice, and just because the iron and clay will not amalgamate. The Eurasian, in his physical aspect alone, provides (even when social disabilities are discounted) an example of the evils arising from racial promiscuity. It is therefore clear that relative purity is something to be desired.[90]

Here 'ugliness', the highly visible alterity of the 'Eurasian', is deployed to reinforce the 'notoriety' of hybridity and the 'evils' of 'in-betweenness'.

Many of the white women that Chinese men married were poor; many, indeed, were ethnically Irish. Often family reactions were hostile. In Chinatown women's stories collected by Maria Wong, one Chinese-Liverpudlian woman recounts

[89] *Ibid.* 590.
[90] G.R. Gair, *Liverpool Review* vol. IX, no. 1 (January 1934) 12.

the story of her childhood experience of rejection by her white grandparents;

> My mum took me to [meet] my grandfather and he said 'What are you doing, bringing your shame over here?' And I knew he wasn't referring to my mum, he was referring to me. . . . I must have been very small, just started school. And I kept saying. . . 'Mum what's a shame?'[91]

In America in 1922, Congress passed the Cable Act removing citizenship from a woman if she married an alien Chinese, Korean or Japanese. In Britain the immigration laws were just as severe. A woman forfeited her citizenship by marrying a foreigner and was required to register as an alien in her own country. This legal fiction aimed to resolve the problem of hybridity by means of a legal instrument, an Act of Parliament. British women who married Chinese men were no longer British. They had been 'unEnglish'. They were excised from the national body, and the body was thus saved from contamination.

While racist myths and practices may have been dominant, there always have been those who gave the lie to English racial purity. In 1701, many years before the advent of scientific racism, and before the creation of Robinson Crusoe and Man Friday, Daniel Defoe had satirised in his poem *The True-Born Englishman* the notion of English superiority derived from the purity of their blood by foregrounding England's hybrid attributes:

> While ev'ry nation that her powers reduced,
> Their languages and manners introduced;
> From whose mix'd relics our compounded breed,
> By spurious generation does succeed;
> Making a race uncertain and uneven,
> Derived from all the nations under heaven.
>
> The Romans first with Julius Caesar came,
> Including all the nations of that name,
> Gauls, Greeks, and Lombards; and by computation,

[91] Wong 71.

Auxiliaries or slaves of ev'ry nation.
With Hengist, Saxons; Danes with Sweno came,
In search of plunder, not in search of fame.
Scots, Picts and Irish from th' Hibernian shore;
And conq'ring William brought the Normans o'er.

All these their barb'rous offspring left behind,
The dregs of armies, they of all mankind;
Blended with Britons, who before were here,
Of whom the Welch ha' blest the character.

....

Thus from a mixture of all kinds began,
That heterogeneous thing, an Englishman.[92]

After the Second World War Liverpool's Chinatown shrank, and new Chinese immigrants coming to Britain settled in other major cities like London and Manchester. Both Chinese men and women came, but mainly from Hong Kong. Individuals intermarried much less frequently, and yet the problems of racism and cultural hybridity remained.

China man angels, American monkey kings

'For I am the sworn poet of every dauntless rebel the world over,
And he going with me leaves peace and routine behind him.'
        —Walt Whitman, 'To a Foil'd European Revolutionaire'[93]

'The society of comrades. That was the American revolutionary dream to which Whitman contributed so powerfully; a dream broken and betrayed long before that of Soviet society's.'
                                        —Gilles Deleuze[94]

[92] *The Novels and Miscellaneous Works of Daniel Defoe*, vol. V (London: G. Bell, 1891) 435, 441.
[93] Sculley Bradley et al., *The Collected Writings of Walt Whitman*, vol. 1 (New York University Press, 1980) 250.
[94] *Critique et Clinique* (Paris: Les Éditions de Minuit, 1993) 80.

'The Monkey is the sign of the inventor, the improviser, and the motivator. . . . No challenge will be too great for him. . . . On the negative side the Monkey has an inborn superiority complex. He doesn't have enough respect for others.'

—Theodora Lau[95]

The English term 'chop suey' is derived from the Cantonese *shap sui*, 'odds and ends'; in northern Chinese, *zá suì*, literally 'mixed bits'. What that definition does not reveal is that chop suey is as American as the hamburger. It is an invention of Chinese in America and an oddity to visitors from China in search of 'authentic' Chinese food. Chop suey is a hybrid dish. Non-Chinese think it's Chinese. The Chinese outside America think it's American. It is neither one thing nor the other: it is hybrid. Hybridity can be uncomfortable for the authentic. The Self is under attack. How can you Otherise the hybrid when *you* are contained within it? The lack of purity, the lack of authenticity, the 'in-between state' can disturb, or be made to disturb, profoundly.

Parallel to, and laid over, racial hybridity is cultural hybridity. Maxine Hong Kingston's monkey directly addresses such questions. He is the Chinese monkey of the 'classic' Chinese novel *Journey to the West* and, more generally and democratically, of popular legend. But he is also an American monkey. Monkey refuses to be suppressed, monkey will not be denied what others have. Rebellious, subversive monkey, monkey as Robin Hood, incarnates the democratic impulse of the Vietnam War era protagonist of Hong Kingston's *Tripmaster Monkey*, Wittman, named by his semi-literate father for the great American patriot-patriarch-poet, Walt Whitman.[96] 'And I will report all heroism from an American point of view,' sings Walt Whitman.[97] Yet the Chinese American Whitman/Wittman is also celebrating the richness of ethnic

---

[95] *The Handbook of Chinese Horoscopes* (London: Fontana, 1991) 206.

[96] Maxine Hong Kingston, *Tripmaster Monkey: His Fake Book* (New York: Vintage, 1990) 161.

[97] 'Starting from Paumanok' (part 6), *Leaves of Grass*, in Walt Whitman, *Complete Poetry and Selected Prose* (Cambridge, MA: Riverside Press, 1959) 17.

Chinese culture. His immediate aim is to see Chinese theatre, which had existed for decades in nineteenth-century California, rise phoenix-like from the ashes. And yet he also wants to be treated and accepted as American, all American; Chinese American, yes, but Chinese American 'without the hyphen'. He declares, at the end of his Halloween-night theatrical production, paternalistically praised by the local press:

Without a born-and-belong-in-the-USA name, they can't praise us correctly. There's a favourable review here of our 'SINO-AMERICAN' theater. When the United States doesn't recognize a foreign communist country [the story is set in the 1960s], that's Sino-American. There is no such *person* as a Sino-American.[98]

Our Wittman, like the Walt Whitman of 'Song of Myself', looks idealistically to an American-ness that disregards colour. In 'Song of Myself' even the grass sprouting from the earth is a great democratic leveller: 'Growing among black folks as among white.'[99]

The nature of the Asian American identity is something Hong Kingston attempts to interrogate, negotiate and construct in her novel. There are numerous references to the earliest Chinese immigrants. Wittman contemplates San Francisco Bay and Alcatraz: 'And Angel Island too, waiting for us to come back and make a theater out of the Wooden House, where our seraphic ancestors did time. Desolation China Man angels.'[100]

Today many Americans celebrate another and more famous island, Ellis Island. Tourists make the ferry trip from Manhattan, by way of the Statue of Liberty, to visit this essential artefact of the American dream. A line of prose in the chronology displayed on one of the walls of the exhibition halls mentions briefly the anti-Chinese exclusion laws of 1882. But the Chinese are not part of the Ellis Island narrative. They are excluded from the Ellis Island narrative just as they were

---

[98] Kingston 307.
[99] Part 6, *Complete Poetry* 28.
[100] Kingston 161.

excluded from America itself. Ellis Island is narrated by a television bard, news anchorman Tom Brokaw, on a recorded 'audio tour' of the Immigration Museum: 'The story of Ellis Island in English, Español, Deutsch, Français and Italiano'.[101] There is no need of a Chinese soundtrack; for all the time that Ellis Island processed would-be immigrants – from 1892 till 1938 – Chinese people were excluded from America.

It is in the Ellis Island gift shop that the absence of Chinese and China is most marked. On sale is an array of golden medallions, one each for many of the world's nations. On one side of the coin is a racially stereotypical representation of a head belonging to one of that nation's immigrants, while on the other side is embossed the number of immigrants admitted to America from that country. There is even a Japanese face, for it was not until 1908 that the so-called Gentleman's Agreement officially restricted immigration from Japan. But there is no Chinese head. Next to the medallions are the posters and coffee-table books showing white, honest-looking turn-of-the-century European immigrants; described famous-ly by Emma Lazarus in 1883 as 'huddled masses yearning to breathe free', they are depicted staring into the eyes of the 'Mother of Exiles', the Statue of Liberty. The Chinese had been excluded in 1882.

Ellis Island is commemorated, and for sale, on souvenirs which range from plastic back-scratchers to the video narrated by the late Greek-American television and film star Telly Savalas, *Remembering Ellis Island: Everyman's Monument*. The video plays repeatedly on the overhead monitor. There are glass display cases full of 'authentic' goods from Italy, Ukraine, Israel – plates, embroideries, Russian wooden dolls: folklore from the old country. Prominently displayed is the official souvenir ceramic tile ('decorative – useful', 'protects your fur-niture – a lasting remembrance' reads the lettering on the box). The tile sports a representation of Ellis Island's main hall, the words 'DESTINATION: AMERICA' emblazoned across it, and

---

[101] ARA Leisure Services, 'Audio Tour of Ellis Island with Tom Brokaw' leaflet.

above the lettering are the flags of Finland, Germany, France, Italy, Sweden, Britain, Poland, Iceland, Japan, Spain, Mexico, Greece and Holland. On the other side of the tile is a small sticker: 'Made in Taiwan'.

On the other side of America there was a less proud detention centre – the wooden house – on Angel Island: the Ellis Island of the 'Chinaman', the back-door Ellis Island, the Ellis Island of the official Other. In the structure of the wooden house the early Chinese immigrants carved their anonymous poems, inscribed their desolation. These are the texts of the first Chinese American writers, unknown 'Desolation China Man angels ' – generations before Maxine Hong Kingston and Amy Tan. Some were related to early pre-Exclusion Act immigrants; some were impostors: economic desperation in China led them to pose as the relatives of Chinese Americans. They bought and internalised the identities of others in order to emigrate to the Gold Mountain.

Angel Island became home to the wooden barracks in 1910. The would-be immigrants endured physical examinations and harsh interrogations. Those who passed the test were allowed to cross the bay; those who failed were deported back to China. Suicides occurred, poems were written:

> The moment I hear
> We've entered port,
> I am all ready:
> My belongings wrapped in bundle.
> Who would have expected joy to become sorrow:
> Detained in a dark, crude, and filthy room?
>
> What can I do?
> Cruel treatment, not one restful breath of air,
> Scarcity of food, severe restrictions – all unbearable.
> Here even a proud man bows his head.[102]

While the racism institutionalised in the immigration policies of the nineteenth and twentieth centuries may be

---

[102] Marlon K. Hom (ed.), *Songs of Gold Mountain* (Berkeley: California University Press, 1987) 75.

elided in the collective memory, here at Angel Island the suffering that exclusion caused is made concrete, inscribed. Ultimately, the silent and silenced become voiced. This was one of the first modern detention centres; it was followed by that twentieth-century phenomenon, the camp.

Yuri Kochiyama, a Japanese American, writes in her autobiographical essay 'Then Came the War', that knowledge and understanding of one's own past should not be merely a form of self-defence, of ensuring one's own ethnic group is not persecuted once again. It should also lead to solidarity with other oppressed groups.[103] Her experience of internment during the war in an American concentration camp – 'we feel it is apropos to call them concentration camps' – and her struggle for redress led her to conclude:

Historically, Americans have always been putting people behind walls. First there were the American Indians who were put on reservations, Africans in slavery, their lives on plantations, Chicanos doing migratory work, and the kinds of camps they lived in. . . dispossessed people – disempowered.[104]

The whole Japanese American redress movement itself was 'very good because it was a learning experience. We could get out into our communities and speak about what happened to us and link it with experiences of other people.' Yet Yuri Kochiyama is critical of the collective self-interest and ethnocentrism of many Japanese Americans who 'didn't even learn that part', who 'don't even see other ethnic groups who have gone through it'.[105] One of the paradoxes of the experience of racism is how often the lesson is not learnt.

Just as many Japanese Americans have essentialised their experience, there is a danger of essentialising the Chinese American experience to the extent that exclusion and marginalisation, rather than being overturned, may be reinforced. Hong Kingston's Wittman Ah Sing clearly is made to voice

[103] In Joann Faung Jean Lee, *Asian Americans* (New York: New Press, 1992) 10–18.
[104] *Ibid.* 18.
[105] *Ibid.*

that danger. There is a very moving soliloquy towards the end of the novel when he seeks to deny the Chineseness of his cultural production, and even its hybrid status: 'There is no East here. West is meeting West. This was all West. All you saw was West. This is The Journey *In* the West.'[106]

But if this is the West, this can no longer be the West as it has been. Wittman's story foregrounds the confrontation and disjuncture between Chinese ethnicity and culture, and non-Chinese American culture. Wittman struggles to write and stage an American drama based on Chinese myths with a multi-racial cast of actors. It is Chineseness and hybridity out of which Maxine Hong Kingston constructs her narrative. She is not after all writing about the Pilgrim Fathers or Ellis Island. And yet, while she may not write about white America and its cultural mythology it is always there, the ever present Self against which she invents and reinvents the Other of her stories.

One of the contradictions generated by the category 'Chinese America' is that Chinese American identity, and its literary representation, cannot be historically fixed in one defining moment to the satisfaction of all who are determined by it. New immigrants come to America from China. Their ancestors did not suffer Angel Island. They come from the People's Republic of China, Hong Kong, Taiwan, South-East Asia. If there is a commonality beyond a vague and general shared culture, it is surely the experience of racism. Throughout the Chinese diaspora, Chinese people have long been victims of racism and there are always new Angel Islands. In 1993 Chinese would-be immigrants were deported back to China from North America. Those who successfully smuggle themselves into the United States suffer financial, sexual and racial abuse.

The category of 'Asian American' is no less problematic. Is it in any sense more inclusive than Chinese American? Should Asian Americans be prepared to be homogenised? Why should

[106] Kingston 308.

Japanese and Korean and other 'Orientals', yesterday's 'Mongolians', come together because the white man who cannot tell the difference puts them together? In *Tripmaster*, the question is posed even of the supposedly homogeneous Chinese Americans: '[W]hy should they greet each other? Because your parents and grandparents would have run up yelling to one another and shouted genealogies of relatives and friends and hometowns until they connected up.'[107]

There is then a natural tendency to question homogenising projects, but just as disturbing in this last decade of the twentieth century is the phenomenon of petty nationalisms and sub-nationalisms. Of course, the Korean American, the Japanese American, the Philippine American and the Chinese American – and within that category why not the Cantonese American, the Taiwanese American?–each should have the right to assert cultural autonomy; as should the other twenty or so distinct Asian American ethnic groups categorised and marginalised within the designation Asian American. The white man's criteria need not be accommodated. But the realities of racism can be faced in common:

If we can see the connections, of how often this happens in history, we can stem the tide of these things happening again by speaking out against them. . . . [G]et out into our communities and speak about what happened to us, and link it with the experiences of other people.[108]

Still eating cats – or Charlie Chan may be dead but is Fu-Manchu?

'I'm not the oppressor,
I don't want to be your foe
I'm not proud of our Colonial past.
Great Britain, the Empire –
what a farce
But whatever I do can't put past wrongs right
so all I can say is,

[107] *Ibid.* 59.
[108] Yuri Kochiyama in Joann Lee 18.

sometimes, I'm ashamed
of being white.'

—Jennifer Pedler[109]

'What are names for?
They are given to us
so we know who we are.

But who are we?
Ah, that's the question
that brings the police to the door
at three o'clock in the morning
BANG. BANG. BANG.'

—Richard Brown[110]

At the latter end of the twentieth century the explicit and
extreme racist discourse of the kind that was to be found in
mainstream newspapers and church journals is now largely
consigned to the newspapers of the extreme right. But the
extreme right accounts for at least 15 per cent of the electorate
in a country such as France, and can command a vast number
of votes in elections in parts of the United States. Moreover,
dominant notions of racism are still current among majority
white populations in the advanced industrialised societies.
Witness the lack of any critique at all of the racist prose of Sax
Rohmer in the preface to the very recent re-publication of
The Mystery of Dr Fu-Manchu. For the writer of the preface,
Granville Wilson, a novelist and journalist, Fu-Manchu may
be 'exaggerated' as a fictional 'personification of evil', but he
states quite without compunction: 'The real world has thrown
up such monstrosities in the past and it may well do so in the
future.' Jessica Hagedorn, alluding to an infamous representation
of a Chinese American, entitled her recent and excellent
selection of Asian American fiction *Charlie Chan is Dead*. It is

[109] 'Trying to Explain', in *Once I was a Washing Machine: An Anthology of Poetry and
Prose* introduction by Ken Worpole (Brighton: Federation of Worker Writers and
Community Publishers/Queen Spark Books, 1989) 153. Jennifer Pedler is a
member of Tottenham Writers, London.
[110] 'Names', in *Once I was a Washing Machine* 165. Richard Brown is a member of
Tower Hamlets Writers, London.

a wonderful title, and it would be comforting to think that such literary and cinematic representations of the Chinese Other really were of the past, but unfortunately in Britain the stereotypical representation of Chinese people is still ingrained in the consciousness of many. Charlie Chan may be dead; Fu-Manchu is alive and well and making profits for publishers.

Far less well publicised than the authors whose work is collected together in *Charlie Chan is Dead* are the lyrics of young British Chinese poets of the 1990s. Their work reveals the alarming degree of racial prejudice and hatred that still exists for the Other in societies like America and Europe. Meiling Jin's poem, 'One of Many', foregrounds the nature and the extent of the marginalisation of Chinese in Britain. It describes how they are excluded and marginalised, constructed as 'on the fringes' and out of fear remain there, 'going about their business', saving white society from the necessity of 'rigorous segregation'. The Chinese Briton – how unusual that sounds, so unlike Chinese American – with no stable identity, tries to all but elide her/himself, become 'thin', become 'transparent', invisible:

> I used to be a Chinese social worker,
> But now I'm just Chinese,
> One of the many
> Living here in Britain.
> We go about our business
> On the fringes
> Trying to make ourselves thin enough
> To slide past your malice
> Or thick enough to absorb your hatred
> Or transparent enough to go unnoticed.
> Some of us are deeply wounded,
> Our bodies litter the landscape,
> We did not make it past your malice
> Our eyes betrayed us,
> And the spikes stuck.[111]

But 'we' never 'go unnoticed', however long one lives as

[111] Lacy *et al*. 11.

Chinese British.[112] Paul Wong's poem, 'The Great Wall',
vividly illustrates the typical, repetitive abuse that 'Chinese' in
Britain live with daily. Not just their bodies, but their cultural
practices and products, in this instance Chinese food, are made
the object of the threatened Self's invective. These lines show
the contradictory demands of the pressure to conform that
comes from immigrant parents with a desire to assimilate:

> Chineeeman! How you doin' yellow-boy? You still eating that
> Nasty smelly stuff and all those
> Flat chickens?
> Nastee, run-over food. . . how did'ya get to be so fat anyways?
> Think you're so fucking brainy and superior, dontcha
> Well you may be Mr. Intellectual but you're still ugly, fat and
> Unpopular.
> What did you call me?!
> You better watch your mouth China boy or else this ape's
> Gonna make those fucked-up teeth of yours even worse
>
> ....
>
> Here comes Fu Manchu. . . where's your moustache then?
> Here comes Bruce Lee. . . show us a bit of your Kung-Fu then
> Hwoar!! Hai-ya!!! Woo, oo, ah, ah, ah,HA!!
>
> ....
>
> You're so weird, son. What is the matter with you nowadays?
> Why don't you want to fit in – what is wrong with
> Conforming?[113]

While first-generation immigrants suffer racism, they do not
suffer the inimitable mental cruelty of the school playground
and frequently are not sensitive to the subtleties of the language
of racist ideology. These poems also reveal how in large
measure the question of hybrid identity is still largely unad-
dressed. There are, of course, strategies for surviving the

---

[112] As I was writing this chapter I had a phone call from my mother, still living in
Liverpool. 'After all these years,' she said, 'who would have thought it? To think
they'd still use that word.' A group of youths had been dawdling on a central
Liverpool street corner, and as she passed one of them remarked in a loud voice to
the others: 'Hey, that's a Chink.'

[113] Lacy *et al.* 58.

prejudices, attitudes and *idées reçues* of the dominant and the
'authentic' culture. In Kim Tan's poem, 'Life as a Banana,
What Does it Mean', both Chinese and white English attitudes
are shown to leave little space for the hybrid subject:

> You go to John Lewis' and some woman asks you which wok to buy
> As if all Chinese people know which one is best
> 'Oh, Meyer's flat bottomed 15 pounds from Argos – doesn't even
>   rust!'
> Got that one sussed.
> It's when you learn a set menu for when you go to yam cha
> so the waiter doesn't give you a bad stare or spit in your food.
> You even tap the table with your fingers when someone pours
>   your tea
> ....
> It's when you hate it when there's a dangling Chinese lantern in
>   everyone's car in Chinatown.
> ....
> It's when you get a headache listening to Chinese music.
> ....
> It's when you wish the little Chinese lady
> Who is shouting in a raucous voice
> Would overdose on MSG
> ....
> It's when you think about arranged marriages
> And whether your future husband would give your family £99
> £999 or £9,999 as a dowry.
> ....
> Oh the joys of being a banana! A banana![114]

Are these subjects marginalised, or are they squeezed between rigid poles? Is there really space there at all? One of these
Chinese 'British' poets finds himself physically, geographically at
the peripheries of two societies. Lab Ky Mo, who lives in
Belfast, speaks English with a Belfast Irish accent. His Chineseness is Cantonese, which is the language he speaks as a second
or foreign language. Hong Kong is further from Beijing than
Belfast is from London, but Lab Ky Mo in his poem 'Chinas
with Belfast accents', like Salinger's Laughing Man, cleaves
himself a space somewhere along the Ulster-Chinese border

[114] *Ibid.* 48-9.

where he maps his own Chinas where his multiple identities
and cultural desires can belong:

> No, indeed, my Chinas need to have Belfast accents and there's not
> a thing I can do about it.
> There's no place in China for them – the Communists wouldn' t have
> it and the EC neither. No, instead, I store them in my head.
>
> I build my Chinas in my head – I make drawings on paper.
> I make drawings on paper and they become maps.
> I am its only Civil Servant – I issue me my own passport
> in fact, I'm a citizen with full rights who doesn't even need
> a passport to travel in and out of the place.
> I am its first President – I get issued free travelcards.
> And their national vocabulary, well it's a marriage of English
> with a Belfast accent.
> They speak a little Hakka too, and Cantonese, only there not too
> good at it.
> And they all understand each other. Do you hear me?[115]

Lab Ky Mo may have imagined his own autonomous zone,
but his poems stand as reminders that there is a reality beyond
race, and nation, and that is a reality marked by a lived sense
of community, a community forged out of a shared class
experience. The poem 'It Was Good to See All My Old
Friends Again, Down at the Bowling' reminds us that the
communities where these poems are produced are communities of working people living in a twilight culture of
exploitation, where even the routine and habit of exploitation
and patriarchal dominance can dull the pain of the particular
alienation felt by those caught in the 'fish and chip shop' culture
of the take-away catering industry of cheap, Chinese food:

> Although younger than I am,
> they all work full-time.
>
> Poor guys.
> Six days a week, they work in the kitchen,
> and on the seventh, the day of rest,
> they just smell of it.
>
> We drove Kenny home that night.

[115] *Ibid.* 18–19.

It was five in the morning,
but Kenny still chose to peel
the potatoes before he went to bed.[116]

But it is during the long days in the 'chip shop' that the white customers invade their lives. With them come the racist insults, the reminder of identity to which colour is the casing and the key ('white fish in yellow batter'), so disturbing to the English Self, so intrusive. Siu Won Ng's poem 'Fish and Chips' shows the deep psychological hurt inflicted by such encounters with the racist neighbourhood bully. 'Bastard' is the important word, the word that is always in the mind, the word that the pens of the racist ideologues long to inscribe. Again the impure, the inauthentic, the mixed is the object of hatred. For this is no common insult, not a straightforward 'Chinese bastard', but rather a more considered, race-inflected and rhetorically nuanced 'bastard Chinese':

White fish covered in white paste
before it is tanned by the burning oil
into a crisp yellow –
so, will you claim that
your meal has been polluted?

You want to know the way to Peking
and your van was stuck in traffic
....
Peking, you stipulated
wanting to know from a bastard Chinese.
....
Was it my face that bothered you?
that made you vomit such words,
you eat Peking duck,
like you do fish and chips.
A great British meal
covered in patriotic red sauce.
....
I could have thrown your fish at you
....
Would you have fought back

               with your stubby fingers
               to a woman heated by your vulgarity?[117]

Facts have never really impeded the construction of racist discourse, and science has frequently been recuperated into the project whose aim is exclusion of the Other, even by means of physical extermination, as is happening at this moment in numerous societies around the globe.

The veracity or otherwise of 'facts' is irrelevant to such a racism. The discursive practice of the Liverpool *Weekly Courier* in 1906 was not impeded by facts. The paper's reporter was supposedly accompanied by an 'Asiatic gentleman' on a tour of Chinatown who allegedly

declared that he had seen a dead cat carried into a restaurant. Alluding to one of the dishes he said that Chop Sooy was not at all bad; it contained chicken finely chopped and other eatables. And cat? I asked. 'Oh, no,' was the reply. 'Cat is a delicacy to be eaten separately!'[118]

Ninety years later the trope of the cat-eating 'Oriental' is as embedded in popular white racist discourse as ever. The stories about cats continue, as do the exclusions and expulsions:

THE FAT MARKET CAT

               Didn't you know?
               She's lost her cat
               The big fat angora
               That she took to market.
               Didn't you know?
               She's lost her cat
               Lost, yes, lost
               I'd say they've stolen it!

---

[117] *Ibid.* 28-9. I remember an occasion in Britain in the 1970s, a time when South Asians were subject to frequent violent racist attacks, known as 'Paki-bashing'. I was in the queue at the local Chinese fish and chip shop when a skinhead came in and lashed out at the Chinese teenage boy behind the counter, shouting 'Paki bastard'. He missed and ran off, leaving the boy in shock, still frying and serving the chips. There weren't many South Asians in Liverpool at the time, and a non-white face was a non-white face.

[118] *Weekly Courier* 8 December 1906, p. 7.

Oh when you see what our neighbourhood's become
No, it's not what it was: it's not surprising.

....

They've stolen her cat
Stolen, yes, stolen. . .
Maybe they've eaten it!
They're capable of anything these foreigners!

Didn't you know?
Now they're stealing the cats
They start with the cats
And then who knows . . .

....

Oh when you see what our neighbourhood's become
Isn't it awful: eating French cats!

Didn't you know?
That's all people are talking about:
The daughter of the woman with the cat
says she's been raped!

....

It seems they drugged her
So as to carry her off to their own country
Oh when you see what our neighbourhood's become
We need more cops on the beat: we're not protected!

Didn't you know
We're forming a committee
To get them expelled
Before there's any more damage

....

Oh when you see what our neighbourhood's become
It was about time: we waited too long!

Didn't you know
She's found her cat!
Her cat? How d'you mean? What cat?
What cat are you talking about?
– The big fat angora
That she took to market!
Oh, the cat at the market. . . yes. . .
I'd forgotten![119]

---

[119] 'Le gros chat du marché', French pop song by Gilbert Lafaille, quoted by permission of Budde Music France (Paris).

8

POETIC ZONES,
AUTONOMOUS MOMENTS

'At what moment was choice postponed? We have let things go.'

—Guy Debord[1]

'People think of oppression as low wages and hard work and then being put on the scrapheap. But there's another kind of oppression: killing their faith in the work of their hands and of their minds.'

—Raymond Williams[2]

'Sales, the ultimate Frontier of the 80's where
everybody drinks the juice of consumption
which has no limit.
I see the black youth running, entering
the local McDonalds – a
place of common ritual meeting I suppose,
where time does not make any sense.'

—Rahul Barot[3]

Claude Sicre, one of the duo which is the Fabulous Trobadors, believes that those who sing about change and action must not only sing but act to change society in society. He is critical of those who do not. By acting he means organising actions and events which change and show how to change communities. In his home town of Toulouse he has organised weekly neighbourhood street suppers where impromptu entertain-

[1] 'Critique of Separation', in *Situationist International Anthology*, ed. and transl. Ken Knabb (Berkeley, CA: Bureau of Public Secrets, 1989; no copyright) 36.

[2] Nesta, the coalminer's daughter, in Raymond Williams's novel *Loyalties* (London: Hogarth Press, 1989) 36.

[3] 'Youth with Black Skin' in *Once I was a Washing Machine: An Anthology of Poetry and Prose, op. cit.* 145-6. Rahul Barot is a member of the Bristol Broadsides writers' group.

ments and political exchanges may take place. On a larger scale
he has organised music and arts festivals for those to whom
such pleasures are normally denied. It is not the case that such
actions are merely idealistic, for they also create, through
moments of practice, understanding of ways in which life may
be lived and not simply survived.

For the last decade an organisation called *Vitécri* has been
organising activities on the under-privileged northern periphery
of Toulouse where unemployment stands at 30 per cent. In
1993 it organised, for the deprived suburban communities of
les Izards, Bourbaki, le Fronton and Négreneys, the third
consecutive festival called *Ça bouge au nord* comprising painting, dancing, street theatre and a great deal of music; 'pleasures
usually denied to them'.[4] One of the main attractions was the
group Zebda; established in the mid-1980s by Magyd Cherfi
when he realised that out of 300 North Africans in his
neighbourhood there was not one musician. The name 'Zebda'
is a play on words. It means 'butter' in Arabic, which is 'beurre'
in French, which is a homophone for the French backslang
term for 'Arab'. Zebda sing about Palestine; the cover of their
latest album, *L'Arène des rumeurs*, includes a photograph of a
Palestinian child.[5] But they are concerned about injustices
closer to home too. They also get involved in making things
happen —*faire bouger les choses* — in their immediate community.
In the drug-ridden *banlieues* north of Toulouse it would be
utopian to expect that summer festivals would permanently
change the lot of its inhabitants. Magyd Cherfi recognises as
much: 'We are dreamers. . . . Maybe the young people we're
helping will come to a bad end, but we'll have done what we
could.'[6] What Cherfi and the others achieve is not insignificant
and goes beyond a mere moment of resistance-cum-pleasure
afforded by their music. The young people who are the
audience themselves are involved in the organisation of the
festival. It is *their* festival, with *their* fences; a festival where they

[4] *Le Monde*, 7 September 1993, p. 16.
[5] Nord-Sud Barclay. 513 787-4, 1992.
[6] *Le Monde*, 7 September 1993, p. 16.

provide the catering and the policing. It is for the week of the festival a truly Temporary Autonomous Zone (TAZ) where the street drug dealers' capitalist dreams of profits are displaced by a sense of community and autonomy. As Cherfi puts it, 'When I see a youth who normally says, "I want a BMW and I don't want to work", proud to spend his whole evening controlling a parking lot, I'm happy'.[7]

This is the kind of popular activity which raises popular consciousness, and which Sicre has been promoting for years. His ideas of regional culture are not narrowly nationalistic and xenophobic. The North Africans, the Spanish, the gypsies are there, so they are part of the local culture. Sicre acknowledges as much in his music, when he borrows North African melodies and rhythms. Zebda in turn have acknowledged him by doing a cover version of his song 'Come on Every Baudis'; a song which is aimed at the centre-right mayor of Toulouse, Dominique Baudis.

Zebda and the Fabulous Trobadors are united, then, in their embracing of a local inclusive culture; marginalised by the nationalist centralism of Paris, they share a marginal space.

Guy Debord has described as 'concentrated' spectacular power 'the ideology condensed around a dictatorial personality', a form of power that had 'accomplished the totalitarian counter-revolution, fascist as well as Stalinist'.[8] The alternative form of spectacular power, the 'diffuse', was that which drove earners to use their 'freedom of choice' to purchase the array of commodities available. Debord arrived at that analysis in 1967. Twenty years later he discerned the emergence of a third and dominant form of spectacular power which would ultimately replace the other forms, a combination of the two based on 'the general victory of the form which had showed stronger: the diffuse. This is the *integrated spectacle*, which has

[7] *Ibid.*

[8] Guy Debord, *Comments on the Society of the Spectacle*, transl. Malcolm Imrie (London and New York: Verso, 1990) 8. Translation of *Commentaires sur la société du spectacle* (Paris: Gérard Lebovici, 1988). Quotes here are taken from the English edition.

since tended to impose itself globally.'⁹ Nowhere has that
integration of the two forms of the spectacle been more
thoroughgoing than in the China of the last decade or so.
While capitalist practices have been entrenched in a society
where there have never been bourgeois forms of democracy,
dictatorial practices have survived. Thus, just as under the
Franco regime (1939-75) in Spain the capitalist market
flourished while accommodating official ideology, so in China
market capitalism and 'freedom of choice' are limited. For
instance, in October and November 1993 the Chinese
authorities implemented a range of censorship measures aimed
at controlling the distribution of information and of cultural
products and practices. Thus the government news agency
Xinhua announced the government's intention to close illegal
dance halls, video game parlours and other types of entertainment deemed harmful to 'the body and mind of the people'.¹⁰
Controls on publishing were also reinforced and publishing
houses were closed down for printing 'anti-government'
books. Meanwhile, many dance and karaoke halls are owned
by government offices or the army. *Xinhua* claimed that 'some
of the profit-oriented entertainment facilities' had been used
as 'gambling dens, brothels and for showing pornographic
videotapes', and that pornographic shots had been inserted
into video games 'to corrupt young games lovers'.¹¹

   Franco did not have to contend with pornographic video
games; banning *Playboy* and Marx was sufficient in the pre-
electronic age. In the last decade of the twentieth century the
Chinese authorities have to attempt to extend their control
over an exploding domain of consumer products and services.
In October 1993 the government banned the use of un-
authorised satellite dishes, estimated to number in the millions,
thus attempting to prevent reception of direct satellite broad-
casts from Hong Kong and elsewhere. In November 1993 it
entrenched its monopoly over other forms of electronic com-

⁹ *Ibid.* 8.
¹⁰ UPI, 28 October 1993.
¹¹ *Ibid.*

munication, including mobile telephones, pagers, telecommunications and radio and television stations; at the end of 1993 there were 460,000 mobile telephones and 6 million radio-pager users.[12]

The ultimate balance of the authoritarian 'concentrated' form of power and the 'diffuse' form, giving full play to commodity capitalism, is still under negotiation, and yet a consolidation leading to what Debord calls an 'integrated' form of the society of the spectacle has certainly occurred. Debord wrote of the development of the 'diffuse' form of spectacular power as an 'Americanisation', as 'a process which in some respect frightened but also successfully seduced those countries where it had been possible to maintain traditional forms of bourgeois democracy'.[13] Now in the 'integrated' society not just economic practices but ideological practices are conflated. Not only is commodity capitalism globalised; so are ideological attempts to control. State authorities are, indeed, desperate and determined to maintain ideological domination. But once again, from Paris to Peru, the only ideology available to them is that of nationalism, which they attempt to nurture and exploit by appeals to patriotic sentimentality and its associated practices.[14] The Chinese state authorities, for instance, recently called for the national flag to be raised and for the national anthem to be sung at all meetings and popular activities.[15] Is this the new 'Americanisation'? Will allegiance to the national flag soon be demanded in all 'integrated' societies of the spectacle?

As a bard of the 'concentrated' spectacular society, Ai Qing in his 1954 poem 'On a Chilean Cigarette Packet' confronts the 'diffuse' spectacular society's culture of total commodification:

[12] UPI, 6 November 1993.

[13] Debord, *Comments* 8.

[14] The official slogan of the right-wing Premier Edouard Balladur's French presidential campaign in 1995 was simply '*Croire en la France*' (Believing in France).

[15] Agence France Presse, 9 November 1993.

On a Chilean cigarette packet,
Is drawn a Goddess of Liberty,
Although she raises high a torch,
She is still just a black shadow;

As a trademark, and an advertisement,
The Goddess of Liberty is allowed a space,
Just a few coins can buy her,
The cigarettes finished, she's gone up in smoke. . .

The packet is thrown by the road side,
 I tread on it, you spit on it,
Whether fact or whether symbol,
The Goddess of Liberty is a mere pack of cigarettes.[16]

The poem bemoans the lack of freedom in Chile by extending the trope of the Goddess of Liberty used as a trade mark on a cigarette packet. This might be interpreted either as a cynical move, given the lack of freedom to engage in similar critique in China, or as an intended irony. The evidence of Ai Qing's later poetry written in support of the regnant authority of the Chinese spectacular society would suggest that this poem is meant to be consumed in China (it was originally published in the state's mass circulation literary magazine *Renmin Wenxue* [People's Literature]) as an ideological commodity. Ai Qing, soon after writing this poem, would in any case spend twenty years banished by the state from the literary and political centre, only to emerge to bolster anew the state's battered ideology: 'Red the pomegranate in May,/Red is the sun at the birth of day./But most beautiful of all, the red flags on forward march!'[17]

Thirty-five years after the publication of 'On a Chilean Cigarette Packet', the sign was reappropriated in China as the Goddess of Democracy, a simulacrum of the Goddess/Statue of Liberty, and reinvested with renewed political meaning. Just what those values were depended on how you read the

[16] August 1954, Santiago de Chile, *Aiqing quanji*, vol. 2 (Shijiazhuang: Huashan wenyi chubanshe, 1991) 185.

[17] *Wenhui bao*, 30 April 1978. Translated by Kai-yu Hsu in his *The Literature of the People's Republic of China* (Bloomington: Indiana University Press, 1980) 917-18.

sign; more than one semiotic interpretation was possible. Was it a symbol of democracy? Was it a concretization of the 'diffuse' spectacular society interjected into the space of the 'concentrated' society of the spectacle? Undoubtedly there were those who read it innocently as a symbol of hope and resistance in the midst of Tiananmen Square, the geographical, institutional and symbolic centre of power, but also a historic site of contestation throughout the twentieth century.

Later in 1989 the interjection of the symbol of the 'diffuse' spectacular society into the space of the mutating, but not yet diffused, 'concentrated' spectacular society inspired the 'fall' of Communist régimes all over Europe. This was the victory of the 'diffuse'. In China the trajectory was different, but the ultimate point of arrival the same: the 'integrated' society.

In the 1990s, as the global integrated society of the spectacle dreams of its destination at the end of the information highway rainbow, the Goddess of Democracy, while still retaining political symbolic value for some, represents for many, and not just the Chinese authorities, a deviation from the business of integrating 'Communism' and 'capitalism', the 'concentrated' and 'diffuse' forms of the society of the spectacle; witness the San Francisco statue affair.[18]

There are multiple ironies involved in the deployment and redeployment of the Statue of Liberty/Goddess of Liberty icon. As mentioned in Chapter 7, for all the years that the Statue of Liberty welcomed immigrants who sailed down the Hudson River to Ellis Island, the Chinese were an excluded race, unfit to be citizens. While in New York, in the words of Emma Lazarus's 1883 poem, there stood a 'mighty woman with a torch' from whose 'beacon-hand/Glows world-wide welcome', in San Francisco there was no welcome for the 'tempest-tost', no lamp lifted 'beside the golden door.' The Statue of Liberty and the dream of freedom lyrically represented in Emma Lazarus's poem constitute one of history's great deceptions. The symbol of welcome to 'huddled masses

---

[18] In 1993 attempts to construct a bronze replica of the Goddess in San Francisco met with resistance and embarrassment. *San Francisco Chronicle*, 6 October 1993.

yearning to breathe free' is simultaneously the symbol of 'John Chinaman's' exclusion. Jean Baudrillard is widely credited with interrogating the reality of America. In fact, he was alluding to the irreality of America's self-representation:

America is neither dream, nor reality, it is hyperreality. It's a hyperreality because it is a utopia which since the beginning was lived as if accomplished. Everything is real, pragmatic, here, and everything leaves you dreaming.[19]

The Statue of Liberty/Goddess of Democracy is the icon of that utopia. What stood in Tiananmen Square was not an emblem of history inflected with hope, but the icon of China's forgotten exclusion from freedom, the representation of deception and a symbol of the success of the American ideology. Effectively, it was the concretisation of the victory of the 'diffuse' spectacular society. In San Francisco – the site of Old Gold Mountain, the first American 'home' of excluded 'John Chinaman' – its arrival would be truly perverse, a genuine irony. As with the cigarette packet, the Goddess of Democracy, the Goddess of Freedom, makes an excellent marketing mechanism for 'utopia'.

'For a few pennies you can buy her', wrote Ai Qing of Emma Lazarus's 'mighty woman', and whether Ai Qing was guilty of bad faith in foregrounding the ignoble fate of the Goddess of Freedom sign in 'On a Chilean Cigarette Packet', the poem nevertheless does accomplish the task of making the reader rethink the icon and its relationship to the American myth, money and modern capitalist society in America's 'backyard'.

In 1989 it was the mythic power of the Goddess of Freedom/Statue of Liberty that was recuperated as an icon of resistance and provocation in Tiananmen Square. Tiananmen (the Gate of Heavenly Peace) was, of course, the focal point for student and popular demonstrations during the spring of that year. It was the centre of the 'action' for the Western

---

[19] Jean Baudrillard, *Amérique* (Paris: Grasset, Livre de Poche, Biblio, Essais, 1986) 32.

media, who hardly bothered to cover events in the rest of Beijing, not to mention the rest of the country. It was ultimately the site of the authorities' 'crackdown', the Tiananmen massacre on the night of 3-4 June, and the place of destruction for the Goddess of Democracy.

The history of numerous important events that have taken place over the century at Tiananmen Square is now effaced, for the word 'Tiananmen' has become synonymous with a ruthless and authoritarian crushing of innocent people. All other associations, the previous Tiananmen demonstrations, have been displaced by the meaning given to Tiananmen by the acts of that night.

Ai Qing wrote of the redeployment by commodifiers of this symbol of 'democracy' to denote a brand of cigarette. It was of a different order altogether from the cynical use of 'Tienanmen' (*sic*) as a brand name in 1990s France, where a foodstuffs company continues to exploit the association of Tiananmen with things Chinese. It does so to sell food: 'Tienanmen' noodles, soy sauce, sweet and sour pork are sold at every good supermarket throughout France. Commodity capitalism has no political or moral code, and no need of history. Even the bourgeois fetish for 'taste' has in the guise of 'post-modernity' succumbed to marketing imperatives. Witness the advertising campaigns of the clothing corporation Benetton which have exploited offensive images, including photographs of AIDS victims and starving children. There are no limits. The Benetton campaigns aim to gain brand recognition by shocking the spectator/consumer. 'Tiananmen', on the other hand, loses its negative historical associations and hence the power to shock. Hence it simply once again conveys a vague sense of 'Oriental', exotic otherness.

Language can conceal, language can disclose. It can do both at the same time. Poetic language can construct and can rent apart the dissimulation of ideology. When, as Guy Debord has demonstrated, history has been effectively neutralised and the contemporary event itself necessarily fades into a condition of the dehistoricised fabulous with its own unverifiable tales and statistics, unrealistic explanations and unsustainable reasoning, there is then a need for a denaturalised language beyond the (un)reassuring discourse of naturalised airline-TV news jargon. When the airline patter of 'at this time' is really no time at all, we need a practice to help us re-establish history, to wake us from the eternal present. Lyricism, as a denaturalised and denaturalising language, may be capable of providing that practice in the age of the spectacle.

Time

> 'Whereas totalitarianism ensures itself against the risk of the fracturing of time by brutally asserting an historical truth which turns future progress into a development of the present. . . , the new ideological discourse takes hold of the signs of the new, cultivates them in order to efface the threat of the historical.'   — Claude Lefort[20]

> 'I have let time slip away. I have lost what I should have defended.'
> —Guy Debord[21]

The Chinese poet Mang Ke in his long poem 'Timeless Time' isolates and negotiates the phenomenon of the space which is beyond, or rather beside time:

> Here feelings grow no more
> Here is a stretch of stark time
> Gloomy and cold
> Still and deserted
> Here is a stretch of dust-covered time
> No more memories, and no more thought
> No more waiting, and no more hoping
> Here is time that has passed your life by
> And time that has passed my life by
> Here is a timeless time
> We are still we

---

[20] *The Political Forms of Modern Society: Bureaucracy, Democracy, Totalitarianism*, ed. and intro. John B. Thompson (Cambridge, MA: MIT Press, 1986) 196. The chapter of the book from which this quotation is taken first appeared in *Les Formes de l'Histoire: essais d'anthropologie politique* (Paris: Gallimard, 1978) 233.

[21] Debord, 'Critique of Separation' in Knabb 36.

> I and I are not divided
> My past remains the mirror of my now
> My now is the inverted image of my future
> Here, the boundary between life and death no longer exists
> I have no need to be terrified by death.[22]

Here we have the sameness of existence, the timelessness of everyday life, time left unhistoricised. This poem addresses directly what poems are about. Bachelard writes of the poem's capacity to 'construct a complex instant', an instant when and where simultaneous moments are 'knotted' together. The poet needs to 'destroy the simple continuity of sequential time'. Thus 'elements of stopped time' are always to be found.[23] Time in poetry is 'vertical', according to Bachelard, that of prose horizontal:[24] 'it is in the vertical time of an immobilised instant that poetry finds its specific dynamism.'[25] The paradox is that poetry's prosody organises itself in sequential units of sound, horizontally. Within that paradox lies the means by which the 'poetic instant' joins up with 'prose', with 'social life' and with 'slipping, linear, continuous life'.[26] Bachelard cites Mallarmé as a poet who 'directly brutalises horizontal time' and 'inverts syntax'. The result is a time in which labour has been invested, a time that has been worked on, *temps travaillé*.[27] Other poets seize the 'stabilised instant' more naturally: Baudelaire, for instance, who in the depths of a lover's eyes sees clearly 'time, always the same, a vast time, solemn, vast as space, without divisions into minutes and seconds – an immobile time which is not marked on clocks.'[28] Paul Virilio has arrived at a description of stopped time,

---

[22] *Mei you shijian de shijian* (Bejing: n.p., 1987).

[23] Gaston Bachelard, *Le droit de rêver* (Paris: Presses Universitaires de France, 1970) 224.

[24] *Ibid.* 225.

[25] *Ibid.* 232.

[26] *Ibid.* 225.

[27] *Ibid.* 227.

[28] *Ibid.* 228; Charles Baudelaire, 'L'Horloge', *Petits poëmes en prose. Oeuvres complètes* (Paris: Éditions du Seuil, 1968) 158.

employing the imagery and imagination of the electronic 'post-modern' age, which was remarkably similar to Bachelard's. Virilio writes of 'a time which exposes itself instantaneously'. He describes 'duration' as becoming the 'support surface of inscription' on the screen of the computer terminal; '*le temps fait surface*' or 'time becomes surface'.[29]

Mang Ke writes of a 'timeless time'. It is timeless, but still it has the semblance of age, is 'dust-covered'. Yet it is an 'immobilised instant'. Future and present are knotted together in that instant; 'all that devalorises at the same time the past and the future is found in the poetic instant.' Readers are not led sequentially from one moment to the next. They descend vertically through the stabilised instant, and then re-ascend.[30] This time is not just a personal time, it is a collective shared time; 'time that has passed your life by/And time that has passed my life by'. In vertical time, the 'I' is unfragmented by the usual alienation between subject and object.[31] 'I and I are not divided.' In this immobilised instant, even death is disempowered. There is no 'boundary between life and death' in the immobilised instant, because there is no sequential dynamic.

The tension between the will to stop time and the traditional associations of regularly measured time are foregrounded and made explicit in the poem 'April', from Mang Ke's undistributed 1989 collection *Mang Ke Shiji*:

> This is April
> April is like other months
> It makes people reminisce, makes people suddenly think of things
> Of yesterday, of far away
> Or think of a winter snowfall
>
> Of course, now long since turned to tears

---

[29] Paul Virilio, *L'Espace critique* (Paris: Christian Bourgois, 1984) 15. This idea is used by Thomas Docherty in his essay 'Ana-; or Postmodernism, Landscape, Seamus Heaney' in Anthony Easthope and John O. Thompson (eds), *Contemporary Poetry Meets Modern Theory* (University of Toronto Press, 1991) 68-80.

[30] Bachelard 229.

[31] *Ibid.* 232.

Or to a flight of doves
Flown who knows where
April, it makes you think of people
Think of those either living
Or already dead
Think of those who are perhaps happy
Of those who are perhaps doomed to tragedy
Think of men and women. . .
This is April
April is like other months
But it forces you to recall things past
Forces you to dive again into the depths of memory
 — That place where the dead are buried
I think that even if you were a standing slab of stone
You would sob.
1983

'April' is the month of death, of remembering the dead, and yet here Mang Ke suggests and deploys horizontal time, while immediately stopping time: 'April is like other months.' This time is ambivalent time. April is specific and special time, but it is time just as in other months. This stabilised instant descends vertically to that repository of time which is memory, 'where the dead are buried'.

The images and metaphors in this poem are both familiar and startling. The 'dead who are buried' are the already dead and those yet to die. As in 'Timeless Time', the inequality between the living and the dead is elided; again there is no division in time between life and death. The modernity of the integrated spectacle 'rushes along linear Time, its glaring beams always thrown forward, extinguishing subtler lights, while behind, a dark void. The dead are consigned to the void.'[32] The dominant forces in society control by dividing. 'The living are divided from the dead. The dead are the history of the living. Cut off from the dead, their history, the living are weakened.'[33] However, in Mang Ke's 'April' the living and

[32] Leo Baxendale, *The Encroachment: Part I* (Stroud, England: Reaper Books, 1988) 44.
[33] *Ibid.*

the dead co-exist in stopped time, in the memory. In 'April' there is a tension between the real time 'of things past', grounded in the context of recent Chinese history, and vertical time that permits language to 'rework' that time, to produce a poetic instant that is a function of *temps travaillé*.

Yet work takes place in historical time. Ultimately *the* work is read in horizontal time. It may make the reader think time differently, seem to stop time, but in the reader's work of reading there has also been an investment of time. Hakim Bey has commented that, like festivals, 'uprisings cannot happen everyday – otherwise they would not be "non-ordinary". But such moments of intensity give shape and meaning to the entirety of a life. . . a *difference* is made.'[34] Similarly with the poetic instant. The return on the investment of real time is the difference that is made to consciousness. The poet makes his or her difference at the point of completion of the poem. The difference is made to and by the reader during the moment of reading, when real time is traded for vertical time.

Thomas Docherty, reading a poem by Seamus Heaney, invokes the concept of 'cinematism', which again can be seen as an attempt to imagine the tension between vertical time and horizontal time. Here is a poem by Duoduo in which there exists just such a temporal tension between the pull of narrative time and the anchoring force of stopped time, between the unreflective glimpses afforded by the rapid succession of images of the cinematic camera and the leisurely perusal provided by the snapshot:

ONE STORY TELLS HIS ENTIRE PAST

When he opens up the windows of his body which give on
    to the ocean
and leaps towards the sound of a thousand knives clashing
one story tells his entire past
when all tongues stretch towards this sound
and suck back the thousands of knives of this clashing sound

---

[34] Hakim Bey, *T.A.Z.: The Temporary Autonomous Zone: Ontological Anarchy, Poetic Terrorism* (Brooklyn, NY: Autonomedia, 1991; 'anti-copyright') 100.

all days will squeeze into one day
thus every day will have an extra day

the last year flips over under the great oak
his memory comes from a cattle pen, above a column of
  undispersed smoke
some children on fire holding hands sing and dance in a circle
  round the kitchen knife
before the flames die down
they persistently rage round the tree
the flames, finally injuring his lungs

and his eyes are the festival days of two hostile towns
his nostrils two enormous tobacco pipes pointed at the sky
women wildly shoot love at his face
forcing his lips agape
any moment, a train travelling in the opposite direction to death
  will pass by
making a morning remain between his outstretched arms
pressing down the sun's head

a silent revolver announces this morning's approach
a morning more cheerless than an empty box thrown to the
  ground
a sound of branches breaking in the forest
a broken pendulum on an old shutter lifted down from the
  funereal street
one story tells his entire past
death, has already become a surplus beat of the heart
when stars dive towards the snake venom-seeking earth
time rots beyond the tick-tocking of the clock
rats shed their milk teeth on the copper coffin's spots of rust
fungi stamp their feet on decaying lichen
the cricket's son does laborious needlework on his body
and then there is evil, tearing apart his face on a drum
his body now filled entirely with death's glory
entirely, one story tells his entire past
one story tells his entire past
one thin lanky man sits resting on a tree stump
the first time the sun reads his eyes closely
and closer still it sits on his knees
the sun makes smoke between his fingers
every night I fix my telescope on that spot
until the moment the sun dies out
a tree stump takes its rest where he sat
more silent than a cabbage patch in May
the horse he drove walks past in the early morning

death has already fragmented into a mound of pure glass
the sun has already become the thunder rolling down the road of
    the mourners returning home
and the children's slender feet tiptoe onto evergreen olive branches
and my head swells up, like millions of horse hooves stamping
    on drums
compared to big, crude, curved knives, death is a mere grain of sand
so one story tells his entire life
so a thousand years turn away their face – look
    1983[35]

This is a pre-exilic poem. The 'story that tells his entire past' is a story told in the language of cinematic montage. Although a single story is sufficient to tell an entire past, there is no regular narrative and any notion of normal time is suspended early in the poem: 'all days will squeeze into one day/thus, every day will have an extra day'. Bachelard's 'stabilised moment', the poetic instant, is instantiated in this poem again and again. In seeking to cleave out of real time a poetic instant in which time moves vertically, the language of the poem deploys metaphors of the body and of motion and stasis to inscribe time's physical arrest: the sun is prevented from rising further, its 'head' is pressed down and a morning is made to remain. Time fails to move on. The pendulum is broken and 'time, rots beyond the tick-tocking of the clock'. And then real time returns as 'every night I fix my telescope on that spot/ until the moment the sun dies out'. In this recounting of a death, a ceremony of one person's or many people's death, historical time, 'a thousand years turn away their face'. Again, time is timeless, and death which marches together with time is a mere 'surplus heartbeat', has 'fragmented', is but a 'grain of sand', as if without real time there is no real death. But after the poetic instant there is the return to real time, and after the worked time which has produced the poetic instant, a heightened sense of death's reality and inevitability.

    Chinese society is now converging with other spectacular societies to become an integrated society of the spectacle. Thus to stop time in the new China is to threaten the newly emerged

---

[35] Duoduo, manuscript.

commodity-oriented society. The spectacle must not, cannot stop. Ordinary time speeds on, from commodity to commodity, from image to image, never proffering the pause of a stabilised moment, so that

> incomprehension is present everywhere in everyday encounters. Something must be specified, made clear, but there's not enough time and you are not sure of having been understood. Before you have done or said what was necessary, you've already gone. Across the street. Overseas. There will never be another chance.[36]

In *Society of the Spectacle*, Debord writes that

> individual experience of separate daily life remains without language, without concept, without critical access to its own past which has been recorded nowhere. It is not communicated. It is not understood and is forgotten to the profit of the false spectacular memory of the unmemorable.[37]

A handful of contemporary Chinese poets are among the few cultural producers who have attempted to record the past of Chinese spectacular society, and just as Marina Tsvetaeva attempted to deploy poetry as a historical and critical discourse, so in China the poets of the 1970s sought to use 'the experience of separate daily life' to recreate a critical language. Perhaps such an attempt can only be made before the 'time of image consumption'.[38] While in China during the first thirty years of the People's Republic there was a surfeit of official spectacle, the dominance of the moving image, of televised spectacle had not been established. Similarly, the poetry that Bachelard employs as his example was produced before the spectacular society had displaced bourgeois society. In the integrated spectacular society, the possibility of effecting a stabilised moment is increasingly rare. In British and American poetic production it has been scarce since the 1950s, since Dylan Thomas's 'Do not go gentle into that good night' raged

---

[36] Debord, 'Critique of Separation' in Knabb 34.

[37] (Detroit: Black and Red, 1983) 157. Translation of *La société du spectacle* (Paris: Buchet-Chastel, 1967).

[38] *Ibid.* 153.

'against the dying of the light' and urged violent, if futile, defiance of time and death.[39]

The reason why death recurs so persistently in the poetry of Mang Ke and Duoduo is not simply a function of the historical trajectory that took them through the Chinese Cultural Revolution when the sight of corpses discarded in the schoolyard or on the street corner was all too common. The preoccupation with death is more than a negotiation of the specificity of recent Chinese history. It is a reaction against the elision of death in all spectacular societies. What is not registered by the spectacular society, either diffuse or concentrated, is precisely death. 'One who has renounced using his life can no longer admit his death.' As Debord explains, death is socially absent just as is life.[40] When the Great Helmsman, Mao Zedong, shone like the sun, radiated his divine aura, death did not happen, its naming was taboo. When in Dengist China the commodity is everything, not even the menace of the death penalty, meted out for a whole range of 'economic' crimes, is sufficient to deter such crimes. That 'life is cheap' in Asia is a popular Orientalist *idée reçue*, which seeks to explain inhumane actions by allusion to a feudal tradition. But China is no longer a feudal society, it has moved forward into the time of spectacular society where the 'spectator's consciousness. . . no longer experiences its life as a passage toward self-realization and toward death.'[41] Hence the importance of the poets', especially Duoduo's, insistence on 'death'. These poems are not simply, if at all, a meditation on or a negotiation of the killing and lived misery of recent Chinese history, but a more general attempt to foreground the 'existence of irreversible time in the expenditure of an in-

[39] *Collected Poems 1934-1952* (London: J.M. Dent, 1972) 159. Paradoxically, Thomas in his brief poetic career exploited to the full the technology of the phonogram and of radio broadcasting, yet missed the full blooming of spectacular society of which he would undoubtedly have been a commodity. It was left to John Betjeman to offer up mundane and safe lyrics to the sterile camera lens of British spectacular society.

[40] Debord, *Society of the Spectacle* 160.

[41] *Ibid.*

dividual life', life which is a 'mere accessory from the point of view of modern production' whether in Detroit or Wuhan.[42] Death, then, is employed as a metaphor, although not in any traditional religious sense, for emancipation. Death is the imagined space that lies beyond the reach of society's dominators, the space that 'makes them hate'.[43] Dylan Thomas established a similar nexus when he seized death in a poetic moment 'as time's jacket or the coat of ice', and froze the instant when 'like a running grave, time tracks you down.' Our relation to Nature measured by time is ineffable in the spectacular society of consumption, in this 'kissproof world' of 'city tar and subway bored to foster/Man through macadam.'[44] 'It is an act of love to think of the dead. It is an act of love to write of the dead', and the society of the spectacle 'knows nothing of love, though the word falls constantly from the lips of its propagandists.'[45]

It is not the death that follows life that inspires dread and anxiety so much as the death that is survival. 'Survival', as Vaneigem insists, 'is centered on negativity'. In China's post-Mao socio-economy, survival has become 'reality reduced to the perspective of the market' whose imperative 'according to the ideology of industrial societies is called "economic necessity" '.[46] After the despair of the Cultural Revolution era, 'emancipation' has given rise to the bondage and negativity of the market. Denying the human and inverting 'human growth this negativity creates a dialectic of death in which every life becomes the nothingness to which it was doomed initially.'[47]

[42] *Ibid.*

[43] Duoduo, *Looking Out From Death: From the Cultural Revolution to Tiananmen Square*, trans. Gregory Lee and John Cayley (London: Bloomsbury, 1989) 81.
[44] 'When, Like a Running Grave', *Collected Poems* 16-17.
[45] Baxendale 44.

[46] Raoul Vaneigem, *The Movement of the Free Spirit: General Considerations and Firsthand Testimony Concerning Some Brief Flowering of Life in the Middle Ages, the Renaissance and, Incidentally, Our Own Time* (New York: Zone Books, 1994) 244.
[47] *Ibid.*

Language, destruction, poetry: 'knocking on hollow words'

'The appropriation of language is both the labyrinth and the Ariadne's thread that lead to the heart of life, to the latencies that wait to be born in each of us, and which economic necessity paralyzes and corrupts with its universal negativity and its fundamental inhumanity.'

—Raoul Vaneigem[48]

Revising an earlier pronouncement in *Critique of Culture and Society*, that 'writing a poem after Auschwitz is barbarous', Adorno in *Negative Dialectics* writes that 'it may have been wrong to say that after Auschwitz you can no longer write poems'. However, Adorno writing as a survivor, with 'the drastic guilt of he who was spared', persists in wondering about the 'less cultural question': 'whether you can go on living'.[49] He reveals a belief that poetry is but a mere 'expression' of life. Henri Meschonnic criticises Adorno for this move, claiming that he 'only aggravates the distance between language and life'.[50]

It was with reinventing language that many of the young urban 'survivors' of the Cultural Revolution chose to renegotiate and re-record the past and to imagine the future. Given 'the irreducible centrality of language in all social acts', its denaturalisation, its 'refashioning' was a priority:[51]

> With refashioned tools refashion language
> with refashioned language
> continue to refashion[52]

Deleuze describes this literary function in language as designing a type of foreign language 'which is not another language, nor a recovered dialect but the becoming-other of

[48] *Ibid.* 243.
[49] Theodor W. Adorno, *Negative Dialectics*, E.B. Ashton (New York: Continuum, 1973) 362-3.
[50] 'Le Langage chez Adorno ou Presque comme dans la musique', *Revue de Sciences Humaines* 229 (January–March 1993), 116.
[51] *Ibid.* 116.
[52] Duoduo, *Looking Out From Death*, 112. Revised translation.

the language, a making minor of this major language.'[53] What
is drawn is a 'sorcerer's line which escapes from the dominant
system.'[54] And the 'becoming of the language' is found in
syntactical creation. While one of the operations of literature
is 'a decomposition or destruction of the mother tongue', a
second aspect is the 'invention of a new language in the
language', achieved by syntactical creation.[55] Deleuze cites
André Dhôtel: 'The only way to defend a language is to attack
it.'[56]

Syntactical creation is the essence of much of the 'unofficial'
Chinese poetic production of the last fifteen years, and in a
number of Duoduo's poems the question of language is made
central. One of his post-exile poems, 'There is No' (*Mei you*),
for instance, constructs a repetitive, rhythmic, pessimistic
negativity of lugubrious silence where communication and
salutation are absent, a space where there are no borders,

> except for language. facing the land with its lost border
> except for the tulips' flourishing fresh flesh, facing windows
>   unclosed into the night
> except for my window, facing my no longer comprehensible language

But the language that resists comprehension is no sooner
invoked than it becomes absent altogether:

> there is no language
>
> there is only light repeatedly grinding, grinding
> that repeatedly worked saw at daybreak.[57]

The poem tells of a process, and the poem itself is part of a
literary process. Language self-consciously tells of its own
disappearance, only to be recreated in the telling of its own
destruction. The poem itself as its descends through vertical

[53] Gilles Deleuze, *Critique et clinique* (Paris: Les Éditions de Minuit, 1993) 15.
[54] *Ibid.*
[55] *Ibid.*
[56] *Ibid.*
[57] *Manhattan Review* 6, 2 (1992).

time traces a 'sorcerer's line' of hope through its own horizontal narrative of negation.

Deleuze indicates a further aspect of literature's work in language that is found on the underside or the outside of language and consists of 'sights and hearings which are no longer a part of any language'.[58] Deleuze's morphology of literature recalls Bachelard's theory of stabilised, poetic moments, when he designates these ideas, heard and seen in the 'interstices of the language, in its gaps', as stationary moments (*haltes*) which are not interruptions of the process, but rather part of it 'like an eternity which can only be revealed in the becoming, a landscape which can only be seen in movement'. These 'ideas' are not outside of language, but *are* its very outside.[59]

Adorno wondered how people could conceive of writing poetry, indeed how they could conceive of living, after knowledge of the concentration camps. Perhaps only the denaturalisation of language, the production of 'poetic instants', can, after such historical moments, provide the means to negotiate sentiment, the means to reorient the mind towards logic and sanity, to replenish the resources of hope we need to carry us through, and more importantly to help us construct the necessary matrices for change. It is in the language of lyrics that such change can be actively imagined. Poetry 'refuses preambles, principles, methods, proofs' and by 'knocking on hollow words, silences prose', writes Bachelard.[60] Such was the objective of the 1970s and 1980s underground or 'unofficial' poetry in China. This need to take back language necessitated a struggle to refuse coherence, to defy eventual naturalisations of the texts. But the reader constantly attempts to make readable these texts. Any reader with an acquaintance with recent Chinese history and society will always be led to historicise and contextualise the texts of contemporary Chinese poetry. Specifically, the reader may try to anchor them in the

[58] Deleuze 16.

[59] *Ibid.*

[60] Bachelard 224.

material reality of the 1970s, 1980s and 1990s. I defend attempts to read them in that way. If the texts defy such readings we can start to ask why and how. But any reader who refuses to attempt such readings should also ask herself or himself: why? Naturally, attempts to read in the light of socio-historical conditions must be tempered by a sensitivity to a wider context and to global phenomena. Modern Chinese poets increasingly write in an economically and semiotically globalised context. They are the poets of (post-)modernity. That is not to say that they write 'world poetry' but each writes a poetry informed by her or his own personal experience of the late twentieth century, which is for some nowadays an exilic experience but in any case a lived experience of turn-of-the-century spectacular society. The questions posed by (post-)modernity are no longer addressed by poets of the 'Western world' alone.

Practice out of poetry: a 'struggle for spiritual liberation'

'What better way could there be of abolishing the poem than realizing it?'

—Raoul Vaneigem[61]

'The medieval assassins founded a "State" which consisted of a network of remote mountain valleys and castles,. . . connected by the information flow of secret agents, at war with all governments, and devoted only to knowledge. Modern technology, culminating in the spy satellite, makes this kind of *autonomy* a romantic dream. No more pirate islands!. . . Are we who live in the present doomed never to experience autonomy, never to stand for one moment on a bit of land ruled over only by freedom?'

—Hakim Bey[62]

Hakim Bey's utopias, what he calls 'pirate utopias', are based on the existence in the eighteenth century of the navigation

---

[61] *The Revolution of Everyday Life* (London: Rebel Press/Left Bank Books, 1994) 202.

[62] Hakim Bey 98.

network, the means by which commerce was pursued. There were many islands in this network, points of replenishment and trade. 'Some of these islands supported "intentional communities", whole mini-societies living consciously outside the law and determined to keep it up, even if only for a short but merry life.'[63]

Bey's response to the loss of pirate utopias suggests that a substitute, a 'kind of "free enclave" is not only possible in our time but also existent'. Bey imagines, with wilful ambiguity, the 'concept of the TEMPORARY AUTONOMOUS ZONE' or TAZ. Tantalisingly Bey proclaims: 'If the phrase became current it would be understood without difficulty. . . understood in action.'[64]

The map of the USA, Bey reminds us, 'is an abstraction', 'a political abstract grid'. But the map is not accurate and 'enfolded immensities escape the measuring rod.' The map of France, the map of Britain, the map of China soon to (re)cover Hong Kong are not accurate either. The isocultural lines on the chart can never accurately map cultural differences. China's regnant authority wants to erase cultural difference, wants China to be a map of rigid grid lines. Such a project is described by Bey as the 'surveying and mapmaking and "psychic imperialism"' of the state.[65] China's and India's concerns over and efforts towards controlling satellite broadcasting are indicative of the state's endeavours to retain a monopoly over such 'psychic imperialism' at a time when it is increasingly usurped by supranational entities whose allegiance is to the new imperialism of the global spectacle whose maps are the footprints of satellite broadcasting. Simply because a map is virtually identical with the territory it shows, it cannot control it; and a satellite footprint is not, at least not yet, commensurate with the tread of the jackboot. So Bey sees the possibility of exploiting '"spaces" (geographical, social, cultural, imaginal)' which have the potential to become

[63] *Ibid.* 97.
[64] *Ibid.* 98-9.
[65] *Ibid.* 103.

autonomous zones. But the mapmakers of the Chinese state, like imperialist states before it, are unlikely to overlook such spaces. Hong Kong is a space which has been subject to the 'surveying and mapmaking and "psychic imperialism" ' of not one but two states. While it is not necessarily territorial space that is coterminous with an autonomous zone, the difficulties that 'unofficial' cultural and political movements have experienced in the People's Republic do not bode well for Hong Kong. Even now TAZs are scarce in Hong Kong. British colonialism, as odious as any colonising structure and ideology the world has known, after being shaken by riots and resistance in the 1960s and 1970s negotiated a spectacular society based on a bonanza of consumption for the colonised and a larger share of the economic pie for the local bourgeoisie. The result is a peculiarly neo-colonialist – Hong Kong has not known and will not know post-colonialism – form of spectacular society in which compliance and silence are purchaseable commodities and where only commodities are negotiable.

Bey's idea of TAZs is problematic, but at least hopeful and applicable to Hong Kong; such zones of autonomy are interjected into spectacular society even if for the briefest moments. At least the theory and practice of TAZs are an imaginable phenomenon in the colony of Hong Kong, whereas the 'modern intellectuals' affirmative version of the "public sphere" ' which is 'increasingly and unfailingly dragged out of retirement' is as inapplicable to Hong Kong as it is to China. It remains a concept 'haunted by the ascetic regime of its architects and only true practitioners – European bourgeois men in the eighteenth century'.[66]

In his essay on Temporary Autonomous Zones, Hakim Bey cites two instances of what may have been historical material instantiations of the poetic instant. Both occurred in the immediate aftermath of the First World War.

In 1919 a poetically inspired revolution established the

[66] Andrew Ross, 'The Rock 'n' Roll Ghost', review of *Lipstick Traces: A Secret History of the Twentieth Century*, by Greil Marcus, *October* 50 (Fall 1989) 108-17.

Revolutionary Republic of Bavaria. The pacifist, independent socialist Kurt Eisner, the founder of the short-lived 1919 Bavarian *Räterepublik*, or Council Republic, which drew its support from Munich's working class and marginalised groups, 'believed quite literally that poets and poetry should form the basis of the revolution'.[67] Eisner, who advocated direct participatory democracy through revolutionary councils, saw politics as a creative process and considered it delusory to believe political ambitions could be realised without 'poetic power'. The victim of an anti-Semitic press campaign, Eisner was assassinated by a young nationalist aristocrat, Count Anton von Arco-Valley.[68] Following weeks of confusion and in the wake of the declaration of a soviet republic in Hungary, the Bavarian soviet republic was declared. Its head was the Expressionist playwright-poet Ernst Toller, its Minister for Education a literary critic and intellectual, the anarcho-socialist Gustav Landauer. The republic was opposed not only by the right but also by the KPD, the German Communist Party.

For a week in early April there was interjected into the Central European heartland not simply a revolutionary moment, but an extended poetic instant. Landauer, whose philosophy was 'essentially a poetic interpretation' of the European anarchist tradition, believed that the language of science was incapable of expressing the essence of reality, which could only be conveyed 'indirectly through poetic language and image'.[69] After six days there was a counter-revolutionary putsch, followed by a workers' action which the Communists exploited to seize power. A Red Army was formed, not around the Communists but around Toller, the pacifist poet, who was acclaimed its commander. After an initial period of sensational victories, the revolution was crushed.[70] Toller was charged with high treason and at his trial

---

[67] Bey 127.

[68] Richard Dove, *He was a German: A Biography of Ernst Toller* (London: Libris, 1990) 67.

[69] *Ibid.* 37-8.

[70] James Joll, *Europe since 1870* (Harmondsworth: Penguin, 1983) 249-50. The

declared: 'You say the revolution is merely a wage struggle by the workers and thus seek to denigrate it. . . . But you will also find a great longing for art and culture, a struggle for spiritual liberation.'[71] He spent five years in gaol. Victor Serge recalled seeing Toller after his release at a Writers' Union meeting in Moscow:

One day in a small, dark meeting-room. . . we heard a report from Averbach on the spirit of the proletariat, the collective farm, and Bolshevism in literature. Lunacharsky, frozen in a stance of weary boredom. . . spoke nothing but a few quasi-official remarks, in terms more intelligent than the official speaker had used. Between the two of us Ernst Toller was seated, lately released from a Bavarian prison. Bit by bit the whole deadening speech was translated for him, and in his great dark eyes, in his face of strength and gentleness, a kind of confusion could be seen. Surely in his years of imprisonment as an insurgent poet, he had pictured the literature of the Soviets as altogether different from this.[72]

Toller and the other leaders of the anti-authoritarian and libertarian Munich revolution had known from the outset that their soviet would be of limited duration, a mere poetic instant incised into the relentless and dominant logic of twentieth-century modernisation.[73] The Bavarian republic, supported by both working class and avant-garde, has been described as 'a little ludicrous', but, as Bey has noted, had the soviet 'lasted even a year, we would weep at the mention of its beauty – but before even the first flowers of that Spring has wilted, the *geist* and the spirit of poetry were crushed, and we have forgotten'.[74]

Communists took over. They in turn were ousted by the army, and the Social Democrats were restored to power.

[71] From the proceedings of the Bavarian *Landtag* session, 21 December 1921, cited in Dove 93.

[72] Victor Serge, *Memoirs of a Revolutionary*, trans. Peter Sedgwick (London: Oxford University Press, 1963; Writers and Readers, 1984) 272. See also Ernst Toller's autobiography *Eine Jugend in Deutschland* (1933) which recounts the story of the Munich Revolution. Toller committed suicide in New York in 1939.

[73] Bey 127.

[74] Joll 249; Bey 127.

The second poetic instant to erupt in post-First World War Europe has been referred to as the 'madcap Republic of Fiume', an interruption of the dominant order that was '*not meant to endure*'.[75] The Adriatic port-city of Fiume, part of Austria-Hungary until 1918, had an ethnically mixed population; two-thirds were Italian, the remainder southern Slavs.[76] At the head of an irregular army, a man known as 'the Poet' took the city by force on 13 September 1919.[77] The independent enclave survived by piracy for over a year. Artists, bohemians, anarchists, stateless persons, homosexuals and other excluded individuals flocked to participate in the new aesthetically oriented republic, which claimed music to be its central principle. The Italian authorities, believing it was denigrating 'the Poet' Gabriele D'Annunzio's action, designated the liberation of Fiume as a 'literary expedition' or 'literary *coup d'état*'.[78]

The lyrical government of Fiume, whose constitution was framed as a revival of medieval Italian communes, devoted itself not to economic or military performance but quite simply to performance: 'Every morning D'Annunzio read poetry and manifestos from his balcony; every evening a concert, then fireworks.'[79] D'Annunzio had long been a showman, and his ideal republic, while equipped with a constitution full of revolutionary intent, was ruled in more dirigiste fashion; indeed the constitution itself allowed for the *Commandante* to be given full powers when the Free State of Fiume was menaced by 'grave peril'.[80] D'Annunzio designed a new

---

[75] Bey 125.

[76] President Wilson at the Versailles peace conference did not extend his principle of self-determination to the residents of Fiume, who had decided on 30 October 1918 to be united with Italy, preferring to bolster the monarchy of Yugoslavia, which wanted a port. The Italian government acquiesced and Italian public opinion turned against it.

[77] Francis Lacassin, preface to Albert Londres, *D'Annunzio, conquérant de Fiume* (Paris: Julliard, 1990) 8-9.

[78] *Ibid.* 9.

[79] Joll 265; Bey 125-6.

[80] Article XLIII, published by Jacques Benoist-Méchin in *La Pensée nationale* (November-December) 1975; reproduced in Londres 247-71.

form of liturgy in Fiume 'which would play a very important role in the evolution of civic festivals and the development of mass politics in the modern world.'[81] D'Annunzio it was who at Fiume reinstated the Roman salute. The performative aspect of D'Annunzio's régime, mimicked by the inventor of Italian Fascism, Mussolini, was also the precursor of a spectacular form of power, and it is unsurprising that D'Annunzio and his ideas were ultimately diverted by *Il Duce*. Nor can it be said that D'Annunzio's patriotism derived from a benign pride for a young nation. His nationalism, as evidenced by his poetic collection *Praise for the Sky, Sea, Earth and Heroes* (1904-12), was fervently 'Latin' and explicitly expansionist, harking back to the Roman empire, and looking forward to an overseas Italian empire. After all, he had initially seized Fiume to reunite it with the new, vigorous Italy. While Bey may be right to describe the Fiume republic as 'the last of the pirate utopias', it is doubtful whether it really was 'very nearly the first modern TAZ'.[82] D'Annunzio was a bellicose patriot and a romantic; choosing his crew for the mellifluence of their names, he once set sail for Venice in a boat named, in homage to Shelley, *Lady Clara*.[83] The Expressionist anarcho-socialist, pacifist and reluctant military commander, Toller, on the other hand, participated in a moment of a different sort of poetry – surely the precursor of really autonomous zones.

Old utopias, new zones

Baudrillard describes America as 'utopia realised'; a society founded on the idea that it is 'the realisation of what all the others have dreamed about'.[84] For the French, at least, 'America' seems to have furnished a space of mediation

[81] Michael A. Ledeen, *The First Duce* (Baltimore, MD: Johns Hopkins University Press, 1977) 148.
[82] Bey 126.
[83] Londres 10.
[84] Baudrillard 76-7.

beyond the mundane imbalanced dualities of Paris – province, centre – region. Claude Sicre, of Toulouse/Tolosa, discussing the relationship between provincial culture and that of the France of the dominant centralising French ideology, explains: 'We did not belong to that world, and our prejudices even prevented us from seeing its successes where they occurred'. Blind and deaf to everything (Parisian) French, just as Parisians were to everything 'provincial', there was 'one common point for dialogue, Amerika [Américke]'.[85] American (or rather utopian Amerikan) culture thus provided the contentious nexus between centre and region, and yet the resultant mimicry was sterile and disillusioning:

As it is always with all these abstractions and 'incommunications' thousands of kids cast aside thousands of guitars every year, genuinely disappointed not to have become the great Rolling Stones, or more simple little Ferrés, unable for a moment to imagine that there could be other models, other ways out.[86]

Rejecting the statism of the 'eternal France of official lies', Sicre is also wary of the lure of a bourgeois Occitania, of the folklore of a bygone ruralism, and 'its ally, academic ethnology', coupled with a 'mystical call to modernity'. That way lies the route to another nationalism along the lines of Catalonia, behind which, as Sicre shrewdly discerns, lies the French centralising model itself. Is the only alternative then 'a vague space of an even vaguer melting pot', the renunciation of identity?[87] The alternative Sicre proposes is not Occitan nationalism but Occitan culture; to which he imputes the function of contesting that which refuses it as culture. Occitan culture can be instrumental in reformulating, reimagining France and Frenchness: 'Occitan culture does not contest any France, since it is itself French. . . Occitan culture is the future of French culture.'[88] Occitania is France's unconscious. But

[85] Claude Sicre, *Vive l'Américke!* (Paris and Toulouse: Publisud, Collection les Pierres du Temps, 1988) 29.
[86] *Ibid.*
[87] *Ibid.* 33.
[88] *Ibid.* 43-4.

aware of the danger of substituting one totalising ideology for another, Sicre adds that the unconscious of Occitania is Normandy, Picardy and 'all above the Loire that gets confused with Paris in the nordic fog'.[89]

This is not a multi-culturalism, but a pluri-culturalism which if restricted to mere *tolerance* for 'peripheral particularisms' would be devoid of sense, would fall into the trap of reproducing in communities a 'nationalism *à la française*' and of 'employing as a mirror that which ought to be rejected'.[90] Yet the contemporary reality of 'injustice done to indigenous and immigrant cultures in France can only be revealed' by the blues and the Occitan language, not through 'traditional music'.[91] 'The Occitan blues is the only hope, the last hope, for the Francophone author-composer-singer.'[92] The hybrid Occitan blues, the *blues d'oc*, a music of *ouverture totale* (complete opening up), operates like a poetry effecting a stabilised moment. 'The adversary of all ethnocentrism, of all racisms, of all inquisitions, of all dictatorships, of all unitarisms', the *blues d'oc* when taken to the local communities of Occitania has the power to surprise, open people's minds and give voice to the dumb. Occitan folklore is no more; it is not even a reinvented folklore. There is simply a 'will', *une volonté*, a space for the 'great people of cut-off languages to awake, polyglot'.[93]

If Occitania is France's unconscious, can we imagine a Chinese unconscious? Where would it be located if not in Hong Kong? Cantonese Hong Kong and Mandarin Beijing are the north-south poles of China.

Is there an emancipatory and hopeful 'hybridity' which is not the hybridity negatively critiqued by Rey Chow but which has the features of that 'alternative community' she

---

[89] *Ibid.* 44.
[90] *Ibid.*
[91] *Ibid.* 44-6.
[92] *Ibid.* 75.
[93] *Ibid.* 51.

describes as containing 'neither roots nor hybrids'?[94] I think that there could be and it would have much to do with the potential and space afforded by Hong Kong's own language, a language which is neither English nor standard Chinese (Mandarin/Putonghua), but 'the "vulgar" language in practical daily use – a combination of Cantonese, broken English, and written Chinese, a language that is often enunciated with jovial irony and cynicism'.[95] Hong Kong's young generations are not sufficiently well trained in standard written Chinese, and there is even less prospect of a written Cantonese attaining authority outside comic books and popular romances. Cantonese culture, then, is largely mass culture; and given the popularity of Hong Kong film and music, it is overwhelmingly a visual and aural culture. The still largely colonialist and élitist cultural institutions of Hong Kong, its schools and universities, do not valorise the serious study of popular culture, and so the value and significance of Hong Kong culture itself are elided. Even those whose intention it is to introduce Western cultural theory to Hong Kong dismiss Hong Kong's culture as 'low brow'. The 'civilising mission' of the coloniser is the still dominant mentality of many a colonialist educator.

If Hong Kong could efface this élitist colonisation of the mind before a new cultural centralising force is substituted for it, the interjection of the necessary conditions for the proliferation of TAZs and the eventual overturning of the culture of survival might yet be possible. However, as things stand, the culture of survival is barely challenged. Made more palatable by the provision of the 'pleasures' of gluttonous consumption, the taming of Hong Kong has been achieved through the reduction of human beings to an automatised existence predicated upon extreme forms of alienation both in terms of relations between people and the dominative relation of

[94] Rey Chow, 'Between Colonizers: Hong Kong's Postcolonial Self-Writing in the 1990s', *Diaspora*, 2, 2 (1992) 163.
[95] *Ibid.* 154-5.

people to Nature, which has embroiled Hong Kong in the production of a social and ecological Hades.

While the possibility of its being realised presently seems slight, the potential for cultural and social decentralisation does exist. The reality of cultural life in China, the spread of audio-visual technology, a burgeoning urban class from Taiwan to Shanghai will surely disintegrate the monologic and monolingual frame the centre has imposed for so many decades. There is no reason why Cantonese should not be China's 'unconscious', no reason why Hong Kong should not perform a more critical and emancipatory function as the temporary locomotive of decentralisation for the other communities of non-Mandarin-speaking China, indeed for all Chinese communities looking for an anti-hegemonic model. Surely that is the very reason why the Beijing authorities are obliged to seek to suffocate, as in Macao, a real post-colonial future for a truly decolonised post-imperialist Hong Kong.

If the majority of Hong Kong's people were not faced with such an uncertain future, if the virus of impotence were not endemic, if colonialist educators would retreat or facilitate the valorisation of their student's culture rather than seek to embed themselves and their values, if the colonialist custodians of cultural authenticity would abandon the implantation of the colonialist classical canon rather than merely seek to reauthorise and supplement it by means of post-modern theory, then I would more confidently propose that it is precisely the very unterritoriality, and the lack of concern with political authority (and lack of *political* power with which to defy it), which could be deployed in a way analogous to Sicre's imagined future for Occitan culture. Just as 'Occitan culture does not contest any France, since it is itself French', Hong Kong culture cannot contest any China.[96] It is this superficial lack of contestatory power that could be Hong Kong's strength. Certainly, Hong Kong's menace to Beijing stems from its cultural otherness. That otherness is what I would

[96] Sicre 43-4.

refer to as a hybrid otherness, not what Chow interprets as 'post-modern hybridity' but rather what she calls 'inter-semioticity' and which she sees in the pop singer-songwriter Luo Dayou's recent work. What I find valuable in her reading of his lyrics, and which is very similar to the intersemioticity of Claude Sicre's *blues d'oc*, is his 'articulation of an alternative community'.[97] Luo Dayou's music rejects the 'themes of tradition versus modernity, and ethnicity versus inter-nationalism' in its concern for the social problems that Hong Kong shares with the other cities of the world.[98] Similarly, Sicre rejects a folkloric nostalgia for a medieval Occitania, which of course as a political entity never existed, instead privileging a contemporary conceptual network of Occitan cities and their satellite towns and villages. Sicre promotes a progressive hybridity, an intersemioticity of a local culture resistant to the metropolis; a culture in parallel, and indebted, to an already intersemiotic and hybrid musical and spiritual tradition of poor American blacks:

The blues, musical language of the poor old blacks of the rural South, children of slaves in the richest country in the world, becoming in three decades, step by step, the musical model for the wealthy, urban, white youth of all the Western Norths and industrial capitals, the source and sustenance of a cultural revolution the world over.

The Occitan language, language of the lowest of the plebs and of a few regionalists without power (in the face of the latest street slang); literary language (concealed by the textbooks) of the idealist, self-taught (in the face of the worldly academic of the capital), provincial intellectual (the last thing to be!); forgotten language of all the provincial Rastignacs in search of salons, plural (multiplicity of *parlers*) anti-academic language, language fixed in time, *finally and above all a classless and stateless language*. . . which has nothing to lose and absolutely *nothing to gain*. . . language of realisable dreams. . . Dragging in its wake all the indigenous

[97] Chow 164.

[98] *Ibid.* 163-4. The fact that Luo Dayou no longer lives and works permanently in Hong Kong, although he does continue to produce and distribute his music there, has been understood by some as an abandonment or betrayal of Hong Kong. In fact, it reveals that he refuses to reinscribe the stasis of the traditional 'patriotic' Chinese cultural producer by investing all his creative energies in one 'cause' and one territory. Luo Dayou and Hong Kong shared a moment; he participated in a TAZ.

or immigrant languages and cultures of France to sow the seed of a new *universalist thought*. A revolution through poetry, philosophy, imagination and laughter under the reign of economism and merchandise of class, State, region.[99]

Both the kind of 'alternative community' that Chow discerns as Luo Dayou's project and Sicre's promotion of a non-nationalistic space called Occitania relate to and depend on real and extant cultural communities. These are marginalised and bastard communities, which know the meaning of past and present injustices. These are what I intend by 'hybrid' communities. They are not national cultural communities; but then, as Todorov has demonstrated, a common culture is not necessarily national and generally is 'of a smaller size', and moreover 'it can also be transnational'.[100]

Like Occitan (a 'language which doesn't know and has never known *its own name*'), the language of Hong Kong has 'nothing to lose and absolutely nothing to gain', yet its speakers may have a great deal to gain in asserting the cultural currency of their language. While Sicre's strategy – challenging dominant power by not directly challenging it on its own terms – may seem utopian, he and those like Zebda whom he has inspired have already had success in establishing at least moments and spaces of autonomy. Such temporary and not so temporary communities constitute an answer to Hakim Bey's concern over the lack of contemporary potential for the assertion of autonomy, and whether 'we who live in the present [are] doomed never to experience autonomy, never to stand for one moment on a bit of land ruled over only by freedom'.[101] The post-colonial city, the currently British 'dependent territory' (a euphemism for the now ineffable but still very real 'colony'), the future 'special administrative region' of Hong Kong may offer, as Chow suggests, 'a third space

[99] Sicre 91; Rastignac is a character in Balzac's *Comédie humaine*; an impoverished provincial noble.

[100] Tzvetan Todorov, *Nous et les autres. La réflexion française sur la diversité humaine* (Paris: Editions du Seuil, 1989) 241.

[101] Sicre 91; Bey 98.

between the colonizer and the dominative native culture', a space which foregrounds concerns 'which exceed national boundaries'.[102] While it may be too early to judge, it may also be too late.

Over the last few decades, a distinct culture has developed in Hong Kong which is a hybridisation of local and transnational cultures. It may overlap with the Chinese nation-state's culture, but it is already something else. The Chinese 'nation-as-state, a country separated from others by political frontiers' will in all probability culturally as well as politically incorporate Hong Kong within its boundaries. However, in doing so it will reveal the abstract quality of the cartography of its cultural imaginary and expose even more clearly that the 'nation-as-state' only partly coincides with the 'nation-as-culture'. Despite previously somewhat successful attempts to impose a national cultural consciousness, the disjuncture that is already evident elsewhere in China, manifested both in local cultural communities and in 'national' sub-cultural divergence, will be intensified. What we already know, that while the state and the cultural 'nation' are frequently connected 'the concepts themselves are independent, and to a certain degree opposed', will be reaffirmed.[103]

'Here we are, the dead of all times, dying once again, but now with the objective of living.'

—Zapatista communiqué[104]

'The appearance of new necessities', wrote Debord and Wolman in 1956, 'outmodes previous "inspired" works. . . . We have to go beyond them.'[105] Not only in the sphere of theory

[102] Chow 158.

[103] Todorov 241.

[104] Statement of 6 January 1994. Cited in Marc Cooper, *The Zapatistas: Starting from Chiapas* (Westfield, NJ: Open Magazine pamphlet series, no. 30, February 1994) 14.

[105] Guy Debord and Gil J. Wolman, 'Methods of Detournment', *Les Lèvres nues* 8 May 1956 in Knabb 9.

but also in praxis, *bricolage* (patching things up, concocting something new out of what is to hand) ought to be regnant. 'Any elements, no matter where they are taken from, can serve in making new combinations. . . . Anything can be used.'[106] It is no mere coincidence that Debord and Wolman in their advocacy of a methodology of mimicry, parody and plagiarism should cite the instance of modern poetry whose discoveries 'regarding the analogical structure of images demonstrate that when two objects are brought together, no matter how far apart their original contexts may be, a relationship is always formed.'[107] We ought not to set out to pay attention to lyrics in order to discern an author's intentions, or to critique the failings and lacunae of a text, or simply to praise what we like, but rather in order to help ourselves imagine and reimagine. This 'reading', then, is active; it is to raid, to redeploy, to recontextualise the reflections and meditations of others. This activity in itself produces a hybridity, but then every mind, every social imaginary is surely a hybrid fabric of ideas and hopes and dreams. It is not the hybrid that is impure and inauthentic, but the idea of 'authenticity' and 'purity' that is a deception which leads ineluctably to fanaticism, exclusion and genocide.

The processes of hybridity, as I understand them, are the processes of renewal and of meaningful and emancipatory change. The deployment of a strategy of intersemiotic hybridity is, it seems to me, the way forward culturally and politically to greater and more frequent zone-moments of autonomy. The seemingly 'politically' powerless, for instance Occitania, the internally colonised dominated by one of the most centralising and interventionist states in modern history, subjected to an imposed, dominant national and international culture, has successfully begun the process of asserting divergent and alternative cultures. Such cultural power is exceptionally effective politically in confronting a state whose

[106] Ibid.
[107] *Ibid.*

power depends on its historico-cultural claims to legitimacy. Similarly, the poetic moment produced by the 'refashioned' poetic language of Duoduo, Mang Ke and others slits open the veils of the once concentrated, now integrated spectacular society, exposing the inherent conservatism and nostalgia of an ideology shrouded in the threadbare clothes of an increasingly feeble nationalism and dedicated to a preservation of the present and its order.

Where the process of the eventual abolition of poetry through its realisation will start is not known – perhaps in China, perhaps in France, perhaps in the Mexican Chiapas – but the poem when made will without doubt be a hybrid epic of life and not an 'authentic' dirge of survival. In conclusion, I leave the reader with these sanguine words of Raoul Vaneigem:

After 10,000 years of lamentation and a few years of bankruptcy... it may occur to late twentieth-century consciousness that the true meaning of destiny is to create life and increase its enjoyment, not to accumulate devalued money, boast about the impotence of power and produce an ever growing volume of misery.[108]

---

[108] Vaneigem, *Movement of the Free Spirit* 244.

INDEX